T0330056

Public Private Partnerships

Governing Common Interests

Sara Valaguzza

Full Professor of Administrative and Environmental Law, University of Milan, Italy

Eduardo Parisi

Postdoctoral Research Fellow in Administrative Law, University of Milan, Italy

 Edward Elgar
PUBLISHING

Cheltenham, UK • Northampton, MA, USA

Published by
Edward Elgar Publishing Limited
The Lypiatts
15 Lansdown Road
Cheltenham
Glos GL50 2JA
UK

Edward Elgar Publishing, Inc.
William Pratt House
9 Dewey Court
Northampton
Massachusetts 01060
USA

A catalogue record for this book
is available from the British Library

Library of Congress Control Number: 2019951891

This book is available electronically in the **Elgar**online
Law subject collection
DOI 10.4337/9781789903737

ISBN 978 1 78990 372 0 (cased)
ISBN 978 1 78990 373 7 (eBook)

Printed and bound in Great Britain by TJ International Ltd, Padstow

Contents

About the authors   vi
Acknowledgments   viii
Introduction   x

PART I

1   Public private partnership: first steps towards a juridical
     definition   2

2   Public private partnership's juridical identity: the
     international dimension   30

3   Public private partnership's juridical identity: the local
     dimension   56

4   Clearing up the picture: overcoming common misperceptions   81

PART II

5   Reconstructing the juridical identity of public private
     partnership   103

6   From public interest to common interests   116

7   Conclusion   138

Bibliography   174
Index   221

About the authors

Sara Valaguzza is Full Professor at the University of Milan and the founding president of the European Association of Public Private Partnership. She is also the director of the Italian Centre of Construction Law & Management, constituted by the University of Milan, the Polytechnic of Milan and the University of Brescia.

She is serving in the University of Milan Foundation as a member of the board of directors.

She is involved in several public private partnership initiatives advising public authorities and local governments and piloting case studies for improving public value.

Professor Valaguzza is a leading expert on administrative and environmental law.

She has written six monographs, both in Italian and in English, and more than 50 essays on administrative law topics. She has written extensively on institutional design, public procurement, administrative procedure, European multilevel governance, sustainable development, *res iudicata* and judicial review.

Her books *Alliancing in public sector* (2019) and *Governing by contract – Procuring for Value* (2018), are recognized by the academic community as a deep analysis of the fragmented situation of public organizations and a starting point for reforming frameworks and tools for outsourcing. Recently, as one of the first European scholars expert on collaborative behaviours in public sector, she authored a chapter in the book *Collaborative Construction Procurement*, by David Mosey (2019), about the civil law countries' approach to alliancing and collaborative procurement.

She also practices as attorney for Italian and international clients and leads a research group to promote collaborative procurement in public and private sector, reaching environmental and social targets and producing added value.

She is a founding member of the Transnational Alliancing Group, an international group of academics and practitioners constituted in 2018 for the research and dissemination of collaborative frameworks all around the world.

Eduardo Parisi is Postdoctoral Research Fellow in Administrative Law at the University of Milan where he carries out a research project on alliancing and collaborative behaviours in contractual relationships.

During his PhD on Administrative Law (University of Milan – 2014–2017) he deepened the subject of co-administration among public institutions at the European level.

He holds an LLM in Legal Theory – NYU School of Law. His research focus was on environmental law and global administrative law.

He is the Responsible for the International Relationships of the European Association of Public Private Partnership and contributes to the initiatives of the network lecturing at international conferences on the issues of public private partnership.

As a founding member of the Transnational Alliancing Group, he is working with several academics and professionals on construction procurements in a global perspective.

As an attorney at law, he worked with numerous public administrations, on projects of public procurement and public private partnership.

Acknowledgments

The most fascinating aspect of our work is being in contact with people who are sometimes truly exceptional, who contribute to enriching and improving our thinking. The dialogue in which we are involved as law professors and researchers is an experience of continuous growth both in our studies and our lives.

The exchange of ideas, cultures, sensibilities and experiences between different people, in different countries, in various contexts, is the engine of the research carried out for this book during the last three years.

We have greatly benefited from the insights and ideas provided by international academics, colleagues and students about the topic of the relationship between government and society and especially on public private partnering. Some of these colleagues are part of our everyday life, others are unaware they have contributed to our reflections with their works.

We would therefore like to take this opportunity to express our heartfelt gratitude to all the leading academics, researchers, colleagues, practitioners and students, in presence or in spirit, who have supported, encouraged and inspired our research with their writings.

In particular, we would like to acknowledge the benefits we received from the interactions and networking of the European Association of Public Private Partnership – EAPPP, established in Milan in 2016, which has been essential for this book because it inspired the idea of combining a strong theoretical background to actual case studies on the use of public private partnership in the world. A special thanks goes to those who joined us as founding members of EAPPP: Professors Annamaria La Chimia from the University of Nottingham; Raquel Carvalho from the Universidade Católica Portuguesa – Centro Regional do Porto; Ymre Schuurmans from Leiden University; Francesco Goisis from the University of Milan; Mauro Renna from the Cathlolic University of Milan; Adriana Spassova and the Bulgarian Society of Construction Law; Alessandra Canuti and Luca La Camera, Attorneys at Law; Maria Rita Surano, Attorney at Law and guardian angel, all special colleagues and friends.

Part of our inspiration also came from the amazing place where we live, Milan, which in the last decade has grown very fast, thanks to the efforts of businesses and the local administration. We met excellent public managers there. Among the many, a special thanks for the energy they spend in improving public value in public private partnership goes to Christian Malangone, city manager, Filippo Salucci, director of environmental transition, Francesco Tarricone, director of social housing, Mariangela Zaccaria, deputy secretary of the Municipality, and Salvatore Barbara, who leads the concession for the two new subway lines under construction in Milan.

We have also benefited from the interactions with the Public Procurement Research Group of Nottingham University, led by Professor Sue Arrowsmith, from the talks with Professors Christopher Yukins and Steven Schooner from the George Washington University, and with Professors Richard Stewart and Katrina Wyman from the New York University School of Law: their pragmatic attitude made us look at juridical structures in terms of 'simple' tools to help innovation and growth.

The spread of research activities allowed us to listen to hundreds of speeches and get in touch with extraordinary human beings, such as Professors Steven Kelman, Jody Freeman and Cass Sunstein, leading scholars and generous minds. We also had the chance to start important relationships and friendships, like the one with Professor David Mosey, from King's College, London, whose persistence and love for law are a precious example of integrity and passion.

Finally, a special thanks also goes to all the students of the course on Public Private Partnership for Sustainable Development, held at the faculty of law of the University of Milan: we are grateful for all questions and contributions they have made during classes.

Milan, 30 June 2019

Introduction

1   SETTING THE SCENE

Visitors leaving the John F Kennedy International Airport in New York are greeted with several signs asking them to 'adopt a highway'. One of them reads: 'Next 1 Mile – Jet Blue'. One could ironically say that American highways have many fathers.

This programme is an interesting example of public private partnership, which we can define, in a preliminary way, as a particular juridical arrangement in which one or more public authorities cooperate with private operators to carry out an activity of public importance, with substantial private financing and assumption of risk.[1]

In the case of the New York highways, which can stand as an example for many similar adopt-a-highway programmes all over the world, a private operator – here, an airline company – cooperates with a public authority – here, the New York City Department of Transportation – to carry out a publicly significant activity, such as the maintenance of a stretch of highway near the airport. In exchange for the economic investment and the operational contribution, the private sponsor receives the benefit of promoting its logo on the signs located at the sponsored highway section.

These road signs indicate a synergy between the public and the private spheres; they are the result of an agreement through which public infrastructures are maintained by a private operator.[2]

---

[1]   Since this is an introduction to the topics of the book, the readers will not find a detailed and exhaustive description of the juridical concepts dealt with at this point. For now, it is best to follow our reasoning, which uses examples taken from cases, legislation and experience, to enter into conceptual contact with public private cooperation.

[2]   The adopt-a-highway programmes are a type of public private agreement that are quite widespread in the United States of America, through which public authorities in charge of the management of stretches of highway promote litter control and reduce the expenditure of public funds for litter control. These kinds of programmes are quite appreciated as they foster citizenship participation and a strong sense of community. The juridical outline of said programmes and the implications for the re-definition of the line between public and private governance of common goods are tackled in Martha Minow, 'Partners, not rivals: redrawing the lines between public and private, non-profit,

As a consequence of the public private partnership, the public authority benefits from an entrepreneurial project which generates public value, sharing responsibility to meet the needs of the community. At the same time, the private operator profits from the involvement in an otherwise inaccessible dimension, namely the tasks reserved for public administrations.

The adopt-a-highway programme is only one example of the many positive synergies between public entities and the business world which universally satisfy common needs in different spheres of the economy, from infrastructure to education, environmental protection and cultural heritage.[3] Some other examples are presented below.

The women's literacy programme named '*Projet d'Alphabétisation Priorité Femme*', launched by the Senegalese government in the late 1990s,[4] is an interesting case from the field of education. This programme involved many small

---

and secular and religious' (2002) BU Law Review 1061. For an account of the difficulties that may be caused by the flanking of certain private organizations with public authorities, see the legal dispute that arose in 1996 regarding the request of the Ku Klux Klan to adopt a section of the Interstate 55 near St. Louis, Missouri. The refusal of the Missouri Department of Transportation to accept the application of this group, based on the history of unlawful violent and criminal behaviour of the Klan, was repealed in two grades of trial on constitutional grounds. See *Cuffley v. Mickes* (1999) 44 F.Supp.2d 1023; *Cuffley v. Mickes* (2000) 208 F.3d 702. The decision of the Courts was respected but the Missouri Legislature decided to name the stretch of highway adopted by the KKK the 'Rosa Parks Highway', in honour of the civil rights heroine from Alabama whose refusal to give up her bus seat to a white passenger in 1955 led to a boycott of the Montgomery's bus system and the start of the civil rights movement. For a comment, see Suzanne Stone Montgomery, 'When the Klan adopts-a-highway: the weaknesses of the public forum doctrine exposed' (1999) Wash. U. Law. Q. 557; Ray Leeper, 'The Ku Klux Klan, public highways and the public forum' (2000) Communications and the Law 39; Marybeth Herald, 'Licensed to speak: the case of vanity plates' (2001) U. Colo. Law Review 595; Mary Jean Dolan, 'Government speech' (2003–2004) Hastings Const. Law Q. 71; Alyssa Graham, 'The government speech doctrine and its effects on the democratic process' (2011) Suffolk U. Law Review 703.

[3]   To introduce the reasoning on public private partnership, we chose to propose a selection of examples of successful projects in different economic fields. The cases presented have been chosen from experiences of public private partnership carried out around the world in the last thirty years, on the basis of their capacity to represent a concrete answer to the needs of local communities. Many more recent public private partnership projects have been launched after the ones cited in the text. Nevertheless, we chose to consider the ones with concrete results for the affected communities that could be evaluated and assessed by the scientific community.

[4]   Bjorn H Nordtveit, 'Managing Public-private partnership. Lessons from literacy education in Senegal' (The World Bank, 2004); Helen Abadzi, 'Improving adult literacy outcomes: lessons from cognitive research for developing countries' (The World Bank, 2003); Peter Easton, 'Enhancing the contributions of adult and non-formal education to achievement of education for all and millennium development goals: Vol. I.

local providers, consisting mainly of local community-based organizations, both profit and non-profit, in implementing small-scale literacy projects covering courses in reading, writing, health and hygiene for local women in different villages. The private providers took on the costs of the organization and teaching, whereas the government's literacy department maintained responsibility for policy formulation, monitoring and evaluation,[5] as well as the authority to approve single projects. Because of its accomplishments, in terms of number of projects approved and women educated, the programme was taken as a best practice and replicated in Gambia, Burkina Faso and Guinea.[6]

In the arena of environmental and endangered species protection, in 2005 the International Finance Corporation – the private sector arm of the World Bank Group – signed a $5 million grant for a public private partnership aiming at ensuring sustainable financing for the Komodo National Park in Indonesia.[7] The goal of the initiative was to protect the park's biodiversity, particularly the endangered species of the *Varanus komodoensis*, while providing tourist attractions for visitors wanting to explore the site, declared a World Heritage Site and a Man and Biosphere Reserve by the United Nations Educational Scientific and Cultural Organization (UNESCO).[8] The grant was provided to an Indonesian limited liability company jointly owned by The Nature Conservancy – an international non-profit organization active in the field of the preservation of diversity of life on earth – and an Indonesian private

---

Finding improved means of service provision in adult and non-formal education' (The World Bank, 2004).

[5]   Nordtveit (n 4) 1.

[6]   Bjorn H Nordtveit, 'Use of public-private partnerships to deliver social services: advantages and drawbacks' (Centre for International Education Faculty Publications, 2004). In order to face what the United Nations Educational Scientific and Cultural Organization (UNESCO) has labelled as a 'global learning crisis' and to provide children of rural and indigenous populations, cultural minorities and conflict-affected countries with their fundamental right to education, many governments (such as Colombia, Pakistan, Peru, Philippines, Sierra Leone, Uganda and Venezuela) have engaged in the non-public sector to build schools and to manage the educational services. See: UNESCO, 'The global learning crisis: why every child deserves a quality education' (Program and Meeting Document, 2013).

[7]   International Finance Cooperation, 'IFC supports management of Komodo National Park in Indonesia' (27 June 2005) https://ifcextapps.ifc.org/ifcext/Pressroom/IFCPressRoom.nsf/0/7B5F1CD246F58BA18525702D004B681E?OpenDocument, accessed 11 January 2019.

[8]   Viviana Lujan Gallegos et al., 'Sustainable financing for marine protected areas: lessons from Indonesian MPAs. Case studies: Komodo and Ujung Kulon National Parks' (Environmental and Resource Management, 2005) http://www.selfpas.it/libreria/Sustainable_Financing_of_MPAs-Komodo.pdf, accessed 11 March 2019. See also Johannes Subijanto, 'Towards a sustainable Komodo National Park Management: a 2002 progress report' (The Nature Conservancy, 2002).

tourism enterprise which entered into an agreement with the Indonesian government, the park authority and the local communities to promote the park as a tourist destination and increase the net benefits to conservation and local development.[9]

As for the field of cultural heritage, a fruitful public private partnership was recently carried out by the Australian Federal Government. In this case, the project called for the requalification and reuse of the North Head Quarantine Station, a 30-hectare area outside Sidney of great historical and social significance containing many aboriginal sites. This was made possible thanks to a 20-year lease by the Federal Government and the public National Parks and Wildlife Service to a private investment group, which took on the responsibility of investing approximately $6 million for the conservation of buildings, cultural landscape, infrastructure and movable heritage collection, as well as setting up a retreat centre, two restaurants, a conference and visitor centre, a theatre and parking spots.[10]

The above examples bring us close to the subject of our analysis, as they show forms of cooperation between the public and the private sector carried out in order to satisfy a community's needs (transport, education, environmental protection, culture) which can be easily qualified – at least in its general sense – as forms of public private partnerships. Said agreements allow public authorities to draw near to the administered communities as they enable governmental authorities to receive inputs from market operators or members of society, in a 'bottom-up' approach. Public private partnerships drag public administrations out from the isolation where they end up when they act with authoritative modalities and as 'monopolists' of the management of publicly relevant activities.

From an academic point of view, the blend between public and private inevitably also produces a juridical contamination of values, dynamics, principles, rules of action and parameters of responsibility, which has not been fully investigated by the literature on public private partnership. Our contribution is to analyse and decipher the elements and consequences of said interaction.

More precisely, this book intends to take a further step in this direction, providing a theoretical account of public private partnership as an instrument

---

[9] International Finance Cooperation, n 7.

[10] Susan Macdonald and Caroline Cheong, 'The role of public-private partnerships and the third sector in conserving heritage buildings, sites, and historic urban areas' (The Getty Conservation Institute, 2014) 22. Different forms of PPP are commonly adopted in numerous parts of the world to enhance the value of historical and cultural assets. On the topic, see UNESCO, 'The Hangzhou Declaration placing culture at the heart of sustainable development policies' (Adopted in Hangzhou, People's Republic of China, on 17 May 2013).

of governance able to bend some of the principles of administrative action that are often unquestionably accepted across the board and, at the same time, to absorb the private sectors into a social dimension in which the subjective differences of the public and the private operators are blended, leaving space for the community's needs.

The path taken also leads our line of reasoning to analyse deeply the notion of 'public interest'.

In particular, we question whether said concept is still current and truly representative of a concerted public and private action through which the private actors' spontaneous ventures promote the protection of common goods.

Anticipating the outcomes of our researches on this specific aspect, we will argue for the need to overcome some of the dichotomies of the past, i.e. market versus government; public versus private; public values versus private values; economy versus protection of community's interest. We will relocate these features in a new environment and introduce the more 'subjectively neutral' dynamic of what we call 'governing common interest'. We will not only detect the need for a terminological change in the public law discourse. Rather, we will analyse the juridical – and formalistic – consequences of the shift provoked by public private partnership in relation to the principles governing the administrative action.

We will mention the 'community' on different occasions throughout the book, in relation to interests, initiatives and needs. We intend to clarify that in all those cases we will intentionally refer to an undetermined object, different from the concepts of citizenship.

Using the term 'community' we intend to bring public private partnership into a dimension of social and political inclusion. In fact, we think that in the context of globalization, migratory flows and economic and cultural circulation, the role of public institutions transcends formal distinctions.

Public authorities, both local and central, are at the front lines in ensuring that 'primary goods' such as health, equality and human dignity, as well as public values like justice and solidarity, are recognized among all persons employed in the public authority sphere of competence and surveillance. Therefore, when we refer to common interest or common needs in the text, we refer to a category of people – not necessarily citizens – that are in a determined space and time, as direct recipients (and, through public private partnership, active protagonists) of welfare production.

2 THE ACADEMIC LINES OF REASONING ON PUBLIC PRIVATE PARTNERSHIP

The literature examining public private partnerships is largely concerned with the economic and social aspects of the phenomenon.[11]

Some recurring questions that have inspired academic investigation are: in which sector of the economy is public private partnership most commonly adopted? In which countries was public private partnership most successful? Which type of enterprise most often seems to be a suitable partner for the administration? Which economic results have public private partnership delivered in a specific sector?

Research has shown that, for instance, infrastructure and energy contexts are particularly interesting test fields for public private partnership, especially in developing countries, and that, in a global perspective, big enterprises are more suited to maximizing the value resulting in a partnership with the public sphere.

Starting from the observation of public private partnership's massive spread in the modern economy and of the intrinsic complexity in terms of variety of juridical schemes and interactions among the involved parties, the legal liter-

---

[11] Among the most noteworthy monographs are: Pauline Vaillancourt Rosenau (ed.), *Public-private policy partnerships* (MIT Press, 2000); Akintola Akintoye, Matthias Beck, and Cliff Hardcastle, *Public-private partnerships: managing risks and opportunities* (Wiley-Blackwell, 2003); Darrin Grimsey and Mervyn Lewis (eds), *The economics of public private partnerships* (Edward Elgar, 2005); Akintola Akintoye and Matthias Beck, *Policy, management and finance of public-private partnerships* (Wiley-Blackwell, 2008); Abdelhalim Boussabaine, *Risk pricing strategies for public-private partnership projects* (Wiley-Blackwell, 2013); David Maurrasse, *Strategic public private partnership* (Edward Elgar, 2013); Eduardo Engel, Ronald Fischer, and Alexander Galetovic, *The economics of public-private partnerships: a basic guide* (CUP, 2014); Mark Claypool and John McLaughlin, *We are in this together: public-private partnerships in special and at-risk-education* (Rowman and Littlefield, 2015); Malcolm Morley, *The public-private partnership handbook: how to maximize value from joint working* (Kogan Page, 2015); Carsten Greve and Graeme Hodge (eds), *Rethinking public-private partnerships: strategies for turbulent times* (Routledge, 2016). A more technical approach is taken in Herbert Robinson et al., *Governance and knowledge management for public-private partnerships* (Wiley-Blackwell, 2009); Graeme Hodge, Carsten Greve, and Anthony Boardman (eds), *International handbook on public-private partnerships* (Edward Elgar, 2010); Cyril Chern, *Public private partnerships: practice and procedures* (Routledge, 2017). The social element of the analysis is predominant in Nikolai Mouraviev and Nada Kakabadse (eds), *Public-private partnerships in transitional nations: policy, governance and praxis* (Cambridge Scholars Publishing, 2017); Adam Masters, *Cultural influences on public-private partnerships in global governance* (Palgrave Macmillan, 2018).

ature has also recently shown a keen interest in the phenomenon, which has been studied from different perspectives.

International law experts have underlined how public private partnership has been increasingly adopted as a new mechanism to solve governance deficits in dealing with pressing global issues, with special reference to the Sustainable Development Goals.[12]

Noting that transnational public private partnerships are commonly used as methods to carry out activities that normally fall within the domain of states and international organizations – for example, improving water infrastructures, protecting endangered species, fighting the growing risks of diseases – some scholars have questioned the democratic legitimacy of said alliances[13] and analysed their consequences in terms of responsibility under international public law.[14]

Significant findings resulting from this research show that the problem-solving capacities and effectiveness of public private partnership are an important source of legitimacy and accountability, and that the source of democratic legitimacy, even in transnational hybrid forms of cooperation, lies within the public law type of rules that apply to the decisions taken and the activities carried out.[15]

---

[12]   Particularly interesting, in this perspective, is the systematic analysis conducted in Philipp Pattberg et al. (eds), *Public-private partnership for sustainable development* (Edward Elgar, 2012). See also Harsh Singh, *Creating vibrant public-private panchayat partnership (PPPP) for inclusive growth through inclusive governance* (Academic Foundation, 2010).

[13]   Pattberg et al., n 12, 165ff.; Nikiforos Meletiadis, *Public private partnerships and constitutional law: accountability in the United Kingdom* (Routledge, 2018).

[14]   Lisa Clarke, *Public-private partnerships and responsibility under international law: a global health perspective* (Routledge, 2016). For a discussion on how public private partnerships are treated in WTO litigation, see Gregory Shaffer, 'Defending interests: public-private partnerships in WTO litigation' (2004) TDM 4; Amrita Bahri, *Public private partnership for WTO dispute settlement* (Edward Elgar, 2018).

[15]   Muhittin Acar, *Accountability in Public-private partnerships: perspectives, practices, problems, and prospects* (Verlag Dr Müller, 2009); Magdalena Bexell and Ulrika Mörth (eds), *Democracy and public-private partnerships in global governance* (Palgrave Macmillan, 2010). Other publications provide a comprehensive account of public private partnership in terms of policy management, capturing its main strengths and flaws as a juridical instrument. See Abby Ghobadian et al. (eds), *Public-private partnership: policy and experience* (Palgrave Macmillan, 2004); Graeme Hodge and Carsten Greve, *The challenge of public-private partnership* (Edward Elgar, 2005); Yseult Marique, *Public private partnerships and the law* (Edward Elgar, 2014); Christopher Bovis, *Public-private partnership in the European Union* (Routledge, 2018); Margaret Chon et al., *The handbook of public-private partnerships, intellectual property governance, and sustainable development* (CUP, 2018). As for the Italian literature, an insightful study on the state and quality of the modern national democracy is

Other authors have preferred a case-study approach, focusing their attention on a specific ambit of public private partnership applications to tackle the practical sector-specific issues posed by this instrument and to provide suggestions for policy improvements.[16]

The studies on public private partnership in the sectors of transport and energy infrastructures,[17] affordable housing,[18] sport facilities,[19] homeland security,[20] health care[21] and water management[22] have demonstrated the versatility and flexibility of said juridical arrangement and normalized it as a method of governance in the most diverse areas of public activity.

The scholars who attempted a more theoretical reconstruction focused their attention on the progressive erosion of the boundaries that traditionally separate public and private law.

The intersection between public and private is a relatively recent but already widely discussed phenomenon.

The spill-over of the public into the private and vice versa has contaminated the theories, which have consequently started to identify and articulate

---

contained in Franco Bassanini et al. (eds), *Il mostro effimero. Democrazia, economia e corpi intermedi* (il Mulino, 2019).

[16] See, *inter alia*, Duncan Cartlidge, *Public private partnership in construction* (CRC Press, 2006); Julian Teicher and Bernadine Van Gramberg (eds), *Sharing concerns: country case studies in public-private partnerships* (Cambridge Scholars Publishing, 2013); Joshua Newman, *Governing public-private partnership* (MQUP, 2017); Domenico Crocco (ed.), *Public private partnerships: the PPP guide* (Cedam, 2018).

[17] Among the many publications, we cite Germa Bel, Trevor Brown, and Rui Cunha Marques (eds), *Public-private partnership: infrastructure, transportation and local services* (Routledge, 2014); Stefano Caselli, Veronica Vecchi, and Guido Corbetta (eds), *Public private partnership for infrastructure and business development: principles, practices, and perspectives* (Palgrave Macmillan, 2015); Athena Roumboutsos (ed.), *Public private partnerships in transport: trends and theory* (Routledge, 2015); Jeffrey Delmon, *Public-private partnership projects in infrastructure: an essential guide for policy makers* (2nd edition, CUP, 2017).

[18] Geoffrey Payne (ed.), *Making common ground: public-private partnerships in land for housing* (London, Practical Action, 1999); Nestor Davidson, *Affordable housing and public-private partnership* (Intermediate Technology Publications Ltd, 2016).

[19] Judith Grant Long, *Public-private partnerships for major league sports facilities* (Routledge, 2012).

[20] Nathan Busch and Austen Givens, *The business of counterterrorism: public-private partnerships in homeland security* (Peter Lang, 2014).

[21] Heather Whiteside, *Purchase for profit: public-private partnerships and Canada's public health care system* (University of Toronto Press, 2015).

[22] Rui Cunha Marques and Carlos Oliveira Cruz, *Public-private partnership in the water sector: from theory to practice* (IWA, 2018).

a common ground of principles and a shared area, where the traditional public private dichotomy is brought into harmony.

The European administrative law literature has considered the progressive mutual approach of the public and private sectors as a method applied by public administrations to answer the so-called '*crise de la modernité jurid-ique*'.[23] This crisis is characterized by the demise of some of the fundamental conceptual pillars of public law, such as the supremacy of the state as inter-preter of the community's interests,[24] the completeness and self-sufficiency of the normative framework,[25] and the necessity for public administration to refer only to hierarchical methods of action.[26]

Prominent scholars have underlined that the dissatisfaction with the effi-ciency of administrative actions brought a radical shift from the hierarchical and imperative paradigms and top-down logics to more fluid and horizontal paradigms. From the organizational point of view, some renowned French scholars have remarked that network schemes have substituted pyramid-style

---

[23]   The expression is taken from Pascal Idoux, 'Dynamique contractuelle et dynam-ique délibérative dans le renouvellement des méthodes d'action publique' in Guylain Clamour and Marion Ubaud-Bergeron (eds), *Contrats publics: Mélanges en l'honneur du professeur Michel Guibal* (Montpellier Université, II, 2006). On the same topic, see also Paul Amselek, 'L'évolution générale de la technique juridique dans les sociétés occidentales' (1982) RD Publ. 275.

[24]   The issue is looked at more closely in Jacques Chevallier, *L'État post-moderne* (LGDJ, 2008) 139ff.; Thierry Revet, 'Droit législatif, droit réglementaire et droit néo-corporatif du contrat' (2004) Revue des contrats 607. See also Paolo Grossi, *L'ordine giuridico medievale* (Laterza, 1995) and Paolo Grossi, *L'invenzione del diritto* (Laterza, 2017), where the author states that the law is not something that is imposed on the community from the top down, but it naturally springs from a society, coming from its history, values and collective consciousness.

[25]   The theory of institutionalism, firstly elaborated in Santi Romano, *L'ordinamento giuridico* (Quodlibet, 1917), contributed to design the idea of a legal framework com-posed not only of normative commands but of plural entities emerging naturally from society. For a modern comment, see Norberto Bobbio, 'Teoria e ideologia nella dottrina di Santi Romano' in Norberto Bobbio, *Dalla struttura alla funzione* (Laterza, 1977) 168ff.; Massimo La Torre, *Norme, istituzioni, valori: Per una teoria istituzionalistica del diritto* (Laterza, 1999); Giuseppe Lorini, *Dimensioni giuridiche dell'istituzionale* (CEDAM, 2000); Maria Lucia Tarantini, *Istituzionalismo e neoistituzionalismo: ques-tioni e figure* (Giuffrè, 2011).

[26]   Antonio Amorth provided a first deep and comprehensive account of the private law activity of public administrations as a typical method of administrative action in Antonio Amorth, 'Osservazioni sui limiti dell'attività amministrativa di diritto privato' (1939) Archivio di diritto pubblico 89. According to the author's view, administrative activity could not be considered as a unity, being necessary to distinguish between the activity directed at obtaining a certain public interest and the residual one, where it was possible to admit the dominance of private law.

schemes,[27] as external private stakeholders become involved in the public domain through mechanisms of consensus and negotiation.[28]

In parallel, several fundamental Italian works have delved deeper into the models of administrative action,[29] analysing how imperative measures have ceded the stage to new models based on the value of the participation in the administrative procedure,[30] administrative discretion[31] and on agreement.[32]

---

[27] Jean-Marie Pontier, *Le droit administratif et la complexité* (AJDA, 2000) 187; François Ost and Michael van de Kerchove, *De la pyramide au réseau? Pour une théorie dialectique du droit* (FUSL, 2002).

[28] André de Laubadère, 'Administration et contrat' in *Mélanges offerts à Jean Brethe de La Gressaye* (Editions Bière, 1967) 453. Giandomenico Falcon underlined the importance of the application of the principles and rules of public law to the conclusion of an agreement by a public administration in Giandomenico Falcon, *Le convenzioni pubblicistiche: Ammissibilità e caratteri* (Giuffrè, 1984); Giandomenico Falcon, 'Convenzioni e accordi amministrativi', *Enciclopedia Giuridica Treccani*, IX (1988) 4. See also Yves Jégouzo, 'L'administration contractuelle en question' in *Mouvement du droit public, Mélanges F. Moderne* (Dalloz, 2004) 547; Yves Gaudemet, 'Pour une nouvelle théorie générale du droit des contrats administratifs: mesurer les difficultés d'une entreprise nécessaire' (2010) RD Publ. 313; Mathias Amilhat, 'Contractualisation, négociation, consensualisme: nouvelles approches du droit public' (2018) Revue française de droit administratif 1.

[29] Mario Nigro's attention to the subjective position of the private in front of the exercise of administrative power, both during the administrative procedure and in the judicial review are pivotal to this process. See Mario Nigro, *Le decisioni amministrative* (Jovene, 1953); Mario Nigro, *Giustizia amministrativa* (Il Mulino, 1976); Mario Nigro, 'Procedimento amministrativo e tutela giurisdizionale contro la pubblica amministrazione (il problema di una legge generale sul procedimento amministrativo)' (1980) (now in Mario Nigro, *Scritti giuridici*, Giuffrè, 1996, II, 1427). The author was also one of the first to rightly express the possibility that public administration could choose to adhere to private law rules, as appears clearly in Mario Nigro, 'L'amministrazione tra diritto pubblico e diritto privato: a proposito di condizioni legali' (1961) Foro it. (now in Mario Nigro, *Scritti giuridici*, Giuffrè 1996, I, 495). In this regard, it also seems necessary to recall Riccardo Villata, *Autorizzazioni amministrative e iniziativa economica privata: Profili generali* (Giuffrè, 1974), which represents an essential contribution to understanding how administrative power can impact on the free economic initiative of the market.

[30] Feliciano Benvenuti contributed to affirming an equal role of the private actor and of the public authority, even in the context of the administrative procedure, thanks to the warranties imposed by the administrative law, in Feliciano Benvenuti, 'Eccesso di potere amministrativo per vizio della funzione' (1950) Rass. dir. pubbl. 1; Feliciano Benvenuti, 'Funzione amministrativa, procedimento, processo' (1952) Rivista trimestrale di diritto pubblico 118.

[31] The elaboration of the concept of administrative discretion which currently dominates the way in which the Italian academia refers to the relationship between law and exercise of public power can be found in Massimo Severo Giannini, *Il potere discrezionale della Pubblica Amministrazione: concetto e poteri* (Giuffrè, 1939).

[32] In the Italian literature, particular attention to the modern legal issues posed by the new forms of public private interaction is already personally devoted in Sara

Moreover, the erosion of the boundaries between the public and the private sphere that has affected numerous aspects of the administrative organization and activity has prompted academics to ask questions about the modernity of traditional concepts and views, characterized by an outdated and limited perception of the forms of governance.

The struggle with the absence of a structured theoretical framework in which to insert new hybrid forms of governance can be detected, above all, in the studies regarding the private management of 'common goods', which has been defined not in relation to their private or public ownership but to their functionality to satisfy the needs of the community.[33]

Said writings deal with the specific arena that we intend to examine more closely; therefore, they are an important point of reference for comparison and inspiration in the part of this book in which we reconstruct the essential fea-

---

Valaguzza, 'Pubblico e privato nell'organizzazione' in Barbara Marchetti (ed.), *Pubblico e privato oltre i confini dell'amministrazione tradizionale* (Cedam, 2013) 99 and – with specific reference to public private partnership – in Sara Valaguzza, *Sustainable development in public contracts: an example of strategic regulation* (Editoriale Scientifica, 2016) 18. On the same topic see Giampaolo Rossi, 'Pubblico e privato nell'economia semi-globalizzata. L'impresa pubblica nei sistemi permeabili e in competizione' (2014) Rivista Italiana di Diritto Pubblico Comunitario 1.

[33]   In the international literature, the topic was elaborated on the basis of the fundamental argument of Elinor Ostrom, *Governing the commons: the evolution of institutions for collective action* (Political Economy of Institutions and Decisions, 1990); Elinor Ostrom, Roy Gardner, and James Walker, *Rules, games and common-pool resources* (The University of Michigan Press, 1994); Elinor Ostrom, 'Reflections on the commons' in John Baden and Douglas Noonan (eds), *Managing the commons* (Indiana University Press, 1998) 95; Elinor Ostrom, *Design principles and threats to sustainable organizations that manage commons* (Bloomington, 1999); Elinor Ostrom et al., *The future of the commons: beyond market failure and government regulation* (The Institute of Economic Affairs, 2012). For a comment, see, *inter alia*, Fred Foldvary, *Public goods and private communities* (Edward Elgar, 1994); Simon Kemp, *Public goods and private wants* (Edward Elgar, 2002); Amy Ludlow, *Privatising public prisons: labour law and the public procurement process* (Hart, 2015); Brigitte Unger, Daan van der Linde, and Michale Getzner (eds), *Public or private goods?* (Edward Elgar, 2017). As for the Italian account, we mention the recent works of Stefano Nespor, 'Tragedie e commedie nel nuovo mondo dei beni comuni' (2013) Riv. giur. ambiente 665; Dereck Wall, *The sustainable economics of Elinor Ostrom: commons, contestation and craft* (Routledge, 2014); Marco Bombardelli (ed.), *Prendersi cura dei beni comuni per uscire dalla crisi: Nuove risorse e nuovi modelli di amministrazione* (Università degli Studi di Trento, 2016); Daniel Cole and Michael McGinnis (eds), *Elinor Ostrom at the Bloomington School of Political Economy: Vol. 3, A framework for policy analysis* (Lexington Books, 2017); Marco Bombardelli, 'La cura dei beni comuni: esperienze e prospettive' (2018) Giorn. dir. amm. 559; Gianfrancesco Fidone, *Proprietà pubblica e beni comuni* (ETS, 2017); Calogero Miccichè, *Beni comuni: risorse per lo sviluppo sostenibile* (Editoriale Scientifica, 2018).

tures of public private partnership and of the consequent activity of governance of common interests.

3   THE STARTING POINT: THE PROBLEMATIC DEFINITION OF PUBLIC PRIVATE PARTNERSHIP

Numerous international documents, monographic works or scientific articles on public private partnership start with a simple question: what is public private partnership?

The need to define this concept is emblematic, if we think that it is neither new – some examples of the phenomenon can be traced back to the nineteenth century[34] – nor unknown.

Yet, the question is not without meaning, considering that public private partnership is a complex phenomenon, present in many forms and in different jurisdictions all over the world.

The need to set a common ground of understanding is therefore essential to develop a line of reasoning on the theoretical aspects of the concept.

Nevertheless, the attempt to define public private partnership is complicated by the fact that the institution rose and spread from the physiological and, in our view, positive interactions between market, society, businesses, community – as a whole and individuals – the public sphere and its institutions and public bodies.

In this perspective, the issue of the definition of public private partnership is as important as it is complex. Indeed, to define public private partnership requires us to have initially dealt with and resolved the most delicate relationships of modern democracies, namely the ones between economic activity and public bodies, between private and public values, between autonomous and external management of the community's needs, and between public interest and private interests.

Given the above-mentioned complexity, for decades public private partnership initiatives have been carried out without a specific discipline, on the sole basis of an instinctive interpretation of the general principles of good administration.

The subsequently enacted laws, regulations and acts of soft law thus mirror the elasticity of the concept, which leaves the market operators free to propose innovative solutions that fall within the general category of public private

---

[34]   An interesting summary of the historical context of the birth of public private partnership can be found in Newman, n 16, 34. See also Joseph Jones, *The politics of transport in twentieth-century France* (MQUP, 1984).

partnership. As a matter of fact, the involvement of private solutions in the management of public tasks requires a departure from the rigid regulations imposed for public procurement.

The above-described approach is particularly evident in the European dimension, where instead of a general regulation on public private partnership it is possible to find practical recommendations contained in acts of soft law. Since 2003, the European Commission has enacted guidelines,[35] green papers[36] and acts of soft law to describe the state of the art regarding the application of public private partnerships in the Member States on the basis of the analysis of practical cases, providing general indications to administrations and financial institutions, more than a structured discipline. Among the most relevant recommendations is the indication of the altered role of public administrations, from 'actors' to 'supervisors'; the need to ensure competition in the selection of the private partner; and the problematic protection of public interests from the requests of the financing entities.

Some relevant aspects of public private partnership were then expanded on by green papers that considered public private partnership as an efficient tool for procurement.[37]

Lastly, in 2014 the European legislator in Directive 2014/23/EU set out rules for the awarding of concession contracts for works and services, considering it neither feasible nor useful to provide a general and unitary discipline of the *genus* public private partnership in the presence of a solid framework for its most basic types, namely concession contracts.[38]

Even outside the European context, in many jurisdictions the definitions of public private partnership are either so wide that they can comprehend basically any form of public private cooperation – as for example in the United Kingdom, where in 2008 HM Treasury affirmed that 'PPPs are

---

[35]   Commission, 'Guidelines for a successful public-private partnership', COM (2005) 569.

[36]   Commission, 'Green paper on public-private partnership and community law on public contracts and concessions', COM (2004) 345.

[37]   Commission, 'Interpretative communication on the application of community law on public procurement and concessions to institutionalised public-private partnerships', COM (2007) 6661; Commission, 'Mobilising private and public investment for recovery and long term structural change: developing public private partnerships', COM (2009) 615; Commission, 'Green paper on the modernisation of EU public procurement policy: towards a more efficient European procurement market', COM (2011) 15 final; European Parliament, 'Resolution on public-private partnerships and Community law on public procurement and concessions' (2006/2043(INI)).

[38]   Mario Pilade Chiti, 'Il partenariato pubblico-privato e la nuova direttiva concessioni' in Gian Franco Cartei and Massimo Ricchi (eds), *Finanza di Progetto e PPP: temi europei, istituti nazionali e operatività* (Editoriale Scientifica, 2015), 12.

arrangements typified by joint working between the public and private sectors. In their broadest sense, they can cover all types of collaboration across the private-public sector interface involving collaborative working together and risk sharing to deliver policies, services and infrastructure'[39] – or limited to specific contractual forms, such as concessions, as in Cambodian, Chilean, Chinese, Costa Rican, Croatian, Liberian and Lithuanian law.[40]

Generally speaking, the idea of public private partnership revolves around the concept of 'cooperation' to deliver services and infrastructures. Something that, although it points the questioner in the right direction, is not adequately able to distinguish the phenomenon of public private partnership from other forms of collaborative delivery of works and services, carried out through public procurement contracts, in the forms of collaborative contracting.[41]

---

[39] HM Treasury, 'Infrastructure procurement: delivering long-term value' (2008).

[40] Two additional examples are the Japanese Act on Promotion of PFI enacted in July 1998 (see Fumio Shinohara, *Perspectives on private finance initiative (PFI) in Japan: the impact on administrative reform* (1998) Social Infrastructure and Public Services. NLI Research, 117 and Turkey, where the legislation on public private partnership is still highly fragmented, despite the vitality of the instrument, especially in the infrastructure sector. See Uğur Emek, 'Turkish experience with public private partnerships in infrastructure: opportunities and challenges' (2015) Utilities Policy 120. A few legislations only consider public private partnership as applied in some strategic sectors: this is the case, for example, in Indonesia where the presidential regulation No. 67 only allows partnerships for transportation; roads; water; potable water distribution; waste water; telecommunications; electric power; oil and natural gas. In other countries such as Singapore or Colombia a threshold of a minimum value is set for projects considered by the specific discipline as PPPs. The Colombian legislator established a specific discipline of PPP as a tool mainly aimed at the realization of infrastructure. Article 1 of Law No. 1508 of 2012 defines PPPs as 'a private capital linkage instrument, which are embodied in a contract between a state entity and a natural or legal person under private law, for the provision of public goods and their related services, which involves the retention and transfer of risks between the parties and payment mechanisms related to the availability and level of service of the infrastructure and/or service'. Articles 3 and 6 of the mentioned law limit the field of application of the rules there contained to building contracts and management of infrastructure, above a specific threshold and for the minimum duration of 30 years.

[41] In the United Kingdom, numerous standard models of collaborative contracts were drafted in order to produce synergies between the client, the contractor, the designer, the subcontractor and the other actors of a specific project or programme. If applied to public procurement, said contracts would produce a collaborative and integrated environment, similar to the one that is possible to imagine when describing public private partnership. For a more thorough account, see David Mosey, *Early contractor involvement in building procurement: contracts, partnering and project management* (Wiley-Blackwell, 2009); David Mosey, 'The origins and purposes of the FAC-1 framework alliance contracts' (2017) International Construction Law Review. For an Italian perspective of the application of said contract types to public procure-

This is why, as we affirm starting in Chapter 1, additional elements are needed to give a precise account of the specific features of public private partnership, provided that the intention is to characterize it as an autonomous juridical concept, encompassing different *species* of the same *genus*.

Therefore, we will not limit the concept of public private partnership to the concept of concession, which is only one of the many *species* of partnership agreement. We will analyse how public private partnership exhibits logical and juridical features that justify the existence of a specific juridical category.

In this regard, the international legal framework has helped provide relevant content for the definitions.

As discussed in Chapter 2, after the 2002 Johannesburg World Summit on Sustainable Development, public private partnership was enthusiastically recognized as a tool for sustainable development, especially useful in trans-national partnerships for the provision of essential infrastructures in less developed countries.[42]

The international debate clearly shaped the national discipline of the concept, as highlighted in Chapter 3. In some jurisdictions, the potential of public private partnership in producing value for the community according to the sustainable development principle has been highly exploited, giving importance to bottom-up initiatives of common goods management and service provision.

These interesting experiences demonstrate the need for a definition able to include different perspectives and conceptualizations.

This is evident, for instance, in France, where the legislation of 2015 – now embedded in the '*Code de la commande publique*'[43] – modified the concept of '*marché de partenariat*' in order to be applicable to diversified types of contracts, not necessarily characterized by private investments, and in Italy, whose discipline of public private partnership can be considered particularly advanced, since it disciplines the many different modalities of public private interaction aimed at satisfying public interests.

As we will see, however, in most cases, the definitions of public private partnership provided by the national legislators still do not adequately reflect the complexity of the phenomenon.[44]

---

ment, please refer to Sara Valaguzza, *Collaborare nell'interesse pubblico: Perché passare dai modelli antagonisti ai contratti collaborativi* (Editoriale Scientifica, 2019).

[42]   United Nations, 'Report of the World Summit on Sustainable Development' (New York, 2002).

[43]   See Ordonnance No. 2018-1074 of 26 November 2018.

[44]   Only a few definitions of public private partnership consider the relevance of the public interest which the economic operation should be intended to satisfy. This is the

In particular, what is missing is a thorough analysis of the intricacies deriving from what we consider the most interesting feature of public private partnership, namely the mixture of tasks and responsibilities resulting from the involvement of citizens and economic operators in the performance of administrative activities directed at the satisfaction of the community's interests.

This is the reason why, in the coming pages, the definitions of public private partnership will be analysed and re-discussed with a critical perspective, on the basis of a theoretical reconstruction of the issues embedded in the concept, in order to capture its essential juridical identity. In doing so, we will try to be neither imprisoned nor influenced by the myopic approaches we have frequently faced in dealing with public private partnership, also at a regulatory level.

4   THE PERSPECTIVE ADOPTED IN THE BOOK

Unlike other forms of private involvement in publicly significant activities, such as volunteer work, which are aimed at taking care of the community's interests from the 'demand' side, in public private partnerships the private operator shifts to the 'supply' side as it works alongside the public administration entrusted with a specific task to carry out an activity that satisfies a need of the community.

Thus, after a reconstruction of a satisfying juridical definition of 'public private partnership', the most significant aspect that we want to investigate in this book is the genetic mutation created by the fusion between the public and the private spheres.

In particular, we are interested in a deeper look at the process by which public administration shares portions of authority and responsibility with a private operator, in the performance of a publicly significant activity.

The following questions inspired our research and will run through the narrative: what is a public private partnership? What distinguishes public private partnership from other forms of public private cooperation? How can private operators act within an ambit that is usually reserved for the exercise of public power? Can public administrations renounce their function of protector of the public interest, and share this function with a private operator? If so, how does administrative law integrate the changes produced by a different management of the public interest? Is the notion of public interest still capable of representing this modification? Can a private entity pursue an interest which is different

---

case of the Russian Federal Law No. 224/2005, the Slovenian public private partnership Act (ZJZP) of 2006, and the Brazilian PPP law No. 12.111/2009. See Chapters 3 and 4.

from the corporate one? How can private operators act in pursuit of common interests?

In order to answer these questions, we logically divide our line of reasoning into two parts: the first includes a detailed description of the phenomenon, and the second is devoted to reconstructing its theoretical foundations and to presenting a systematic reconstruction of public private partnership.

We start from a semantic approach, examining the meaning of the terms composing the expression 'public private partnership' and consequently putting them in the context of socio-economic and institutional relationships.

This approach leads us to highlight the reasons and advantages for embarking on a public private partnership, from both the public and the private side (Chapter 1).

Subsequently, we conduct a complex analysis in order to capture the juridical meaning of public private partnership as applied in both the international (Chapter 2) and national (Chapter 3) dimensions. In doing so, we are able to detect some characteristic but general elements which compose public private partnerships as a juridical phenomenon.

Given the global dimension of the phenomenon and the across-the-board juridical characteristics that appear in jurisdictions of different legal traditions, we do not limit our analysis to the European dimension; instead we try to build a broader theoretical reasoning on the basis of the common characteristics of public private partnership drawn from the transnational laws, regulations and experiences that we considered more relevant to our dissertation.

The assessment of the central features of public private partnership opens a second field of analysis related to the definition of the concept by comparing and contrasting it with similar figures (Chapter 4).

With the distinctive elements detected in Chapters 1, 2, 3 and 4, we introduce a schematic and very technical proposal identifying all the singular components able to constitute an authentic definition of public private partnership. Our proposal builds a step-by-step definition that comprehensively mirrors all the multiple dimensions in which the phenomenon is present (Chapter 5).

The definition reached therefore paves the way for examining the remaining problem of defining the roles of private and public parties in relation to the concept of 'public interest'.

In verifying whether the merging of the public interest with private ones can bring about a new category of interest, we critically discuss whether the expression can be aligned with the conceptual revolution provoked by the spread of public private partnership (Chapter 6). We then argue that there is a need to look for a new category, which is objectively characterized by its relevance to the community's interests more than by the public subjective element that belongs to the administration involved in the partnership.

We name this new category of interests 'common', in order to stress its objective qualification. In this perspective, 'common interests' are shared between public administrations and private operators and determined, in their genetic essence, by the interaction between the public authority and the social and economic reality.

Finally, we develop the conclusion of the research, analysing the consequences that the spread of public private partnership has on administrative action and principles at large (Chapter 7). In the last chapter, all the outcomes of the multiple parts of the juridical reasoning we analysed more closely are circularly re-examined and deployed in a systematic approach to the phenomenon.

Generally, we notice that through public private partnership a new form of interaction between public and private spheres emerges which implies the abandonment of the traditional isolation of the public administration in managing the needs of the community. Public private partnership gives birth to a relationship as complex and thrilling as often found in business, team game or love affairs, all situations in which sharing of information, common planning and mutual satisfaction should be present.

Even though the entire book is a result of the authors' common ideas and shared approach, Chapters 1, 6 and 7 are attributable to Sara Valaguzza, while Chapters 2, 3 and 4 are attributable to Eduardo Parisi, with the Introduction and Chapter 5 jointly attributable.

PART I

1. Public private partnership: first steps towards a juridical definition

1 BACKGROUND: THE PUBLIC PRIVATE PARTNERSHIP'S REVOLUTION – STRENGTHS AND WEAKNESSES

Public private partnership is the modern revolution of governance.[1]

Even in the uncertainty of its precise juridical definition, scholars agree on the fact that the 'cooperative venture between the state [*rectius*, the government] and private businesses'[2] – as public private partnership can be essen-

---

[1]   The innovative character of public private partnership in relation to methods of administrative action is particularly evident in Harvey Brooks, Lance Liebman, and Corinne Schelling (eds), *Public-private partnership: new opportunities for meeting social needs* (Bellinger, 1984); Guy Peters, *The future of governing: four emerging models* (University Press of Kansas, 1996); Jody Freeman, 'The private role in public governance' (2000) NYULR 543; Donald Kettl, *The global public management revolution: a report on the transformation of governance* (Brookings Institution Press, 2000); Stephen Osborne, 'Understanding public-private partnerships in international perspective: globally convergent or nationally divergent phenomena?' in Stephen Osborne (ed.), *Public-private partnerships: theory and practice in international perspective* (Routledge, 2000) 1; Pauline Vaillancourt Rosenau (ed.), *Public-private policy partnerships* (MIT Press, 2000); Darrin Grimsey and Mervyn Lewis, *Public private partnerships: the worldwide revolution in infrastructure provision and project finance* (Edward Elgar, 2004); William Novak, 'Public-private governance: a historical introduction' in Jody Freeman and Martha Minow (eds), *Government by contract: outsourcing and American democracy* (Harvard University Press, 2009) 23; Harsh Singh, *Creating vibrant public-private-panchayat partnership (PPPP) for inclusive growth through inclusive governance* (Academic Foundation, 2010); Derick Brinkerhoff and Jennifer Brinkerhoff, 'Public-private partnerships: perspectives on purposes, publicness and good governance' (2011) Public Administration and Development 2; Carsten Greve and Graeme Hodge, 'Contemporary public-private partnership: towards a global research agenda' (2018) Financial Acc. and Man. 3; Philipp Pattberg et al. (eds), *Public-private partnership for sustainable development* (Edward Elgar, 2012); Lisa Clarke, *Public-private partnerships and responsibility under international law: a global health perspective* (Routledge, 2016).
[2]   Stephen H Linder, 'Coming to terms with the public-private partnership: a grammar of multiple meanings' in Pauline Vaillancourt Rosenau (ed.), n 1, 19.

tially described – has the radical force to break the historic dichotomy between the public and private sectors.[3]

Since the Justinian demarcation of public and private law,[4] the public private distinction has divided the juridical world 'into two separate spheres that at least purport to be mutually-exclusive – something designated as public cannot at the same time be deemed to be private, and vice versa'.[5]

The idea of the public and private sectors merging and steadily cooperating is revolutionary, as it is based on – and fosters – the blending of the juridical schemes that represent the traditional distinction.

Indeed, public private partnership requires 'government actors ... to think and behave like entrepreneurs, and business actors ... to embrace public interest considerations and expect greater public accountability'.[6]

The reported statement can be accepted, in our view, in the sense that there will never be equivalence between the scopes and modalities of public and private actions. However, it is necessary to specify that in a public private partnership there is a sharing of aims and the common elaboration of the activity of public interest. Still, the lucrative perspective that guides the businesses will never be the decisive element that moves the public administration in its decisions, which are always oriented to the pursuit of the general interests of the administrative community.

From another perspective, scholars outline that public private partnership grows in the crisis of the sovereignty of states over public law.[7] This crisis, from one side, leaves spaces for international actors: the international context is dominated by a network of public, private and non-profit entities cooperating for the implementation of commonly accepted values. In parallel, from another side, the national context asks for public private partnership to solve the issues of the lack of resources and skills necessary to respond to the

---

[3]   Ibid, 22; Novak, n 1, 25; Gavin Drewry, 'Public-private partnerships: rethinking the boundary between public and private law' in Osborne (ed.), *Public-private partnerships*, n 1, 57.

[4]   Norberto Bobbio, *Democracy and dictatorship: the nature and limits of state power* (University of Minnesota Press, 1989) 1ff.

[5]   Novak, n 1, 24.

[6]   Linder, n 2, 20–1.

[7]   The issue is explored by the Italian literature: Sabino Cassese, *Universalità del diritto* (Editoriale Scientifica, 2005); Sabino Cassese, *La crisi dello Stato* (Laterza, 2002); Sabino Cassese, *Lo spazio giuridico globale* (Laterza, 2003); Maria Rosaria Ferrarese, *Diritto sconfinato: Inventiva giuridica e spazi nel mondo globale* (Laterza, 2006); Luisa Torchia (ed.), *Attraversare i confini del diritto: Giornata di studio dedicata a Sabino Cassese* (Il Mulino, 2016).

increasing and pressing demands deriving from the population and to enhance private enterprises' initiatives as a form of social and economic inclusion.[8]

In truth, the cooperation between the public and the private sector is an old phenomenon.[9]

For centuries, public private partnership allowed public administrations to carry out their tasks, availing themselves of businesses' funding, experience and creativity. Since the nineteenth century, public private partnership has made it possible to complete works and provide services of public relevance: in France, national railways were built thanks to forms of cooperation between private and public bodies.[10] In the same period in the United Kingdom, building and management concessions were used to construct lighthouses.[11] In the 1930s, the construction of the first oil wells in Texas and Oklahoma was carried out through rudimentary forms of private finance initiative projects.[12]

However, the shift from cooperation, as a generic form of coordinated action between public and private entities, or of delegation of public power to private operators, to partnership as a juridical and logic structure, is far more recent.

The involvement of private actors in the shaping of public policies and in performing administrative activities began a slogan, theoretically supported

---

[8]   The issue is noteworthy in those jurisdictions where normative limits have been internationally imposed to the debt capacity of the States. As a consequence of the economic crisis of 2008, many legislators established major expenditure restrictions to public administrations, which were forced to reduce their costs and state debt. In the European context, the Treaty on Stability, Coordination and Governance in the Economic and Monetary Union (TSCG), formally concluded on 2 March 2012, and effective on 1 January 2013, has imposed on all signatory states to enact rules in their national legal systems complying with the principles of the so-called 'balanced budget', according to which the amount of public expenditure of the state and of other public entities must correspond to tax revenues. This naturally imposes strict expenditure rules on administrations. In some European states this principle has also been enshrined in constitutional regulations. In Italy, for instance, Article 97 of the Constitution was amended with a further paragraph that states: 'public administration, being compliant with the legal system of the European Constitution, ensure a balanced budget and the public debt sustainability'. The same happened, for example, in Slovenia, where Article 148, para 2 of the Constitution, modified in 2013, stipulates that 'Revenues and expenditures of the budgets of the state must be balanced in the medium-term without borrowing, or revenues must exceed expenditures. Temporary deviation from this principle is only allowed when exceptional circumstances affect the state.'

[9]   Joshua Newman, *Governing public-private partnership* (MQUP, 2017) 34ff.

[10]   Joseph Jones, *The politics of transport in twentieth-century France, Montreal and Kingston* (MQUP, 1984).

[11]   See Grimsey and Lewis, n 1.

[12]   Federica Fabi, Renato Loiero, and Francesco Profiti, *Il partenariato pubblico-privato nell'ordinamento giuridico nazionale, comunitario ed internazionale* (Dike giuridica, 2015) 29.

by the New Public Management theories, which aimed to benefit from private sector innovation, to generate radical new synergies between the design and operation of assets, and to take advantage of private sector commercial discipline, so helping to modernize public services and obtain better value.[13]

In this context, and especially after the launch of the Private Finance Initiative in the United Kingdom in the 1990s,[14] public private partnership exploded globally as a method of governance of the community's needs, in a wide variety of sectors.[15]

The public private partnership's revolution was welcomed with enthusiasm by those who underlined the advantages of allowing the private sector to enter the management of ambits that were previously exclusively managed by public administrations, which forced public and private market operators to compare their procedures,[16] operational process and organizational structures and to generate pro-competitive behaviours, to reduce costs and to expand the coverage and quality of services.[17]

---

[13] Giulio Napolitano, *Diritto amministrativo comparato* (Giuffrè, 2007) 241. Some fundamental contributions on the basic features of new public management theories are David Osborne and Ted Gaebler, *Reinventing government* (Ingrid Schneider Clemson University, 1992); Donald F Kettl, *The global public management revolution: a report on the transformation of governance* (Brookings Institution Press, 2000); Muhammad Shamsul Haque, 'New public management: origin, dimensions and critical implications' (2007) Journal of Public Administration and Public Policy 1; Christopher Pollitt, 'The new public management: an overview of the current status' (2017) Journal of Public Management 110.

[14] On the Private Finance Initiative in the United Kingdom see Richard Thomas, 'Private finance initiative: government by contract' (1997) EPL 519; Stephen Cirell, John Bennett, and Robert Hann, *Private finance initiative and local government* (London, 1997); Penny Badcoe (ed.), *Public private partnerships and PFI* (Sweet and Maxwell, 1999); Sue Arrowsmith, 'Public private partnerships and the European procurement rules: EU policies in conflict?' (2000) CML Review 709; Christopher Bovis, 'The private finance initiative (PFI) as the prelude of public private partnerships (PPPs)' (2006) European Public Private Partnership Law Review 24.

[15] John Dixon and Rhys Dogan, 'Hierarchies, networks and markets: responses to societal governance failure' (2002) Administrative Theory and Praxis 175; Jean-Etienne de Bettignies and Thomas W Ross, 'The economics of public-private partnerships' (2004) Canadian Public Policy 135.

[16] This element is also stressed in Canadian Council for Public-Private Partnerships, 'Public sector accounting for public-private partnership transactions in Canada' (Position Paper by the Accounting Task Force of the Canadian Council for Public-Private Partnerships, 2008).

[17] Lisa Grazzini and Alessandro Petretto, 'Public-private partnership and competition in health-care and education' (2014) Italian Antitrust Review 91. On the topic, see also Ake Blomqvist and Emmanuel Jimenez, 'The Public role in private post-secondary education: a review of issues and options' (Policy Research Working Paper 240, The World Bank, 1989); Harry A Patrinos, Felipe Barrera-Osorio, and Juliana Guàqueta,

In the United States, public private partnership was considered valuable as capable of mitigating the phenomena of bad management in public administrations and limiting the selfishness of business.[18] In this perspective, public private partnership has been intended as an instrument to support the constitutional value to 'separate, divide, balance and most importantly distribute power'; and the counterbalance of public private initiatives providing services and goods to the administrated community has been considered as a 'constitutional means of distributing authority ... offsetting public power with private distribution and checking private jurisdiction with public regulation'.[19]

With more practical justifications, public private partnership has been appreciated as a functional mechanism to access private capital for the construction of infrastructure and for transferring the management and the risk of the provision of public services to the private sector.[20]

'The role and impact of public-private partnerships in education' (The International Bank for Reconstruction and Development; The World Bank, 2009).

[18]   The perspective is thoroughly examined in Freeman and Minow (eds), n 1, 33.

[19]   William J Novak, 'Public private governance: a historical introduction' in Freeman and Minow, n 1, 33.

[20]   Among the more comprehensive studies on the topic, it is possible to quote Sanford Berg, Michael Pollitt and Masatsugu Tsuji (eds), *Private initiatives in infrastructure: priorities, incentives and performance* (Edward Elgar, 2002); Darrin Grimsey and Mervyn Lewis, 'Evaluating the risk of public private partnership for infrastructure projects' (2002) International Journal of Project Management 107; Li-Yin Shen, Andrew Platten, and Xiaopeng Deng, 'Role of public private partnerships to manage risks in public sector projects in Hong Kong' (2006) International Journal of Project Management 587; Grimsey and Lewis (eds), n 1; Ana Belen Alonso-Conde, Christine Brown, and Javier Rojo-Suarez, 'Public private partnerships: incentives, risk transfer and real options' (2007) Review of Financial Economics 335; Angie Ng and Martin Loosemore, 'Risk allocation in the private provision of public infrastructure' (2007) International Journal of Project Management 66; Francesca Medda, 'A game theory approach for the allocation of risks in transport public private partnerships' (2007) International Journal of Project Management 213; Efraim Sadka, 'Public-private partnership: a public economics perspective' (2007) CESifo Economic Studies 466; Gerd Schwartz, Ana Corbacho, and Katja Funke (eds), *Public investment and public-private partnership: addressing infrastructure challenges and managing fiscal risks* (Palgrave Macmillan, 2008); Germa Bel, Trevor Brown, and Rui Cunha Marques (eds), *Public-private partnership: infrastructure, transportation and local services* (Routledge, 2014); Stefano Caselli, Veronica Vecchi, and Guido Corbetta (eds), *Public private partnership for infrastructure and business development: principles, practices, and perspectives* (Palgrave Macmillan, 2015); Athena Roumboutsos (ed.), *Public private partnerships in transport: trends and theory* (Routledge, 2015); Jeffrey Delmon, *Public-private partnership projects in infrastructure: an essential guide for policy makers* (2nd edition, CUP, 2017).

Some commentators stretched the concept of benefits received by public authorities from the private side through public private partnerships.[21]

In particular, it has been underlined that public authorities may profit not only from the receipt of private investments but also from the acquisition of the cognitive heritage composed of technical and scientific knowledge developed by private companies, which constitutes an enrichment of the public know-how and supports the efficiency of public administrations in the provision of services or in the realization of public works.[22]

More recently, however, faith in public private partnership has been questioned, on the basis of evidence of poorly managed projects which resulted in failures to deliver the expected result, both in economic and in social terms.[23]

The authors that have deepened the socio-economic aspects of the cases analysed have criticized public private partnership for being too privately oriented and not able to guarantee higher quality service provision, if compared to other more traditional public contracts.[24]

---

[21]   Enthusiasm for public private partnership as a beneficial instrument of development is shown *ex multis* in Alan Harding, 'Public-private partnership in urban regeneration' in Mike Campbell (ed.), *Local economic policy* (Cassell, 1990) 89; Adrian Webb, 'Co-ordination: a problem in public sector management' (1991) Policy and Politics 19; Philip Kotler, Donald H. Haider, and Irving Rein, *Marketing places* (Free Press, 1993); Ronald McQuaid et al., 'European economic development partnerships: the case of Eastern Scotland European Partnership' in Luiz Montanheiro et al. (eds), *Public and private sector partnerships: fostering enterprise* (Sheffield Hallam University Press, 1998) 355; Ramina Samii, Luk van Wassenhove, and Shantanu Bhattacharya, 'An innovative public–private partnership: new approach to development' (2002) GSDCR 991; Chris Huxham and Siv Vangen, *Managing to collaborate: theory and practice of collaborative advantage* (Routledge, 2005); John Hall, 'Private opportunity, public benefit?' (2005) Fiscal Studies 7; Timothy Besley, 'Public-private partnership for the provision of public goods: theory and an application to NGOs' (LSE STICERD Research Paper DEDPS No. 17, London 2008); Pattberg et al. (eds), n 1.

[22]   The point was stated for instance by the Italian Consiglio di Stato in Cons. Stato, Adunanza Plenaria, 3 March 2008, No. 1.

[23]   Among the others, see Carsten Greve and Graeme Hodge, 'Public-private partnership and public governance challenges' in Stephen Osborne (ed.), *The new public governance' emerging perspectives on the theory and practice of public governance* (Routledge, 2010) 149; Graeme Hodge, 'The risky business of public-private partnerships' (2004) Australian Journal of Public Administration 37; Judith Richter, '"We the Peoples" or "We the Corporations"? Critical reflections on UN-business "partnerships"' (IBFAN, Geneva, 2003).

[24]   On these points, see Stephen Syrett, 'The politics of partnership: the role of social partners in local economic development in Portugal' (1997) European Urban and Regional Studies 99; Robert Bennett and Andrew McCoshan, *Enterprise and human resource development* (Paul Chapman, 1993); John Bryson and William Roering, 'Applying private sector strategic planning to the public sector' (1987) Journal of the American Planning Association 9; Geert Teisman and Erik-Hans Klijn,

Even the capacity of public private partnership to bring innovation has been questioned on the basis of reports showing that, just as with public procurement, the private side, if not controlled, may seek shortcuts to maximize profits.

More generally, public private partnership has been regarded as a potentially disruptive instrument by those who fear that the entrustment of the private sector with public tasks could pose a threat to the pursuit of public values, given that businesses are eminently selfish and oriented towards outcomes that depart from the community's welfare.[25]

In the optic of public law researchers this is probably the harshest point to solve, as it is directly connected to the difficulty of overcoming the institutional distinction between public and private sectors with which we started this chapter.

Given that Western juridical society has developed on the basis of the dichotomy between the public and private spheres, how can the two dimensions coexist in a public private partnership and improve values for the community? Which parameters will have to change if we need to accept public private partnership as an institutional form of governance?

Our research agenda is directed to answering these questions, in order to contribute to a solution of the conundrum posed by the revolutionary institution of public private partnership.

Still, we deem it necessary to start from the analysis of the juridical essence of public private partnership and to provide a definition that is consistent with the modern evolution of the institution, which – as we will clarify over the next pages – can no longer be considered as limited to concession contracts.

With the described background behind us, we now take our first steps toward the (re)definition of the concept of public private partnership.

'Partnership arrangements: governmental rhetoric or governance scheme?' (2002) Public Administration Review 197; Michael Spackman, 'Public-private partnerships: lessons from the British approach' (2002) Economic Systems 283; John Greenway, Brian Salter, and Stella Hart, 'How policy networks can damage democratic health: a case study in the government of governance' (2007) Public Administration 717; Lynne Sagalyn, 'Public private development. lessons from history, research and practice' (2007) Journal of the American Planning Association 7; Guido Codecasa and Davide Ponzini, 'Public-private partnership: A delusion for urban regeneration? Evidence from Italy' (2011) European Planning Studies 647.

[25]   See Max Stephenson, 'Whither the public private partnership: a critical overview' (1991) Urban Affairs Review 109; Hodge, n 23; Carsten Greve and Graeme Hodge, 'On Public-private partnership performance: a contemporary review' (2017) Public Works Management and Policy 55.

2 THE VAGUENESS OF THE DISCOURSE ON PUBLIC PRIVATE PARTNERSHIP AND THE NEED TO RE-GAIN JURIDICAL PRECISION: LIGHTS AND SHADOWS OF PUBLIC PRIVATE PARTNERSHIP

As mentioned from the Introduction to this book, public private partnership is often discussed without the due juridical precision. The flexibility that characterizes the instrument, as well as its transnational character, make it extremely difficult to provide an unanimously accepted notion of the concept.[26] Moreover, public private partnership has been studied mostly under a technical or economic perspective,[27] which has contributed to the vagueness of its juridical debate. Yet, if we intend to assume an academic approach, we cannot avoid clarifying the conceptual framework in precise terms, taking back control of a concept that for decades has been discussed only in economic, technical or, at most, sociological terms. Re-appropriating (legally) precise definitions of public private partnership is therefore one of the first steps that we consider necessary to advance the reasoning on the dynamics and the consequents that it generates. This conceptual operation is extremely important to set the correct frame in which to develop our reasoning, which has to be carried out in an objective way, without ideological conditionings. In this regard, it is pivotal to stress that public private partnership is often at the centre of political discussions, being taken as an example of innovative governance.

Public private partnership often recurs in legislative slogans, debates, government initiatives and electoral speeches, being promoted as the new frontier of governance.[28] It is easy to understand why it is politically used: it conveys a positive image of mutual assistance and harmony, in which both the public and private sectors benefit from a fruitful relationship, acting in favour of the community's need. In essence, in public private partnership the public administration is regarded as modern and efficient, whereas the private operator carries out socially valuable activities. The optimism that surrounds

---

[26] Interesting accounts on this point can be found in Carsten Greve and Graeme Hodge, 'Public-private partnerships: governance scheme or language game?' (2010) Australian Journal of Public Administration 8; Linder, n 2.

[27] See Introduction.

[28] For example, the French president Emmanuel Macron, in his speech at Sorbonne University on 26 September 2017 talked about partnership as a key element of the cooperation within the Eurozone. In the literature, an interesting account of the political dimension of public private partnership in the United Kingdom can be found in Matthew Flinders, 'The politics of public-private partnership' (2005) The British Journal of Politics and International Relations 215.

the concept is mirrored in the vocabulary that generally accompanies it: the expressions 'cooperation', 'agreement', 'efficiency', 'risk allocation', 'fruitful relationship', 'participation', 'common goals' and 'exchange of expertise' help promote the positive image of public private partnership as an emblem of progress and a good practice for public administrations. Nevertheless, if we intend to set up a theoretical discussion around the concept, we need to go beyond a general optimism, asking ourselves if public private partnership is just an evocative word or if it can be intended as a specific legal institution, with precise consequences and implications.

Evidence for a positive answer to this question, and, more generally, to the need to consider public private partnership as an autonomous legal concept, consists in the bewildering amount of legislation, regulations, guidelines and recommendations that globally treat public private partnership as a proper juridical phenomenon.[29]

Said juridical documents provide some important distinctive feature of public private partnership as a category of agreements that present recurring features, provoke precise consequences in the dynamics between the public and the private sphere, and require the application of common principles. These, in turn, impose a particular attention to the terms implied when discussing public private partnership, in order to avoid possible terminological misunderstanding.

An example of how the debate on public private partnership may be conditioned by a different terminological idea of the same item is provided by the recent critiques of public private partnership in Europe, at both a political and an institutional level.

As already anticipated, a certain scepticism towards public private partnership recently arose from the evidence of the difficulty faced by administrative authorities in efficiently managing this juridical instrument and transferring to the private sector substantial portions of the projects' risks.

Recently, at a European level the ability of public private partnership to produce value and to be efficiently implemented by public institutions was strongly questioned.

The harshest opposition came in March 2018 from the European Court of Auditors, which published the Special Report No. 9/2018 entitled 'Public Private Partnerships in the EU: Widespread Shortcomings and Limited Benefits', warning public administrations to enter into public private partner-

---

[29]   A comprehensive list of public private partnership and concession legislations is provided by the Public Private Partnership Legal Resource Center of the World Bank Group at https://ppp.worldbank.org/public-private-partnership/, accessed 13 March 2019.

ship agreements only if sufficiently equipped and after a serious consideration of its most recurring issues, such as incorrect risk allocation, increase of costs due to financial renegotiations and diminished competition.[30]

Although said critiques have been directed at public private partnership in general, looking more closely at this report, as well as at many political debates over the failure of public private partnership, we see they only refer to one specific category of public private partnership: privately funded build and operate concession contracts. Said contracts have been for a long time identified with public private partnership due to their popularity in the United Kingdom, where privately funded projects to build, operate and maintain public infrastructures have been strongly adopted since the launch of the Private Finance Initiative in the 1990s.[31]

The terminological overlap between public private partnership and privately funded build and operate concession contracts – managed as Private Finance Initiative projects – is the consequences of a certain vagueness in the discourse of public private partnership which has allowed dangerous and ambiguous generalizations.

In hindsight, the issues pointed out in the mentioned Court of Auditor's Report No. 9/2018 strongly resemble the ones raised by the British Parliament in the last five years, which brought about the adoption of the Private Finance 2 Initiative.[32] Private finance initiative projects (and, analogically, public private partnership ones) have been criticized for increasing costs of finance

---

[30] The report was anticipated by a few local Court of Auditors' accounts on the possible flaws of public private partnership. For example, in December 2017, the French Cour des Comptes published a report highlighting the inadequacy of the public private partnership policy adopted between 2006 and 2014 by the French Ministry of Justice for the construction and management of prison facilities; Cour des Comptes, 'La Politique Immobilière du Ministère de la Justice, Mettre fin à la fuite en avant' (Rapport public thématique, December 2017).

[31] Private Finance Initiative projects are described in the UK as follows: 'a company called a Special Purpose Vehicle (SPV) is set up by private sector investors. The SPV is responsible for the financing, construction and maintenance of an asset such as a school or hospital. The SPV borrows from banks et al. and contracts with construction and facilities management companies (who will often also be investors in the SPV). Once the asset is constructed, the public sector then pays back the SPV over the period of the contract (typically 25 to 30 years)'. UK House of Commons. Public Administration and Constitutional Affairs Committee, 'After Carillion: public sector outsourcing and contracting' (HC 748, published on 9 July 2018) https://publications.parliament.uk/pa/cm201719/cmselect/cmpubadm/748/748.pdf, accessed 13 March 2019.

[32] HM Treasury, 'PFI and PF2' (Report by the Comptroller and Auditor General, HC 718 Session 2017–2019, 18 January 2018).

for public investments;[33] leaving the substantial risks of the operation with the public authorities;[34] providing huge profits for the private operator without proper counterbalancing of public benefits;[35] being subject to frequent costly renegotiations;[36] and being extremely complex and long, thus implying high transaction costs.[37]

However, these critiques only concern private finance initiative projects and not public private partnership as an instrument of cooperation between the public and the private sector as a whole.

Furthermore, it is necessary to underline that, in the public contracts sector, private finance initiative projects are the types of agreement that most closely resembles public procurement.[38] Therefore, the mentioned critiques could

---

[33]   In 2011 a review by the UK parliament's Treasury Committee found that 'The use of PFI has the effect of increasing the cost of finance for public investments relative to what would be available to the government if it borrowed on its own account'; Treasury Committee, 'Private finance initiative' (17th Report of Session 2010–12, HC 1146) 55.

[34]   UK House of Commons. Public Administration and Constitutional Affairs Committee, 'Sourcing public services: lessons to be learned from the collapse of Carillion' (HC 748, published on 9 July 2018) https://publications.parliament.uk/pa/cm201719/cmselect/cmpubadm/748/748.pdf, accessed 13 March 2019.

[35]   It is asserted that 'Early PFI projects often reported huge profits for investors who made money when they refinanced the project after the asset had been built. Once the asset is built and the project has moved to the maintenance phase, risk diminishes so that banks were willing to offer a lower interest rate for the project debt'. UK House of Commons. Public Administration and Constitutional Affairs Committee, 'After Carillion: public sector outsourcing and contracting', n 31. See also Comptroller and Auditor General, 'The refinancing of the Fazakerley PFI Prison contract' (Report by the Comptroller and Auditor General, HC 584 Session 1999–2000, 29 June 2000).

[36]   Ibid, 26.

[37]   HM Treasury, 'The choice of finance for capital investment' (Briefing by the National Audit Office, March 2015).

[38]   Indeed, as the most advanced literature on European public procurement has noticed in relation to the differentiation of procedures between the award of concessions from the ones related to public procurement (see Directive 2014/23/EU) 'concessions do not have special features that distinguish them in principle from other arrangements' and 'the general procedures, which already apply to non-concession arrangements with the same features, are adequate, and certainty could have been made clearly so simply by making available for all concessions the well-known negotiated procedure with a call for competition'. Sue Arrowsmith, 'Revisiting the case against a separate concessions regime in the light of the concessions directive: a specific directive without specificities?' in Fabian Amtenbrink et al. (eds), *The internal market and the future of European integration: Essays in Honour of Laurence W. Gormley* (CUP, 2019) 370, 395. As the author correctly points out, the specificities of concessions mentioned also in Recital 2 of Directive No. 23/2014, namely 'the exposure of the contractor to the economic risk of providing the services, long average duration, greater complexity and important contract value', can be found in many non-concession public

paradoxically be more easily referred to the public procurement sector rather than to forms of public private partnership different from concession-type contracts.

Indeed, concessions are defined by the European Commission as contracts 'of the same type as a public contract except for the fact that the consideration for the works to be carried out or the services to be provided consists either solely in the right to exploit the construction or service, or in this right together with payment'.[39]

Therefore, they are usually affected by the same flaws as public procurement contracts: construction delays, renegotiations, claims and cost increases are factors that are typical across the entire sector of construction of public works.

Public private partnership is much more than that. It is a flexible concept that encompasses both concessions for infrastructure projects and social partnerships, along with sponsorships, forms of public private companies, joint ventures, management-and-operating contracts and leases.

Anticipating a more precise analysis that will be carried out in Chapters 4 and 5, we can affirm now that public private partnership differs from public procurement methods – and, to some extents, from concessions themselves – because it is capable of generating value for the community from the mutual undertaking of public and private actors in carrying out activities deriving from private initiatives and resources.

In public private partnership, the private sector becomes a valuable asset for the pursuit of public interests as it is the primary interpreter of the community's interests. For this reason, it is involved by public authorities in the selection of the relevant interests and in the design of the answers to peoples' needs.

As will be further debated, the recent national and international contexts of public private partnership forbid understanding public private partnership as limited to concession contracts or to the infrastructure sector.

The complexity of the juridical definition of 'public private partnership' should be treated with the due distinctions and the referred critique should

---

contracts. Indeed, some privately financed infrastructure projects may not involve 'sufficient risk overall for a concession' whereas 'important complexity and trust issues arise with many other contracts involving service provision to the public – for example, for housing management'. Ibid, 377. On this topic, see also, Sue Arrowsmith, *The law of public and utilities procurement* (2nd edition, Sweet and Maxwell, 2006) 6; Sue Arrowsmith, 'Modernising the EU's public procurement regime: a blueprint for real simplicity and flexibility' (2012) Public Procurement Law Review 71.

[39] Commission, 'Public private partnerships and Community law on public contracts and concessions', COM (2004) 327 final, 5.

be more correctly intended to be addressed at concessions rather than public private partnership as a juridical concept.

Thus, we consider it important to regain the precision that is needed to correctly understand the juridical essence of public private partnership in all its contractual types. To this end, we begin our analysis with a semantic approach, deepening the meaning of the words that compose the expression 'public private partnership' and their conceptual background.

3   MOVING TOWARDS LEGAL PRECISION: A SEMANTIC APPROACH

3.1   The Notion of 'Partnership': Cooperation versus Juxtaposition

The word 'partnership' is commonly used to indicate a cooperation between individuals that share resources and activities to achieve a common goal.[40]

In the social sphere, a partner is a life companion.

In the business world, the partner is a shareholder of the risks of a given undertaking.

In games, the partner is the one that forms a group with another player.

In international politics, the term is used to represent a form of integration.[41]

All these meanings have in common the stipulation of an agreement establishing a more or less structured and long-lasting cooperation between two or more entities which are undertaking mutual obligations and responsibilities in support of the alliance.

---

[40]   This notion has been further examined in different contexts, from economics to political sciences and psychology. See for example, Jakki Mohr and Robert Spekman, 'Characteristics of partnership success: partnership attributes, communication behaviour, and conflict resolution techniques' (1994) Strategic Management Journal 135.

[41]   Several international treaties take this perspective: the North Atlantic Treaty establishing the North Atlantic Treaty Organization, in which Member States agreed to a mutual defence in response to an attack by an external nation because of a common goal of long-lasting peace, the Euro-Mediterranean partnership, the Lisbon Treaty, the EU-Russia Partnership and Cooperation Agreement as well as other regional policies that identify partnership as a fundamental tool of cooperation and socio-economic cohesion. Even the European Union has been considered by the doctrine as a form of partnership between countries. On this topic, see Gianni Bonvicini et al. (eds), *A renewed partnership for Europe* (Nomos Verlag, 1996), who highlights the importance of the notion of partnership in the 'Europeanization' process, and even considers the mass synonyms while referring to the discipline of the Structural Funds. The Cooperation between the Mediterranean Countries was determined by the 1995 Barcelona Declaration. In Italy, the Euro-Mediterranean partnership was deepened by Annalisa di Giovanni, *Il contratto di partenariato pubblico-privato tra sussidiarietà e solidarietà* (Giappichelli, 2012) 5ff.

This feature can be easily transferred to the juridical context as well.

Indeed, we could affirm that the word 'partnership' is used in a legal sense to identify a structured form of economic cooperation: partnership has been legislatively defined as 'the relation which subsists between persons carrying on a business in common with a view of profit'.[42]

The concept of partnership implies a few common characteristics, that can be traced in the legal literature.

Above all, a partnership evokes a strong form of agreement which binds the parties towards a common objective.

The partners are not interchangeable with external parties: 'no one can substitute a stranger in his place without the consent of the others'.[43] This element makes the agreement as stable as an association where 'two or more persons ... jointly own and carry on a business for profit'.[44] In the association, the parties coexist with their own roles and responsibilities and work together for the realization of the object of their contract, sharing roles, responsibilities and, eventually, losses.[45]

It is thus possible to state that the logic behind the legal concept of 'partnership' implies a cooperation, instead of a juxtaposition. In a cooperation, two or more parties commonly set objectives, timeframes, responsibilities and

---

[42]   UK Partnership Act, 1890, sec. 1.

[43]   Mick Woodley, 'Partnership' in *Osborn's concise law dictionary* (11th edition, Thomson Reuters, 2009) 300. Interestingly, some authors underline that the partnership has a strong objective connotation, blurring the subjective features of the members that compose it into the performance of activities related to a specific project, which assumes defining relevance. See, on this point, James Dunn, 'Transportation: policy-level partnerships and project-based partnerships' in Vaillancourt Rosenau (ed.), n 1, 77; Joop Koppenjan and Bert Enserink, 'Public-private partnerships in urban infrastructures: reconciling private sector participation and sustainability' (2009) Public Administration Review 284.

[44]   Brian A Garner, 'Partnership' in *Black's law dictionary* (9th edition, Thomson Reuters, 2009) 1230. The concept of mutual benefit implied in the partnership is evident in the definition provided by Robert Holland, 'The new era in public-private partnership' in Paul Porter and David Sweet (eds), *Rebuilding America's cities: roads to recovery* (Center for Urban Policy Research, 1984). Other definitions underline a more altruistic aim of the partnership, oriented towards the enhancement of general welfare: see Harding, n 21; Nick Bailey, 'Towards a research agenda for public-private partnerships in the 1990s' (1994) Local Economy 292.

[45]   Mick Woodley, 'Partnership' in *Osborn's concise law dictionary* (11th edition, Thomson Reuters, 2009) 300. See also Nathaniel Lindley, *A treatise on the law of partnership* (1881, 8th edition, Sweet and Maxwell, 1912), where it is argued that 'an agreement that something shall be attempted with a view to gain, and that the gain shall be shared by the parties to the agreement, is the grand characteristic of every partnership', 1. The element of risk sharing is evident in the definition provided by John Allan, *Public-private partnership: a review of literature and practice* (Regina, 2001).

activities; they join forces and exploit the different competences and experiences; they share a common goal, work towards the same achievements, solve together the issues that may arise and decide how to share risks and benefits. There is no substitution of tasks and responsibilities but a coexistence of both.

For this reason, as we will more adequately explain in Chapter 4, public private partnership can be differentiated from the concepts of privatization, contracting out and delegation, which all rely on the substitution of the private sector with the public one. Nevertheless, said alternatives to direct public action do not entail cooperation and joint management with the private sector but only functions of programming and control. In contrast, public private partnership entails a strong involvement of both public authorities and the private sector in the execution of a specific activity, for which the concept has been considered as the successor of privatization.[46]

In this sense, public private partnership can be seen as a modern form of governance which resiliently adapts to the changed dynamics of the society and the legal framework, where the traditional binary separations that dominated the legal debate for centuries can no longer hold.[47]

3.2　　The Public Private Antinomy and the Logic of Compromise

The expression 'public private' is a linguistic antinomy, meaning the association of two words of conflicting meaning. As we have already affirmed, the idea of putting the two concepts together is revolutionary as it contrasts with the sharp separation between the public and private worlds.

The term 'public' evokes a collective dimension, the coexistence of a plurality of individuals organized in a social structure. The adjective can be referred to anything 'relating or belonging to an entire community, state or nation'.[48]

In the context of public private partnership, the term refers to public authorities, that is 'bodies or persons exercising functions for public benefit rather than private profit, such as local authorities'.[49] Public bodies are entities that have been entrusted with the care of interests belonging to the community and

---

[46]　Linder, n 2, 20ff.

[47]　On this point, see Jeff Weintraub and Krishan Kumar, *Public and private in thought and practice: perspectives on a grand dichotomy* (University of Chicago Press, 1997).

[48]　Brian A Garner, 'Public' in *Black's law dictionary* (9th edition, Thomson Reuters, 2009) 1348. A similar acceptance of the public partners is assumed by McQuaid et al., n 21. For a broader discussion on the possible definition of public authority, see further n 50.

[49]　Mick Woodley, 'Public authority' in *Osborn's concise law dictionary* (11th edition, Thomson Reuters, 2009) 332.

armed with the power to impact the individuals' sphere of interests in respect of the rule of law. They can only act within the limits of the norms that provide a framework for their activity in the pursuit of the public interest.[50]

By reason of its institutional function, 'the public sector draws attention to public interest, stewardship, and solidarity considerations. It is ... orientated toward social responsibility and environmental awareness ... It has local knowledge and experience with difficult-to-serve populations.'[51]

Conversely, the adjective 'private' refers to a single individual or to its sphere of activities, relationships and interests. The adjective refers to anything 'relating or belonging to an individual, as opposed to the public or the govern-

---

[50] This feature of public authorities can be found in all the legal systems which acknowledge the supremacy of parliament over the government. In common law countries a strong influence was exercised by Albert Venn Dicey, *Introduction to the study of the law of the constitution* (1885, Liberty Fund, 1982), as it is possible to infer from Richard A Cosgrove, *The rule of law: Albert Venn Dicey, Victorian jurist* (The University of North Carolina Press, 1980); Paul Craig, 'Dicey, unitary, self-correcting democracy and public law' (1990) Law Quarterly Report 106. See, for an American account, William F Willoughby, *The government of modern states* (The Century company, 1919); Ernst Freund, *Administrative powers over persons and property: a comparative survey* (University of Chicago Press, 1928); Frank J Goodnow, *Politics and administration: a study in government* (1900, Taylor and Francis, 2017). In Continental Europe, the idea of the legislative power being a condition and a base of administrative activity was affirmed in the nineteenth century, to be deepened and consciously elaborated in the first half of the 1900s. Luca Mannori and Bernardo Sordi, *Storia del diritto amministrativo* (Laterza, 2011) 260ff. On the different receptions of the legality principle, it is possible to refer to the contribution of Charles Eisenmann, 'Le droit administratif et le principe de legalité' (1957) C. d'E., Etudes ed documents 29. A modern account of the principle in the context of the European Union can be found in Alexander Türk, *The concept of legislation in European Community law: a comparative perspective* (Springer, 2006) and, with a more critical approach, in Leonard F M Besselink, Frans Pennings, and Sacha Prechal (eds), *The eclipse of the legality principle in the European Union* (Wolters Kluwer, 2011). For the global perspective see Carol Harlow, 'Global administrative law: the quest for principles and values' (2006) EJIL 187; Giacinto Della Cananea and Aldo Sandulli, *Global standards for public authorities* (Editoriale Scientifica, 2012). That being clarified, it is important to note that the principle of legality is not an obstacle to public authorities' ability to act on the basis of their private law legal capacity, which according to the juridical literature that has looked most closely at these concepts, is to be recognized to all legal entities, both public and private. In this sense, see Sara Valaguzza, *Società miste a partecipazione comunale: ammissibilità e ambiti* (Guiffrè, 2012) and the bibliography cited at 45ff.

[51] Pauline Vaillancourt Rosenau, 'The strengths and weaknesses of public-private policy partnership' in Vaillancourt Rosenau (ed.), n 1, 217, 218. See also David Osborne and Ted Gaebler, *Reinventing government* (Addison-Welsey, 1992) 24.

ment'.[52] In the context of public private partnership, the term refers to private entities, meaning individuals or juridical persons acting in the market on the basis of their free economic initiative, and driven by the interest of making profits.[53]

As has been pointed out in the legal and economic literature, 'the private sector is ... creative and dynamic ... better at performing economic tasks, innovating and replicating successful experiments, adapting to rapid change, abandoning unsuccessful or obsolete activities and performing complex or technical tasks'.[54]

Hence, even at a semantic level, it is possible to detect the fundamental legal issue of public private partnerships: an intrinsically collective and altruistic dimension (the public) encounters an individual and egocentric one (the private).

In any form of partnership, the different inclinations of the parties continue to exist and create both friction and synergies.

When a partnership is 'public private', the friction could become an evident collision, as it brings two spheres that are intrinsically divergent into contact.

In order to achieve a common goal, the two partners must find a compromise, meaning that they have to renounce portions of their interests in order to live together and jointly work in the same direction. The peculiarities of the public and the private spheres will necessarily have to be reciprocally placed in the background if the two parties want to merge in partnership.

A metaphor could be helpful to explain this process: in any love affair, two partners with their own distinct features, beliefs and inclinations must smooth out some aspects of their characters if they willingly decide to agree to live together for a reasonably long period of time. It is a compromise. Likewise, in a public private partnership, the public administrations and the private party must give up bits of their identity if they willingly decide to enter a long-lasting structured legal relationship. Here, though, the 'union' and its compromise are more difficult to achieve, since any jurisdictional limits are imposed by norms and principles that curb the freedom of public administrations to act and that

---

[52] Brian A Garner, 'Private' in *Black's law dictionary* (9th edition, Thomson Reuters, 2009) 1315.

[53] The transnationally accepted constitutional value of economic freedom is particularly evident in Barry R Weingast, 'The economic role of political institutions: market-preserving federalism and economic development' (1995) Journal of Law, Economics, and Organization 1; Bernard H Siegan, *Economic liberties and the constitution* (2nd edition, Routledge, 2009); James Gwartney and Robert Lawson, 'The concept and measurement of economic freedom' (2003) European Journal of Political Economy 405.

[54] Vaillancourt Rosenau (ed.), n 1, 218.

specify the distinctive features and forms of entrepreneurial activity. Still, as we will further analyse (see Chapter 7), public private partnership is able to modify significantly the principles of administrative actions. Indeed, if the public administration welcomes and engages in a common initiative, the rules and principles that guide its actions consequently change.

The study of the modalities, characteristics and limits of said compromise, and of the modifications that it produces on the rules and principles of administrative law, is, in our opinion, one of the most interesting fields for an in-depth legal analysis of public private partnership. Indeed, we believe that it will be possible to comprehend the phenomenon only if we understand the dynamics that bring the public and the private dimensions together and, subsequently, the consequence of said process.

In the modern scenario, characterized by the crisis of the traditional juridical schemes, public and private actors come together driven by centripetal forces.

The failure of the welfare state because of scarcity of resources, loss of national sovereignty and increasing social demands brings public authorities to turn to modern instruments of government and to find allies in the private sector, as well as to escape from a situation of isolation that prevents them performing their tasks.

Conversely, the increasing attention of consumers to the social and environmental issues that are related to production and development necessarily pushes businesses to adopt altruistic approaches and carry out social practices to gain competitive advantage in the market.

Therefore, we could affirm that public authorities seek the private sector to escape from their isolation, which brings about the involvement of private actors in the selection and definition of public interests. Meanwhile, private actors may be interested in carrying out altruistic tasks and taking on policies of corporate social responsibility because the market imposes on them a need to care about social and environmental issues. The mentioned dynamics will be discussed in the following sections.

4   REASONS (AND ADVANTAGES) OF PUBLIC PRIVATE PARTNERSHIP

4.1   Driving Public Authorities out of Their Isolation

Public administrations face numerous issues, such as prioritizing the most significant needs to satisfy an always-increasing public demand; balancing conflicting interests often in a condition of information asymmetry; facing the formalism of regulation and the fragmentation of the normative context; and acting within a lack of economic resources and shortage of personnel.

In order to fulfil their responsibilities, public administrations may find it advantageous to look for additional capacities[55] and to test new institutional arrangements,[56] both by carrying out an inner public reorganization and by initiating alliances with non-governmental actors that see a potential business in taking care of any activities in the interest of the community.

In this way, public private partnership can become a phenomenon that increases the quality and promptness of administrations in fulfilling pressing social demands.[57]

To do so, public administrations open the doors to external entities, asking for help to perform their duties. It is possible to say that public private partnership allows public authorities to get out of their isolation in the satisfaction of public needs.

Indeed, the absolute monopoly over the means to satisfy the ever-increasing requests coming from the administered community, in different public sectors, is a burden for public authorities. Public private partnership offers public administrations an opportunity to share said burden with private actors, which

---

[55]   Frank Biermann and Klaus Dingwerth, 'Global environmental change and the nation state' (2004) Global Environmental Politics 1, 3.

[56]   Frank Biermann et al., 'The overall effects of partnerships for sustainable development: more smoke than fire?' in Philipp Pattberg et al. (eds), *Public-private partnership for sustainable development* (Edward Elgar, 2012) 45. In this perspective, it is worth mentioning the interactive governance theory, which focuses on the connections between public, private and community actors in dealing with the satisfaction of societal needs. The topic is examined more closely in Jurian Edelenbos, 'Institutional implications of interactive governance: insights from Dutch practice' (2005) Governance 111; Tony Bovaird, 'Beyond engagement and participation: user and community co-production of public services' (2007) Public Administration Review 846; Jacob Torfing, *Interactive governance: advancing the paradigm* (Oxford Scholarship, 2012); Jurian Edelenbos and Ingmar van Meerkerk (eds), *Critical reflections on interactive governance: self-organization and participation in public governance* (Edward Elgar, 2016); William Voorberg et al., *Does co-creation impact public service delivery? The importance of state and governance traditions* (2017) Public Money and Management 365.

[57]   On the challenges faced internationally by public administrations underneath the pressure of the public demand for services, see Leigh Robinson, *Following the quality strategy: the reasons for the use of quality management in UK public leisure facilities* (1999) Managing Leisure 201; John I Mwita, 'Performance management model: a systems-based approach to public service quality' (2000) The International Journal of Public Sector Management 19; Sandford Borins, 'Leadership and innovation in the public sector' (2002) Leadership and Organization Development Journal 467; Arawati Agus, Sunita Barker, and Jay Kandampully, 'An exploratory study of service quality in the Malaysian public service sector' (2007) International Journal of Quality and Reliability Management 177; Claudia Carvalho and Carlos Briton, 'Assessing users' perceptions on how to improve public services quality' (2012) Public Management Review 451.

are direct interpreters of the needs of the community (to which they belong) and generally more creative than public entities. In this manner, public administrations find ways to respond to critiques of backwardness and the scarce quality of administrative action.

To exit from responsibility isolation is, from the point of view of the public agent, a fundamental motive to engage in public private partnerships, both in political and managerial terms.

The described process is noteworthy from a public law perspective because it negates the monopoly of government apparatus on the achievement of social outcomes,[58] and, consequently, extends administrative law concepts, such as accountability, to the private sector.[59]

As a matter of fact, through public private partnership private actors share part of their accountability for the care of public tasks on the basis of an agreement with public authorities.[60]

---

[58]   As is evident from the reading of studies on private participation to public policies, among which see: Albert O Hirschman and Robert H Frank, *Shifting involvements: private interest and public action* (Princeton University Press, 2002); Adam McCann et al. (eds), *When private actors contribute to public interests: a law and governance perspective* (Eleven, 2014); Lez Rayman-Bacchus and Philip R Walsh, *Corporate responsibility and sustainable development: exploring the nexus of private and public interests* (Routledge, 2015).

[59]   The issue is underlined especially in Graeme Hodge, 'Accountability in the privatised state' (2004) Alternative Law Journal 4; John Forrer et al., 'Public-private partnerships and the public accountability question' (2010) Public Administration Review 475; Jean Shaoul, Anne Stafford, and Pamela Stapleton, 'Accountability and corporate governance of public private partnerships' (2012) Critical Perspectives on Accounting 213.

[60]   Charles Gilbert, 'The framework of administrative responsibility' (1959) The Journal of Politics 373; Sidney A Shapiro, 'A delegation theory of the APA' (1996) Admin. Law J. Am. U. 89; Björn Bartling and Urs Fischbacher, 'Shifting the blame: on delegation and responsibility' (2012) The Review of Economic Studies 67; Ryan E Carlin and Shane P Singh, 'Executive power and economic accountability' (2015) The Journal of Politics 1031. In this sense, public private partnership is quite different from the experiments of social co-responsibility particularly analysed by the German literature, where the private sector and the public authorities are seen as equally responsible for the actualization of values shared by the community deriving from the pluralistic character of the society and of the juridical framework. See Eberhard Schmidt Aßmann, 'Verwaltungsverantwortung und Verwaltungsgerichtsbarkeit' (1976) VVDStRL 227; Rainer Pitschas, Verwaltungsverantwortung und Verwaltungsverfahren (Monaco, 1990), 235 ss.; Michael Sachs, 'Bürgerverantwortung im demokratischen Verfassungsstaat' (1995) DVBl 873; Andreas Voßkuhle, 'The reform approach in the German science of administrative law' in Matthias Ruffert (ed.), The transformation of administrative law in Europe (Sellier, 2007) 89; Gunnar F Schuppert, 'Verwaltungswissenschaft im Kontext' in Armin von Bogdandy, Sabino Cassese, and Peter M Huber (eds), *Handbuch Ius Publicum Europaeum* (OUP, 2011) 479.

Moreover, if administrative authorities are created and entrusted with power to perform specific tasks of public importance, sharing their power with the private sector means giving up portions of authority in favour of parties that are not democratically accountable and that are motivated by economic interests.

In this sense, it is possible to affirm that public authorities lose portions of their sovereignty in favour of private entities that take on the responsibilities of helping them in the performance of public tasks. Public private partnership makes it acceptable for public authorities to share their powers and responsibilities for the pursuit of public interests with private parties.

This, for many commentators, may pose a threat in terms of subordination of public interest matters to private bias, thus provoking the need for a stronger democratic legitimation of said kinds of juridical operations.[61] And indeed, even in practice it is possible to capture the potential risks of this action by just imagining a private proposal to transform a run-down but historically relevant portion of a city into an amusement park, or to exploit a province's natural resources to produce cosmetic products. In those cases, the economic lever may remove governance over publicly relevant decisions from administrative authority.

Nevertheless, some scholars have stressed how public private partnership is able to promote a new concept of democracy, not pre-legitimized with norms elaborated by elected representatives but arising from the direct consensus of the community towards the outcome of a specific activity:[62] a 'participative' democracy substituted for the representative one.

In this sense, it is necessary to recall that public private partnership is based on the interactions between government and market, between authority and freedom. If the benefits deriving from the unification of public and private strengths are acknowledged, then the way is paved for a common governance in which the community is the protagonist of the management of its own needs.

Moreover, to escape from the isolation in which the public administration is often left, as both victim and perpetrator, means following a strategic and cultural direction that points at preferring cooperation to antagonism, solidarity

---

[61] See William Leach, 'Collaborative public management and democracy: evidence from Western Watershed Partnerships' (2006) Public Administration Review 100; Magdalena Bexell, and Ulrika Mörth (eds), *Democracy and public-private partnerships in global governance* (Palgrave Macmillan, 2010); Pattberg et al., n 1.

[62] See, in particular, Mathias Amilhat, 'Contractualisation, négociation, consensualisme: nouvelles approches du droit public' (2018) Revue française de droit administratif 1, where the process is read in the light of the thoughts expressed in Jürgen Habermas, Isabelle Aubert, and Katia Genel, 'La démocratie a-t-elle encore une dimension épistémique? Recherche empirique et théorie normative' (2013) Participations 151; Jürgen Habermas, *Droit et démocraties* (Nrf Essais, Gallimard, 1997).

and reciprocal satisfaction to selfishness and the contractual creation of value to litigation and inefficiency.

4.1.1 The promotion of participatory democracy

Public private partnership allows public authorities to overcome their limits by establishing fruitful relationships between institutions, economic operators and civil society, thus enabling them to respond to the increasingly complex needs of modern communities.

Public private partnership's ability to involve private operators in the selection of the relevant needs to be satisfied through administrative action implements a more direct approach to the principle of democratic participation.[63]

Indeed, through public private partnership public authorities can involve citizens in political and administrative policy making: citizens and economic operators, as primary interpreters of the needs of the administered community, are able to propose their innovative solutions to public administrations that are competent for their satisfaction.

In this way, private actors become participants of the formation of public interest and promoters of administrative activity, in a virtuous cycle where the supply of public needs is quick and effectively responsive to the demand which generated them. In turn, public administrations find new roads in their duty to govern and in the selection of efficient methods of addressing public needs, relying on the fact that the private company would not generally embark on a counter-productive and inefficient activity.

Through public private partnership, governments are able to face societal complexities by developing interrelations with citizens and organized groups, thus gathering the many different interests and perceptions and more easily evaluating the possible courses of administrative action: 'in these self-organizations, societal actors take the initiative and aim to develop ideas and projects on their own, without (much) interference from governmental and political institutions. In this way, bottom-up initiatives of empowered and highly educated citizens emerge today that are no longer fully initiated,

---

[63] Sherry Arnstein, 'A ladder of citizen participation' (1969) Journal of the American Institute of Planners 216; Carole Pateman, *Participation and democratic theory* (CUP, 1970); Paul Hirst, *Associative democracy: new forms of economic and social* (Wiley-Blackwell, 1994); Benjamin Barber, *Strong democracy* (UC Press, 2004); Donatella della Porta, *Another Europe* (Routledge, 2009); Fabio de Nardis, 'Challenges to democracy and the opportunity of a new participatory governance in the era of trans-local societies' (2014) Journal of Communication 71, 84.

conditioned and controlled by government.'[64] The described dynamics results in a public private co-creation of value.[65]

The last-mentioned concept indicates the production of a benefit for the community which is carried out by public institutions and private actors in partnership. This, according to the authors who have most analysed said forms of governance, produces both social innovation[66] – since new and more efficient answers to the needs of the community derive from the same stakeholders who are the holders of social demands – and government responsiveness, given that the involvement of the 'customers' in the design of the service provision system increases the level of satisfaction.[67]

Indeed, if private companies are excluded from participating in the government of social demands, they will be more inclined to accuse governments of being inefficient and abandon them to face the claims arising from the community alone.

If, on the other hand, private operators are called on through public private partnership to take a leading role in social and economic life, they will be more inclined – also in order to protect their image in the market – to propose innovative solutions and to find synergies rather than generating conflicts.[68]

Responsiveness and effectiveness in delivering answers to social needs thus becomes the method to legitimize public private partnership in a way that puts the authorities responsible for public decisions and the administered community in direct contact.

---

[64]   Jurian Edelenbos and Ingmar van Meerkerk, 'Introduction: three reflecting perspectives on the interactive governance' in Edelenbos and van Meerkerk, n 56, 1, 3.

[65]   Tony Bovaird, 'Beyond engagement and participation: user and community co-production of public services' (2007) Public Administration Review 846; John Alford, *Engaging public sector clients: from service-delivery to co-production* (Palgrave Macmillan, 2009); Bram Verschuere and Victor Pestoff (eds), *New public governance, the third sector and co-production* (Routledge, 2012); John Alford, 'The multiple facets of co-production, building on the work of Elinor Ostrom' (2014) Public Management Review 299; William Voorberg, Victor Bekkers, and Lars Tummers, 'A systematic review of co-creation and co-production, embarking on the social innovation journey' (2015) Public Management Review 1333; William Voorberg et al., 'Does co-creation impact public service delivery? The importance of state and governance traditions' (2017) Public Money and Management 365.

[66]   Eric von Hippel, *Democratizing innovation* (MIT Press, 2005); Christian Bason, *Leading public sector innovation: co-creating for a better society* (The Policy Press, 2010); Eva Sørensen and Jacob Torfing, 'Enhancing collaborative innovation in the public sector' (2011) Administration and Society 842.

[67]   Voorberg, Bekkers and Tummers, n 65.

[68]   Bjorn Nordtveit, 'Use of public-private partnerships to deliver social services: advantages and drawbacks' (Center for International Education Faculty Publications, 2004).

The involvement itself of citizens and private operators in the performance of activities reconnected to public needs is a consequence of a new way of looking at administrative action and the relationship between the public and private spheres. The concepts of authority, imperativeness, self-governance and auto-determination and monopoly over the public interest that have dominated the discourse of administrative law for decades are now giving way to a shared choice and management of public needs.

In this new dimension, the image of an imperative and authoritative public administration, distant and insensitive to private actors' needs gives way to the appreciation of a more harmonious picture in which the differences between public and private actors are not seen as impossible obstacles, but as strengths and instruments of good governance.[69]

4.2   Responsible Enterprises

The business world, as such, is physiologically sensible to society, as it has the role of examining and intercepting the needs and the interests of the community to which it is addressed, intended as a totality of potential addressees of its own activity. Therefore, business may play a fundamental role in pursuing actions that, alongside public authority actions, are directed at the general welfare.

However, the function of businesses is different from those of government and public administrations. If the latter are, as said, institutionally bound to pursue public interests, businesses may or may not carry out activities that intercept the public interest.

This occasional encounter could happen on the basis of a legal obligation, as in the case of legislative obligations to hire a specific number of disabled persons in certain enterprises[70] and of the requirement to acquire certifications of compliance with environmental standards of practices.[71] Also, the mentioned occasional encounter could be provoked by a strategic vision of

---

[69]   See Fritz Scharpf, 'The European social model: coping with the challenges of diversity' (2002) Journal of Common Market Studies 645; Luisa Torchia, *Il governo delle differenze: Il principio di equivalenza nell'ordinamento europeo* (Il Mulino, 2006); Fabio Giglioni, *Governare per differenza: Metodi europei di coordinamento* (Edizioni ETS, 2012).

[70]   For instance, see Italian Law 12 March 1999, No. 68 and Legislative Decree 14 September 2015, No. 151.

[71]   Of the kind discussed in Paul Humphreys et al., 'Integrating environmental criteria into the supplier selection process' (2003) Journal of Materials Processing Technology 349; Anna Nagurney and Fuminori Toyasaki, 'Supply chain supernetworks and environmental criteria' (2003) Transportation Research Part D: Transport and Environment 185.

business. Indeed, enterprises may find it convenient to adhere to said kinds of policy because they may be imposed either by soft regulation or by specific markets, such as the public procurement one. The phenomena of green and social public procurement are indeed based on the concept that enterprises, in order to contract with public administrations imposing specific criteria in their tenders, would be pushed voluntarily to adopt policies and behaviours that are beneficial for the community in which they operate.[72]

Also, businesses may voluntarily direct their efforts to creating social or environmental value because they consider it either convenient for their economic strategy or right from an ethical point of view. Furthermore, economic studies of what is known as corporate social responsibility have highlighted the advantages, both social and economic, that come from the involvement of private operators in initiatives for the community.[73]

According to these findings, especially in times of economic crisis, the enterprises that are better suited to success are the socially responsible ones, meaning the enterprises that, as well as respecting the law, are also strongly accountable towards the community for their work.[74]

---

[72] Among the most complete contributions on the topic, it is possible to quote Charles Edquist et al. (eds), *Public technology procurement and innovation* (Kluwer Academic Publishers, 2000); Christopher McCrudden, 'Using public procurement to achieve social outcomes' (2004) Natural Resources Forum 257; Sue Arrowsmith and Peter Kunzlik (eds), *Social and environmental policies in EC procurement law* (CUP, 2009); Sue Arrowsmith 'A taxonomy of horizontal policies' (2010) Journal of Public Procurement 149; Roberto Caranta and Martin Trybus (eds), *The law of green and social procurement in Europe* (DJØF Publishing, 2010); Geo Quinot, 'Promotion of social policy through public procurement in Africa' in Sue Arrowsmith and Geo Quinot (eds), *Public procurement regulation in Africa* (CUP, 2013).

[73] To cite only a few significant contributions: Archie Carroll, 'Corporate social responsibility: evolution of a definitional construct' (1991) Business and Society 1; Abigail McWilliams and Donald Siegel, 'Corporate social responsibility: a theory of the firm perspective' (2001) Academy of Management Review 1; Dirk Matten and Jeremy Moon, 'Corporate social responsibility' (2004) Journal of Business Ethics 323; Andrew Kakabadse et al. (eds), *Corporate social responsibility: reconciling aspiration with application* (Palgrave Macmillan, 2006); Charlotte Walker-Said and John D Kelly (eds), *Corporate social responsibility? Human rights in the new global economy* (University of Chicago Press, 2015); Andreas Rasche, Mette Morsing, and Jeremy Moon (eds), *Corporate social responsibility: strategy, communication, governance* (CUP, 2017).

[74] Particularly interesting, in the mentioned sense, are the considerations expressed by the Italian literature on the topic. See, in particular, Marco Vitale et al., *Responsabilità nell'impresa* (Piccola Biblioteca d'Impresa Inaz, 2010); Giorgio Carbone, Angelo Ferro, and Marco Vitale, *Spiritualità nell'Impresa* (Piccola Biblioteca d'Impresa Inaz, 2011); Vittorio Coda et al. (eds), *Valori d'impresa in azione* (Egea, 2012). These authors express the view according to which the responsible enterprise is the one which

Studies on corporate social responsibility affirm that the idea that private businesses only pursue the logic of profit is simply wrong. Or, at least, enterprises that only pursue profit do not have a strategic vision for their future and are not able to realize a harmonic complementation between all the dimensions that characterize the society they are part of.[75] Furthermore, enterprises that acknowledge their role as protagonists of the active society and responsible suppliers of social needs are the ones that have a better chance of succeeding in situations of harsh competition.

In the described context, public private partnership is a precious instrument which recognises and promotes businesses as protagonists of society's welfare and creators of public value.

Still, we need to clarify why businesses should be moved to enter into a partnership with public authorities for the creation of public value.

Besides ethical reasons, enterprises may find it convenient to pursue general interests and intercept the public administration responsible for their care.[76] Indeed, private operators may look at public private partnership because they are interested in occupying a sector of the market that otherwise would be reserved to the public authorities.[77] To advance a proposal to an administration gives a strong competitive advantage over competitive enterprises, because of the possibilities disclosed by the partnership with the subject (the public entity) institutionally responsible for the performance of specific public tasks.[78]

---

not only observes the laws but which also embarks in socially valuable activities, being accountable towards the community.

[75] See in particular Marco Vitale, *L'impresa irresponsabile: Nelle antiche radici il suo futuro* (ESD, 2014), where it is affirmed that enterprises that pursue only their profit have a low rate of survival on the long term. Differently, sound businesses are the ethically correct ones.

[76] Julien Damon (ed.), *Intérêt général: Que peut l'entreprise ?* (Institut Montaigne, Paris, 2013) 81.

[77] A similar statement can be found in International Monetary Fund, '*Public-private partnership*' (Washington DC, 2004), where it is affirmed that 'Public-private partnerships (public private partnerships) refer to arrangements where the private sector supplies infrastructure assets and services that traditionally have been provided by the government', 4. Similarly, the European Commission defined public private partnership as '[a]greements that transfer investment projects to the private sector that traditionally have been executed or financed by the public sector'. Commission, Directorate-General for Economic and Financial Affairs 'Public Finances in EMU – 2014' (2014) 144.

[78] The concept is expressed in Peter Drucker, 'Converting social problems into business opportunities: the new meaning of corporate social responsibility' (1984) California Management Review 53; Lance Liebman and Harvey Brooks (eds), *Public private partnership: new opportunities for meeting social needs* (American Academy of Arts and Sciences, 1984).

It is important to stress that this reason is present not only for the realization of infrastructural works. For instance, sponsorship contracts are a clear example of how private operators may abandon the logic of profit maximization to contribute to the creation of public value. In these agreements, businesses intend to exploit a social obligation contracted in favour of society in economic terms. The institution of a local green transportation system or the refurbishment of historic buildings in exchange for the possibility to display its image is an economically valuable bargain for an enterprise willing to expand its social image.

This brief example also brings us to affirm that public private partnership can only thrive between virtuous actors. In theory, no public administration would want to associate its 'public' image with an ethically unsound business. Conversely, no sound business would make any proposal to an inefficient or corrupt administration, because otherwise its company name would be affected by the partnership. In this sense, it is possible to affirm that public private partnership promotes virtuous behaviour, both from the public and the private side.

5   CONCLUSION

Our journey to the exact qualification of the juridical identity of public private partnership – which is useful to avoid the misunderstandings that often populate the debate on said concept – started with the semantic examination of the term 'partnership' and of the public private antinomy.

The first analysis brought us to highlight the revolutionary and 'emotional' strength of public private partnership, which holds together two different and traditionally contrasting dimensions.

The presence of both entities in a partnership requires finding a compromise, the dynamics of which are still unclear and which will be defined only after a reconfiguration of the juridical concept of public private partnership.

In order to start a reasoning on the motives that could bring the two dimensions together, we advanced two theories on why public authorities should involve private actors in the performance of public tasks, and why, conversely, private operators should be interested in pursuing general interests. We proposed that public authorities need to seek aid in the private sector especially to get out of the normative monopoly over the care for specific tasks. Consequently, public authorities allow synergies with the private sector that are legitimized by their efficiency in responding to social needs, according to the idea of participatory democracy.

Furthermore, we affirmed that, based on the economic literature on corporate social responsibility, private operators may have strong economic incentives to associate their images with public authorities, and, more generally, to care about general interests. This, in turn, promotes virtuous behaviour from both sides.

These intuitions can be helpful in setting up the guidelines for our analysis of the features of public private partnership as applied in the economic and juridical context. Given the wide application of public private partnership as a global phenomenon, it is correct, in our opinion, to approach the analytical study from the wider dimension of international relationships, before concentrating on the local scenario. The international dimension of public private partnership is indeed interesting because of the number of relevant legal documents that provide a juridical connotation to the instrument and place it in a strategy achieving public values, within the dimension of sustainable development. Said documents provide a wide and more comprehensive notion of public private partnership, which is less contextualized by the specific features of single jurisdictions, and therefore helps us to set our analysis starting from a wider perspective.

Therefore, we will begin our journey from the international dimension, before tightening our focus on the features of public private partnership in national contexts.

2. Public private partnership's juridical identity: the international dimension

From sustainable development goals to a 'people first' approach

1   INTRODUCTION: PUBLIC PRIVATE
     PARTNERSHIP IN THE INTERNATIONAL
     CONTEXT

For the reasons expressed at the end of the previous chapter, we now begin our investigation, starting from the international dimension.

In the pages of this chapter, we present to the reader the results of our research, highlighting not just the contents of the documents drafted in the context of international collaboration (which will remain the basis of our reasoning), but the spirit that animated and still animates the attention to public private partnership in this dimension.

In the systematic reconstruction of the notion of public private partnership that we are attempting, it is interesting to consider it as an instrument of 'institutional' globalization. With this concept, we intend to describe the spread of international organizations able to study and develop good practices aimed at facilitating the comprehension and the diffusion of juridical and economic tools, based on an informed view derived from the global perspective on their ambit of action.

In the international context, the relevance of public private partnership is mostly political. Public private partnership has been strongly endorsed by international organizations including the United Nations (UN),[1] the Organization

---

[1]   See, United Nations, 'Agenda 21' (United Nations Conference on Environment and Development Rio de Janeiro, Brazil, 3 to 14 June 1992); United Nations General Assembly, 'United Nations Millennium Declaration' (18 September 2000, A/RES/55/2); United Nations, 'Johannesburg Declaration on Sustainable Development' (World Summit on Sustainable Development, September 2002).

for Economic Cooperation and Development,[2] the International Monetary Fund (IMF),[3] UNESCO,[4] and the UN Commission on International Trade Law (UNCITRAL)[5] (to name just a few) as a means to achieve globally significant goals.[6]

According to global sensitivities and policies of international organizations, the promotion of synergies between governments and proactive parts of society has become a primary instrument for sustainable growth.

The strong international appreciation of public private partnership can be explained as a response to the necessity of providing national governments, especially in the most disadvantaged regions, with support in addressing

---

[2]   Organization for Economic Cooperation and Development, 'Participatory Development and good governance, development cooperation guideline series' (OECD Publications, Paris, 1995); Organization for Economic Cooperation and Development, 'Public-private partnerships: in pursuit of risk sharing and value for money' (OECD Publishing, Paris, 2008); Organization for Economic Cooperation and Development, 'Dedicated public-private partnership units: a survey of institutional and governance structures' (OECD Publishing, Paris, 2010); Organization for Economic Cooperation and Development, 'Recommendation of the Council on Principles for Public Governance of Public-Private Partnerships' (Paris, 2012).

[3]   International Monetary Fund, 'Public-private partnerships' (Washington DC, 2004); International Monetary Fund, 'Making public investment more efficient' (Policy Papers, Washington DC, 2015); International Monetary Fund, 'Public-private partnership fiscal risk assessment model: user guide' (Washington DC, 2016); International Monetary Fund, 'IMF Annual report 2017: promoting inclusive growth' (Washington DC, 2017). See also Marco Cangiano et al., 'Public-private partnerships, government guarantees, and fiscal risk' (International Monetary Fund, 2006); Richard Hemming, Gerd Schwartz, and Bernardin Akitoby 'Public investment and public-private partnerships' (International Monetary Fund, 2007); Pawel Gasiorowski and Marian Marian, 'Optimal capital structure of public-private partnerships' (International Monetary Fund, 2008); André de Palma, Guillaume Prunier, and Luc Leruth, 'Towards a principal-agent based typology of risks in public-private partnerships' (International Monetary Fund, 2009); Manabu Nose, 'Enforcing public-private partnership contract: how do fiscal institutions matter?' (International Monetary Fund, 2017); Timothy Irwin, Samah Mazraani, and Sandeep Saxena, 'How to control the fiscal costs of public-private partnerships' (International Monetary Fund, 2018).

[4]   Antoni Verger and Mauro Moschetti, 'Public-private partnerships as an education policy approach: multiple meanings, risks and challenges' (UNESCO Working Paper, 2017).

[5]   United Nations Commission on International Trade Law, 'Model Legislative Provisions on PPPs' and 'Legislative Guide on PPPs', as adopted at the fifty-second session of the Commission (2019).

[6]   For a comprehensive approach, see Benedicte Bull and Desmond McNeill, *Development issues in global governance: public-private partnerships and market multilateralism* (Taylor and Francis, 2006); Liliana Andonova, *Governance entrepreneurs: international organizations and the rise of global public-private partnerships* (CUP, 2017).

globally sensitive goals such as poverty eradication, resource security and environmental protection for the benefit of future generations which, in developing countries, could not be met without an interplay between public action and business involvement.

The international community started to become aware of the value of public and private cooperation to achieve sustainable development goals at the Johannesburg Summit of 2002.[7]

This event was the first time where it was strongly affirmed that the ambitious objectives of poverty eradication, combating climate change, environmental protection, equity promotion and human rights protection could be effectively pursued in public private partnerships based on a 'win-win' logic bringing gains both for the private sector and for public authorities.

The Johannesburg Declaration clearly stated that change in building human dignity and ensuring essential levels of clean water, food, sanitation, adequate shelter and energy could be achieved by investing in 'human solidarity', 'constructive partnerships', and valorization of peoples' differences.[8]

The participation of enterprises, individuals and associations in performing activities of general interest was, in this view, part of a global call for solidarity to people and to the planet in creating the premises for a better world for future generations.

Since then, public private partnership spread across the world, being promoted by a vast array of international organizations as an instrument capable of producing public value through solidarity, until being recognized by the United Nations' 2030 Agenda for Sustainable Development as the principal instrument to achieve globally sustainable development.[9]

---

[7]   Svetalana Maslova, 'The new Russian law on PPP: breakthrough or throwback' (2012) Eur. Procurement and Pub. Private Partnership Law Review 268; John Dernbach, 'Making sustainable development happen: from Johannesburg to Albany' (2004) Alb. Law Envt'l Outlook 173, according to whom 'the intention of the Johannesburg Summit was to encourage partnerships between governments and non-governmental bodies by achieving sustainable development in specific ways and specific places'. See also Jan Martin Witte and Charlotte Streck, 'Introduction to progress or peril? Partnership and networks in Global environmental governance: the post-Johannesburg agenda' (Global Public Policy Institute, Washington DC, 2003); Jacob Scherr and R Juge Gregg, 'Johannesburg and beyond: the 2002 World Summit on Sustainable Development and the rise of partnership' (2006) Geo. Int'l Envt'l Review 425; Henning Grosse Ruse-Khan, 'A real partnership for development: sustainable development as treaty objective in Europe economic partnership agreements and beyond' (2010) J. Int'l Econ. Law 13.
[8]   United Nations, 'The Johannesburg Declaration on Sustainable Development' (Johannesburg, 2002) para 16.
[9]   United Nations, 'Transforming our world: the 2030 Agenda for Sustainable Development' (Resolution adopted by the General Assembly on 25 September 2015).

Therefore, as will be demonstrated, public private partnership in the international sphere is mainly intended as an instrument to achieve precise goals related to sustainable development.

2   PUBLIC PRIVATE PARTNERSHIP FOR SUSTAINABLE DEVELOPMENT

In the international arena, public private partnership is a fundamental instrument of interaction between society – cumulatively considered[10] – and political actors, favouring transnational interventions of interest groups, international organizations and business groups in the production of public value.

Guaranteeing healthy lives, promoting quality education, ensuring access to water and affordable, reliable sustainable and modern energy for all, and making cities inclusive, safe and resilient is not possible without a contribution from the business sector. Yet, especially in developing countries, the economic gap is so critical that it cannot be solved through traditional public procurement methods, as it would impose an excessive burden on the public finances and limit the participation of external investors.[11] So, public private partnership becomes a viable and interesting alternative in order to make progress.

In fact, public private partnership internationally has enabled countries to accomplish fundamental targets of development in almost all the relevant fields of sustainable growth, including agriculture, health care, education and transportation.

At a theoretical level, it must be underlined that public private partnership has been able to adapt to each and every one of its disparate sectors of application, showing distinctive qualities in all of them.

In the agricultural sector, public private partnership is currently widely adopted to develop agricultural value chains, promote research and technology

---

[10]   Transnational partnerships could be both public public and public private: multiple actors of different natures may interact and merge in different forms, to carry out activities that are consistent with international agreements or with the scopes and inclinations of the involved organizations. Nevertheless, in the international context, the subjective connotation of a specific project is linked to its outcomes in terms of the ability to positively affect countries' populations, more than to the public or private nature of the involved actors. The focus then shifts to the objective dimension and, specifically, to the aim of the partnership's object, in terms of satisfaction of relevant interests, becoming intrinsically linked to the goals of sustainable development.

[11]   Irina Zapatrina, 'Sustainable Development Goals for developing economies and public-private partnership' (2006) Eur. Procurement and Pub. Private Partnership Law Review 39.

transfer, build infrastructure and deliver services to farmers and small enter-prises, with the aim of ending hunger and achieving global food security.[12]

Significant projects of public private partnership in the agricultural busi-ness sector have received the direct support of the Food and Agriculture Organization (FAO) for their capacity to stimulate rural economies in remote or socially unstable regions of the world.[13] Such initiatives show the ability of public private partnership to open rural and underdeveloped contexts to the world, calling businesses to a social responsibility which transcends national barriers and bringing them to work in conjunction with local authorities and local communities, for the good of the population.

Health care has also been a primary field of experimentation for public private partnerships, both in building hospitals and in providing medical services.[14]

Concession contracts are broadly used for financing, building, maintaining and managing clinical facilities,[15] and the creativity and organizational capac-ity of businesses have often been exploited themselves by public authorities to provide medical services in publicly owned facilities.

A successful example was carried out in 2015 by the Bangladeshi govern-ment, with the aid of the Finance Corporation of the World Bank, aiming at addressing the shortage of dialysis capacity to treat kidney disease. In this case, the government selected a private operator through public tender, who designed, refurbished and installed more than one hundred dialysis stations in

---

[12]   To cite a few noteworthy contributions on the topic, see: James Clive, 'Agricultural research and development: the need for public-private sector partnerships' (1996) Issues in Agriculture 9; Peter Hazell and Lawrence Haddad, 'Agricultural research and poverty reduction' (International Food Policy Research Institute, Washington, DC, 2001); World Economic Forum, 'African food security: a role for public private part-nership' (World Economic Forum Africa Economic Summit 2003).

[13]   It is possible to refer to Marlo Rankin et al., 'Public-private partnerships for agri-business development: a review of international experiences' (Food and Agriculture Organization of the United Nations, Rome, 2016).

[14]   See, above all, Kent Buse and Gill Walt, 'Global public-private partnerships: part II. What are the health issues for global governance?' (2000) Bulletin of the World Health Organization 699; Roy Widdus, 'Public-private partnerships for health: their main targets, their diversity and their future directions' (2001) Bulletin of the World Health Organization: The International Journal of Public Health 713; Michael Reich (ed.), *Public-private partnerships for public health* (Harvard University Press, 2002).

[15]   The scheme was used, for example, in the case of the Konya Integrated Health Campus in Turkey. See International Bank for Reconstruction and Development, The World Bank, 'Mobilizing Islamic finance for infrastructure public-private partnerships' (Washington DC, 2017) 45ff.

exchange for the operation of the service for patients at a fixed tariff.[16] As this case clearly shows, the emphasis on service quality that public private partnership implicates allows public authorities to match the completion of specific projects with the achievement of policy targets and to enhance the value of their performance, for the benefit of the community.

Quality enhancement of an essential service is evident in the educational sector as well. Here, the promotion of quality in the provision of the service is considered the central goal of public private partnership projects, which implies not only the creation of adequate facilities, but also the application of organizational capacities and amelioration of the level of teaching staff.[17] To this end, public private partnership has been used for the management of schools in schemes that allow governments to reduce investments in the operation and maintenance of educational facilities.[18]

Lastly, the application of public private partnership in the transportation sector allows us to emphasize its ability to achieve multiple values with one single action. Indeed, attaining a smart and modern transportation infrastructure system allows for pollution reduction, greenhouse gas emission reduction, and increases in security and the quality of people's lives, as well as an increase in employment opportunities for local communities, thereby encouraging income equality.

An interesting example here comes from Indonesia: building a rapid transit bus line in Jakarta provided a solution to the city's congestion, reduced emissions of pollutants and greenhouse gases, and increased economic development of the site by providing faster transportation means to the community.[19]

The versatility of public private partnership – that emerges from this discussion – along with its inclusiveness and capacity indirectly to promote socially or environmentally valuable behaviours are precisely the characteristics that led to its adoption as the primary instrument of achieving sustainable development goals. The increasing complexity of goals, interests and values that have to be considered in administrative activity has in turn called for the elaboration of highly detailed contractual schemes.

---

[16]   IFC Advisory Services in Public-Private Partnerships, 'Public-private partnership stories: Bangladesh: Bangladesh dialysis centers' (Washington DC, 2015).

[17]   United Nations Economic and Social Commission for Asia and the Pacific, 'Country guidance: public-private partnerships for sustainable development in Asia and the Pacific' (Washington DC, 2017) 24.

[18]   Monazza Aslam, Shenila Rawal, and Sahar Saeed, 'Public-private partnerships in education in developing countries: a rigorous review of the evidence' (Ark Education Partnerships Group, London, 2017).

[19]   Dail Umamil Asri and Budi Hidayat, 'Current transportation issues in Jakarta and its impacts on environment' (National Development Planning Agency, Republic of Indonesia, Jakarta, 2005).

Public procurement – even 'green' or 'social' – projects[20] are often not comparably able to provide answers to multiple social needs, being characterized by typical contracts and formal procedures.[21]

---

[20]   In the last decade, the public contracts market has been more and more orientated towards strategic objectives of social and environmental relevance. In the European context, contracting authorities have been considered as primary actors in the promotion of 'a highly competitive social market economy, aiming at full employment and social progress, and a high level of protection and improvement of the quality of the environment' (See Article 3, para 3 of the Treaty of the European Union.). The 2014 Directives of public contract are clearly pervaded by the strategic goals of a smart, sustainable and inclusive growth set by the Commission since the Communication of 3 March 2010. See Recital No. 2 of the Directive 2014/24/EU of the European Parliament and of the Council of 26 February 2014. This means that the regulation of the public contracts market is orientated not just (at least not any more) to competition but towards the achievement of specific goals of environmental and social importance. Through public contracts, contracting authorities are indeed able to promote public values, for example by imposing specific technical requirements in the tender or adding value to 'green' solutions (e.g. in works or production). In this regard, it has been noted that 'the European law has developed an approach that is coherent with sustainable development and that has even heled to craft it'. See Sara Valaguzza, *Sustainable development in public contracts: an example of strategic regulation* (Editoriale Scientifica, 2016). Sustainable development has thus become a guiding principle of public contracts; a macro-value that is able to cut through the regulation of the sector, requiring the contracting authority to consider the future social and environmental impact of their procurement choices. On the topic, some of the most comprehensive comments include Gustavo Piga and Tunde Tatrai, *Public procurement policy* (Routledge, 2015); Colleen Theron and Malcolm Dowden, *Strategic sustainable procurement: law and best practice for the public and private sectors* (Routledge, 2017); Gabriel Popescu, *Agrifood economics and sustainable development in contemporary society* (IGI Global, 2019); Rajesh Kumar Shakya (ed.), *Green public procurement strategies for environmental sustainability* (IGI Global, 2019). The described phenomenon is not only limited to Europe. In Asia, the necessity to deal with overpopulation and increasing pollution has recently pushed the most advanced economies of the area (such as China, Japan, and South Korea) to modify public policies and to promote soft regulations in the public procurement sector, to promote the involvement of civil societies to respond to massive urbanization, increasing air pollution and wealth inequalities. See Yong Geng and Brent Doberstein, 'Greening government procurement in developing countries: building capacity in China' (2008) Journal of Environmental Management 932; Linda Ho, Nicholas Dickinson, and Gilbert Chan, 'Green procurement in the Asian public sector and the Hong Kong private sector' (2010) Natural Resources Forum 24; Mengxing Lu, *Corporate social and environmental responsibility: another road to China's sustainable development* (Brill Nijhoff, 2019); Annamaria La Chimia and Peter Trepte (eds), *Public procurement and aid effectiveness: a roadmap under construction* (Hart Publishing, 2019).

[21]   The socially oriented character of the public contracts regulation necessarily requires a certain flexibility and the need to find innovative solutions and model of development, able to improve economic growth in a sustainable manner. For this

In contrast, it is internationally recognized that public private partnership allows the creativity of businesses to express itself in atypical agreements and contractual forms, which consider multiple activities, responsibilities and tasks, to be achieved through the involvement of local communities and governments, thus promoting good governance, stability and social inclusion.[22]

Its intrinsic flexibility and its objective characterization stimulate the finding of new solutions from the market and the participation of stakeholders and international organizations, with supporting and financing roles.

The need to find innovative solutions to issues that fall under the government's responsibility increases the value of partnership with the private sector. In this context, public private cooperation is aimed at researching innovative procedures through recourse to private resources and know-how.

Given that public private partnership does not begin with a pre-determination of technical requirements of the answers to specific needs of the community, the actors of the agreement are pushed to find innovative solutions, unlike those that can be purchased on the market. The confrontation between ideas, skills and techniques belonging to both the government machinery and the private sector enhances innovative thinking and creativity, to the benefit of the beneficiary community.[23]

This is why, especially in the most technologically advanced sectors (e.g. information and communication technologies (ICT), sustainable means of transportation, urban planning, etc.), innovation and efficiency can be achieved through public private partnership.

This application of public private partnership is not new. Already in 2002, the Organization for Economic Cooperation and Development Committee for Science and Technology Policy had already defined public private partnership for innovation as 'any formal relationship or agreement for a fixed or infinite period of time, between public and private actors, in which both sides cooperate in the decision-making process and co-invest limited resources, such as

---

reason, public private partnership is considered a more appropriate instrument to achieve sustainable development. See, in particular, Beate Sjåfjell and Anja Wiesbrock (eds), *Sustainable public procurement under EU law: new perspectives on the state as stakeholder* (CUP, 2016) and Kwame Sundaram Jomo et al., 'Public-private partnerships and the 2030 Agenda for Sustainable Development: fit for purpose?' (UN Department of Economic and Social Affairs (DESA) Working Papers, No. 148, UN, New York, 2016).

[22] Indeed, public private partnership creates 'powerful incentives for job creation, entrepreneurship and innovation development, scientific and technological capacity improvement, forming an agreeable atmosphere in society based on trust and understanding'. Zapatrina, n 11, 40.

[23] Fanny Saruchera and Maxwell Phiri, 'Technological innovations performance and public-private partnerships' (2016) Corporate Ownership and Control 549.

money, personnel, equipment and information, to achieve specific goals in a specific area of science, technology and innovation'.[24]

In this light, public private partnership was intended as an instrument aimed at the development of scientific and technological innovation, through the formation of new ideas via collaboration of government with ICT companies.

In the last decade, innovative forms of governance such as e-governance platforms, remote health care and intelligent transport have been implemented through public private partnership.[25]

In fact, the sustainable development goals which guide the international dimension of public private partnership find an undisputable resource in technologies and innovation as promoters of a smart inclusive and green growth.

Furthermore, public private partnership encourages interested parties to participate in the care of their own needs. Private persons, businesses and stakeholders are not seen just as recipients of commands, sanctions and impositions, but they are directly involved in the discussion and shaping of administrative policy.

This is a very important point to emphasize, because it highlights the positive interaction between the democratic spirit and the global action of international organizations and public private partnership.

With public private partnership, international organizations, local authorities and businesses transversally pursue their mandate by promoting initiatives, suggesting strategies and participating in specific projects with a strong impact on environmental and social targets.

This perspective introduces us to a distinctive feature of public private partnership in the international sphere, namely the presence of an extensive network of actors, at times external to governments and businesses, revolving around a specific project of general relevance.

3   GOAL-ORIENTED NETWORKS

As the United Nations' Agenda 21 stated: 'We are confronted with a perpetuation of disparities between and within nations, a worsening of poverty, hunger,

---

[24]   For a comment, see Elvira Akhmetshina and Ashkar Mustafin, 'Public-private partnership as a tool for development of innovative economy' (2015) Procedia Economics and Finance 35, 36.

[25]   Louis Witters, Revital Marom, and Kurt Steinert, 'The role of public-private partnerships in driving innovation' in Soumitra Dutta, *The Global Innovation Index 2012: stronger innovation linkages for global growth* (INSEAD and World Intellectual Property Organization, 2012) 81. In the report, the authors discuss the cases of three individual cities around the world (namely, Oulu in Finland, Dubuque in the USA, and Beijing in China), which applied public private partnership for urban development.

ill health and illiteracy, and the continuing deterioration of the ecosystems on which we depend for our well-being ... No nation can achieve this on its own; but together we can, in a global partnership for sustainable development.'[26]

The previous statement acknowledges that it is impossible for governments – especially the ones with the most economic and growth disadvantages – to face on their own the problems that humanity is currently confronting.

Thus, it is possible to affirm that public private partnership is a method that allows non-state actors to take part in the dynamics of international relations[27] for the achievement of specific development goals.[28]

In the international arena, therefore, public private partnerships assume a strong 'objective' characterization, being qualified by their final aim.

The stronger the attraction of a project's aim in social terms, the higher the chances of involving interested parties that are transnationally active in representing and promoting specific values.

Consequently, international public private partnership will likely involve not only governments and businesses but also representatives from transnational civil society,[29] advocacy groups,[30] non-governmental entities[31] and international financing institutions.

All these subjects are pulled together by the centripetal force of the aim of the project, which temporarily brings together parties with very different connotations, competences and inclination, for the production of public value.

This feature is a specific characteristic of public private partnership which, more than other forms of procurement,[32] is able to open the doors to positive external contributions.

---

[26] United Nations, 'Agenda 21', n 1, Preamble.

[27] Stephen Linder and Pauline Vaillancourt Rosenau, 'Mapping the terrain of the public-private policy partnership' in Pauline Vaillancourt Rosenau (ed.), *Public-private policy partnerships* (MIT Press, 2000) 1, 5.

[28] Margaret Young and Sebastian Sullivan, 'Evolution through the duty to cooperate: implications of the whaling case at the International Court of Justice' (2015) Melbourne J. of Int'l Law 327; Rebecca Dowd and Jane McAdam, 'International cooperation and responsibility sharing to combat climate change: lessons for international refugee law' (2017) Melbourne J. of Int'l Law 18.

[29] Ann Florini, *The third force: the rise of transnational civil society* (Japan Center for International Exchange – Carnegie Endowment for International Peace, 2000).

[30] See Margaret Keck and Kathryn Sikkink, *Activists beyond borders: transnational advocacy networks in international politics* (Cornell University Press, 1998).

[31] Bas Arts, *The political influence of global NGOs: case studies on the climate and biodiversity conventions* (International Books, 1998).

[32] Public procurement tends to exclude the public administration from exterior inputs: administrative authorities select relevant interests, evaluate and balance different courses of action, and take decisions on the basis of their own knowledge, skills and

As a metaphor, it could be useful to describe international public private partnerships as spontaneous and temporary goal-oriented networks,[33] where 'each participant brings its core competence to [a] temporary organization that will exist until the project that brings the network together is completed'.[34]

In the networks of public private partnership, parties occasionally and temporarily agree to collaborate to achieve a goal of transnational relevance[35] – or even national relevance, but with global implication.

The network creates an alliance of entities with different features, competences, resources and expertise which can pull together energies for the production of a specific outcome. This feature is particularly interesting in the optic of bringing added value to national governments.

Within the network, relationships are not rigid but follow the fluid circulation of knowledge, experiences and information. This is consistent with the scope of international organizations, which are directly involved in overcoming the inflexibilities imposed by official inter-state relationships.

---

expertise. Extensive discussion on the point can be found in Albert Graells, *Public procurement and the EU competition rules* (Hart Publishing, 2011) 33ff.

[33]   The concept of network in the global arena is deepened in particular by Armin von Bogdandy and Philipp Dann, 'International composite administration: conceptualizing multi-level and network aspects in the exercise of international public authority' (2008) German Law Journal 2013; Paul Craig, 'Global networks and shared administration' in Sabino Cassese (ed.), *Research handbook on global administrative law* (Edward Elgar, 2016) 153. For the European declination of the concept, see Tanja Börzel, 'Policy networks, a new paradigm for European governance?' (1997) RSC 5; Renaud Dehousse, 'Regulation by networks in the European Community: the role of European agencies' (1997) JEPP 246; Anne-Marie Slaughter, 'Governing the global economy through government networks' in Michael Byers (ed.), *The role of law in international politics: essays in international relations and international law* (OUP, 2000) 177; Maartje de Visser, 'Network-based governance in EC law: the example of EC competition and EC communications law' (Bloomsbury Professional, 2009). Specifically on public private partnership, see John Kamensky and Thomas Burlin (eds), *Collaborations: using networks and partnerships* (IBM Center for The Business of Government, 2004).

[34]   See Emily Weitzenbock, *A legal framework for emerging business models: dynamic networks as collaborative contracts* (Edward Elgar, 2012) 5. The term 'network' is used, with specific reference to public private partnership, in Renate Mayntz, 'Common goods and governance' in Adrienne Heritier (ed.), *Common goods, reinventing European and international governance* (Rowman and Littlefield) 15 and Tanja Börzel, 'Organizing Babylon: on the different conceptions of policy networks' (1998) Public Administration 253.

[35]   On this point, see Motoko Mekata, 'Building partnerships toward a common goal: experiences of the international campaign to ban landmines' in Ann Florini (ed.), *The third force: the rise of transnational civil society* (Japan Center for International Exchange – Carnegie Endowment for International Peace, 2000) 143.

In this regard, public private partnership has been considered as 'a solution to deadlocked intergovernmental negotiations, to ineffective treaties and overly bureaucratic international organizations, to power-based state policies, corrupt elites and many other real or perceived current problems of sustainability transition'.[36]

In other words, public private partnership can be seen as the modern key to substitute old-fashioned and bureaucratic international relationships, based on hard-law treaties and confrontations among sovereign states, with efficient and non-structured relationships among all the productive components of the international community.

The flexible approach of public private partnership has been particularly appreciated especially after the analysis of the disappointing results of some international treaties in delivering the intended environmental and social results.[37]

Instead of compliance control of binding transnational agreements – often becoming extremely burdensome and scarcely effective – public private partnership offers voluntary allegiance from the private parties, driven by the market to carry out socially and environmentally sound policies.

4   THE ACTORS OF THE INTERNATIONAL PARTNERSHIPS' NETWORKS

It would be neither possible nor consistent with the scope of our research to classify all the possible entities that may participate in an international public

---

[36]   Philipp Pattberg, 'Introduction: partnerships for sustainable development' in Philipp Pattberg et al. (eds), *Public-private partnerships for sustainable development* (Edward Elgar, 2012) 1.

[37]   The reference is, in particular, to the disappointment of the academic world in analysing the results of the Kyoto Protocol. For look at the debate on the outcomes of the Kyoto Protocol as an example of an imperative treaty on environmental issues, see Gene Grossman and Alan Krueger, 'Economic growth and the environment' (1995) Quarterly Journal of Economics 353; Cass Sunstein, 'Of Montreal and Kyoto: a tale of two protocols' (2007) Harvard Environmental Law Review 1; Sammy Zahran et al., 'Ecological development and global climate change: a cross-national study of Kyoto Protocol ratification' (2007) Society and Natural Resources 37; Hiroki Iwata and Keisuke Okada, 'Greenhouse gas emissions and the role of the Kyoto Protocol' (MPRA Paper No. 22299, Munich Personal RePEc Archive, Munich, 2010); Gerald Kutney, *Carbon politics and the failure of the Kyoto protocol* (Routledge, 2014); Amanda Rosen, 'The wrong solution at the right time: the failure of the Kyoto Protocol on Climate Change' (2015) Politics and Policies 30; Nicole Grunewald and Inmaculada Martinez-Zarzoso, 'Did the Kyoto Protocol fail? An evaluation of the effect of the Kyoto Protocol on CO_2 emissions' (2016) Env. and Dev. Econ. 1.

private partnership. Our intention here is to find a conceptualization that expresses general features of their identity.

In this direction, we consider it worthwhile to deepen the analysis of at least two specific kinds of international partnership actor, namely non-governmental organizations and international financial institutions, because both are key players of the international networks of partnership, being respectively the promoters of social and environmental values connected to the project and the providers of financial resources and expertise.

As will be discussed, their relevance in the international dimension of public private partnership transcends the roles they may assume in specific projects; indeed, they are also responsible for the creation and support of an international culture of public private partnership.

4.1   The Role of International Financing Institutions

In conditions of political instability or lack of expertise at the public authorities involved, public private partnerships are usually carried out through the support of international organizations that grant support, counsel and financial resources.

This is why transnational public private partnerships have been increasingly promoted by multilateral development banks[38] such as the World Bank,[39] the

---

[38]   For a comment on the role of multilateral development banks in the public procurement market it is possible to refer to the comprehensive study of Sope Williams-Elegbe, *Public procurement and multilateral development banks* (Hart Publishing, 2017).

[39]   The supporting role played by the World Bank Group in relation to public private partnerships is evident from the reading of World Bank Group, Independent Evaluation Group, 'World Bank Group support to public-private partnerships: lessons from experience in client countries' (Washington DC, 2015). The International Bank for Reconstruction and Development and the World Bank Group also developed an instrument of fundamental importance for practitioners: the 'Public-Private Partnerships. Reference Guide Version 3.0' 3rd edition (2017) and promoted specific projects of research on the topic. See, *inter alia*, Elisabetta Iossa, Giancarlo Spagnolo, and Mercedes Vellez, 'Best practices on contract design in public-private partnerships' (Washington, DC: World Bank, 2007) 40; Edward Farquharson, Clemencia Torres de Mästle, and Edward R Yescombe, 'How to engage with the private sector in public-private partnerships in emerging markets' (The World Bank, 2011) 145; Maria Jose Romero, 'Where is the public in PPPs? Analysing the World Bank's support for public-private partnerships' (Bretton Woods Observer, 2014); Aldo Caliari et al., 'What standards for public-private partnerships (PPPs)? Analysing the role of the World Bank Group' (Bretton Woods Project, 2016); International Bank for Reconstruction and Development, The World Bank. 'Procuring infrastructure public-private partnerships' (Washington DC, 2018).

Asian Development Bank[40] and the European Bank for Reconstruction and Development.[41]

Founded to foster economic and social development by providing financial resources to carry out specific projects that could stimulate economic growth and reduce inequalities, multilateral development banks have been promoting public private partnership as a tool that could reduce governmental and infrastructural gaps, by promoting efficient and quality service delivery.[42]

Public private partnership is particularly appreciated by these institutions because: (1) it delivers an efficient use of resources over the lifetime of a pro-

---

[40] Emblematic is the Asian Development Bank, 'Public-Private Partnership Operational Plan 2012–2020' (2012) 10. On the organization and functioning of the institution, it is worth mentioning the contributions of Robert Nielsen, 'The establishment and operations of the Asian Development Bank' (1970) Colum. J. Transnat'l Law 81; John Boyd, 'From Rio to Johannesburg: a review of Asian Development Bank environmental practice and policy' (2002) Sing. J. Int'l and Comp. Law 723. Specifically on the promotion of public private partnership, see Peter Illig, 'The role of non-government organizations in the development of environmental policy at the Asian Development Bank' (1994) Buff. J. Int'l Law 47; Alfredo Pascual, 'Private sector participation in infrastructure: experience in Asia and the role of the Asian Development Bank.' (2004) Transnat'l Law 107; Ashley Lee, 'Taming Asia's legal frontiers: the Asian Development Bank's General Counsel explains how the bank's technical assistance programmes are improving the investment framework of the region's emerging markets' (2014) Int'l Fin. Law Review 24.

[41] The leading role of the institution in the promotion of public private partnership appears evident in the following contributions: Rebecca Nelson, 'Multilateral development banks, transparency and corporate clients: "public-private partnerships" and public access to information' (2003) Public Administration and Development 249; Darrin Grimsey and Mervyn Lewis, *Public private partnerships: the worldwide revolution in infrastructure provision and project finance* (Edward Elgar, 2004); Gerd Schwartz, Ana Corbacho, and Katja Funke (eds), *Public investment and public-private partnerships* (Palgrave Macmillan, 2008).

[42] See, in particular, Bruce Rich, 'The multilateral development banks, environmental policy, and the United States' (1984) Ecology Law Q. 684; Jose Castaneda, 'The World Bank adopts environmental impact assessments' (1992) Pace Y B Int'l Law 241; Jonathan Sanford, 'US policy toward the multilateral development banks: the role of Congress' (1988) Geo. Wash. J. Int'l Law and Econ. 2; Izelde van Jaarsveld, 'International banking: the world bank and other financial institutions' (2000) Juta's Business Law 160; Sabine Schlemmer-Schulte, 'The impact of civil society on the World Bank, the International Monetary Fund and the World Trade Organization: the case of the World Bank' (2000) ILSA J. Int'l and Comp. Law 401; John Head, 'Law and policy in international financial institutions: the changing role of law in the IMF and the multilateral developments banks' (2007) Kan. J. Law and Pub. Pol'y 201; Leonardo Crippa, 'Multilateral development banks and human rights responsibility' (2010) Am. U. Int'l Law Review 533.

ject;[43] (2) it incentivizes taking into account the costs of the whole life of an asset and thoroughly evaluating the risks;[44] and (3) it is more open to scrutiny than public procurement, since 'the public authority will face scrutiny by parties outside government, such as lenders and investors, whose capital will be at risk over the long term, depending on the performance of service delivery',[45] thus enabling greater levels of quality assurance.

Consequently, multilateral development banks directly promote specific projects that are consistent with the institution's mission of assisting growth in developing countries.[46]

The goal of risk mitigation is usually achieved either by direct financial support from the international institutions or through risk mitigation instruments, which are 'financial instruments that transfer certain defined risks from project financiers (lenders and equity investors) to creditworthy third parties (guarantors and insurers) that have a better capacity to accept such risks'.[47] Said instruments are able to facilitate the mobilization of private capital, especially in those countries that encounter difficulties in acquiring debt.

---

[43]   Indeed, 'the private partner has an incentive to consider the long-term implications of the costs of design and construction quality or the costs of expansion in the case of existing facilities': Farquharson, Torres de Mästle, and Yescombe, n 39, 4.

[44]   Ibid.

[45]   Ibid.

[46]   A leading role in providing technical resources to governments willing to undertake public private partnerships has been recently assumed by the World Bank Group. In this institution's strategies, public private partnership is regarded as a solution to implement policies of infrastructure realization and essential service delivery. Farquharson, Torres de Mästle, and Yescombe, n 39, 145. Within the Group, the Multilateral Investment Guarantees Agency assumes a key role in supporting investments into poor and conflict-afflicted nations. Acting as a catalyst for investments and guaranteeing financial coverage to reduce the risks of transfer restriction, expropriation, war and civil disturbance, said agency is a world leader in the promotion of public private partnerships in developing countries. Recently, the Multilateral Investment Guarantees provided for the building of a 1.5 km bridge in the city of Abidjan, Côte d'Ivoire, that will 'reduce congestion and pollution … and will result in a reduction of carbon dioxide emissions due to lower fuel consumption'. A more technical approach is assumed by the International Finance Corporation, which advises governments of the regions with highest needs on implementing public private partnership, providing technical, legal and economic assistance in projects in the field of agriculture, education, health and water, to name a few. The institution provides assistance to governments in the structuring of the project, in the evaluation of the technical and financial aspects of the agreement, suggesting solutions to make it accountable, sound and sustainable, as well as providing support in the bidding process for the selection of the private partner. Caliari et al., n 39; Romero, n 39.

[47]   Tomoko Matsukawa and Odo Habeck, 'Review of risk mitigation instruments for infrastructure financing and recent trends and developments' (The International Bank for Reconstruction and Development, The World Bank, 2007), xi.

In turn, the participation of multilateral development banks in public private partnership projects is highly valued by public and private parties as it improves the credibility of a project. By assuming portions of a project's risks, financial institutions reassure the private partners on the potential economic returns of their investments.[48]

It has been affirmed that international financing institutions support public private partnership to upgrade the credibility of a specific country as a borrower and to create networks of businesses and organizations interested in promoting development.[49]

However, the academic reasoning on the topic has underlined some issues related to the involvement of multilateral development banks in the financing of procurement projects. In particular, it has been underlined that the method and process for identifying projects that require financing from multilateral development banks is often unclear and that the limited supervision on how the loans are spent 'resulted in the wastage and loss of loans to corruption, theft and incompetent procurement'.[50] This does not affect the borrower's right to repayment but does affect the community as supposed beneficiary of the financed intervention.[51]

Given the strong dependency on international financial institutions' resources and expertise, the mentioned issues can dangerously undermine the possible positive outcomes that public private partnership may have in the international scenario. In this regard, the participation of non-governmental organizations can tame the financing institutions' dominant roles in partnership projects.

4.2   The Role of Non-governmental Organizations

Non-governmental organizations cover the wide area between the market and the state.[52]

---

[48]   Ion Ghizdeanu, 'International experiences to stimulate PPPs' (2012) Rom. Pub.-Priv. Partnership Law Review 36.

[49]   Ibid; Zapatrina, n 11, 40. Here, it is affirmed that businesses and financial institutions invest in countries that they can rely on, in terms of political stability and absence of military conflicts. In this sense, the promotion of international partnerships could have the beneficial outcomes to reduce bribery, to develop transparent and accountable institutions, to build government capacities and to prevent violence and combat terrorism and crime, thus allowing the promotion of peaceful and inclusive societies.

[50]   See Williams-Elegbe, n 38.

[51]   Ibid.

[52]   For this reason, throughout the book, we will refer to the concept also as 'third-sector entities'.

According to the definition provided by the World Bank, non-governmental organizations are 'private organizations that pursue activities to relieve suffering, promote the interests of the poor, protect the environment, provide basic social services or undertake community development'.[53]

In other words, they are voluntary and privately funded organizations that provide social services. By providing services that have been traditionally furnished by the public sector,[54] they contribute to challenging the idea of public interests being fulfilled only by states and public authorities.

As formally private actors but substantially and intrinsically oriented to the pursuit of public interests, non-governmental organizations are particularly suited to the context of public private partnership that we are describing.

Firstly, in the international arena, they are network creators. Indeed, as active protagonists of the international scenario and supporters of values consistent with the sustainable development goals, said actors are often able to connect local realities, businesses and governments by facilitating interactions around specific projects.

Secondly, their specialization, on-the-ground experience and knowledge of the juridical, social, and economic conditions of specific areas of the world, make them leading innovators in proposing projects that evaluate public goods. Some remarkable public private partnerships around the world in the field of education, health and agriculture are indeed a consequence of non-governmental organizations' activism.[55]

Thirdly, they can contribute to specific projects with resources and expertise, with the additional advantage that said organizations, unlike private companies, do not seek private profit but pursue altruistic outcomes: 'the private sector activity in the public good is value-driven [whereas] non-profit organizations are frequently motivated by the desire to help the beneficiaries of the public goods'.[56]

---

[53]   World Bank, 'Working with NGOs: a practical guide to operational collaboration between the World Bank and non-governmental organizations'. Operations Policy Department (World Bank, 1995) 7–9.

[54]   See Tony Bovaird, 'Public-private partnerships: from contested concepts to prevalent practice' (2004) Int. Review Adm. Sci. 199; Jeanne-Etienne de Bettignies and Thomas Ross, 'The economics of public-private partnerships' (2004) Can. Public Policy 135.

[55]   An interesting case of public private partnership in the agricultural sector which was launched in the Philippines by the initiative of a non-governmental organization is discussed in Teresa Encarnaciòn Tadem, 'Transforming the state into a partner in cooperative development: an evaluation of NGO-government partnership in the Philippines' in Stephen Osborne (ed.), *Public-private partnerships: theory and practice in international perspective* (Routledge, 2000) 187.

[56]   Timothy Besley and Maitreesh Ghatak, 'Public-private partnerships for the provision of public goods: theory and an application to NGOs' (2017) Research in Economics 356.

Consequently, they would not expect high returns from the implementation of specific activities, which makes them pivotal protagonists of international partnerships for sustainable development.

The dynamic between the profit-oriented and the value-oriented views of international financing institutions and non-governmental organizations has internationally shaped the juridical and cultural production on public private partnership over the last years. As will be discussed, the context is currently strongly dominated by a predominance of the analysis of the economic and financial aspects of public private partnership, as opposed to a 'people first' approach.

5 SPREADING THE CULTURE OF PUBLIC PRIVATE PARTNERSHIP INTERNATIONALLY: REASONS FOR THE INTERNATIONAL SOFT REGULATION OF THE INSTRUMENT

Over the last decades, the attractiveness of public private partnership as a vehicle that involves both public officials, businesses, financial institutions, interest groups, as well as practitioners and scholars of different disciplines, has produced a global attention to public private partnership as a subject of study and debate. In this debate, international organizations had a primary role, not only in the promotion of public private partnership but also in spreading the culture of cooperation and the elaboration of instruments to facilitate this. In this sense, we can also detect an educational role for the international dimension of the phenomenon. Thanks to the organization of cultural initiatives, fairs and conferences, the last decade has witnessed the autonomous growth of associations promoted by government, academic groups and practitioners around the world. This, in turn, allowed the creation of interconnected networks focused on public private partnership and the circular dissemination of thought and experiences which support the success of public private partnership as a global tool of development.

The main reason for the global spread of knowledge on public private partnership lies in the need to solve the complexity of the instrument, in order to make it easier to implement the public private partnership relationship.[57] For the same reason, some 'regulatory' documents covering public private partnership have been introduced, also at an international level.

Indeed, the intricacy of public private partnership forces public administrations to apply (or to acquire) different forms of knowledge of a technical, managerial, financial, fiscal and juridical type, thus demanding a process of quality enhancement in the public sector, which turns out to be beneficial

---

[57] See, above all, Organization for Economic Cooperation and Development, Principles for Public Governance of Public-Private Partnerships, n 2.

for further administrative activities. Furthermore, the selection of the private party, the technical, juridical and economic analysis of the proposals and the management of a public private partnership contract all require the presence, within public administrations, of highly skilled teams.[58]

Acknowledging the mentioned complexity, international organizations have strongly promoted good practices and confidence and capacity building in the public sector.[59] For international financing institutions, this undertaking was supported by the need to safeguard investments from the risk of poor management, whereas several initiatives have been launched in the spirit of solidarity and aid.

Schools of good governance, courses of good practices and certification programmes on public private partnership have been launched globally to train practitioners in facing possible issues arising from the design and management of complex projects.

In the European context, expertise centres have been created to assist the public sector to overcome shortfalls in public private partnership competences by spreading best practices in project planning and delivery.[60]

Further, the elaboration of practice tools helped the diffusion of standardized assessment procedures and evaluations. This is the case for the 'PPP Fiscal Risk Assessment Model' designed by the IMF in collaboration with the World Bank: an 'analytical tool that quantifies the macro-fiscal impact of PPP projects', helping governmental agencies to 'estimate a PPP's impact on the

---

[58]   'They need the capacity to design projects with a package of risks and incentives that makes them attractive to the private sector. They need to be able to assess the cost to tax-payers, often harder than for traditional projects because of the long-term and often uncertain nature of government commitments. They need contract management skills to oversee these arrangements over the life of the contract. And they need advocacy and outreach skills to build consensus on the role of PPPs and to develop a broad program across different sectors and levels of government'. Mark Dutz et al., 'Public-private partnership units what are they, and what do they do?' (Washington DC, 2006).

[59]   Farquharson, Clemencia Torres de Mästle, and Yescombe, n 39; Ashley Lee, 'Taming Asia's legal frontiers: the Asian Development Bank's General Counsel explains how the bank's technical assistance programmes are improving the investment framework of the region's emerging markets' (2014) Int'l Fin. Law Review 24.

[60]   Consider, for example, the Public-Private Infrastructure Advisory Facility, a multi-donor technical assistance facility established in 1999 as a joint initiative of the governments of Japan and the United Kingdom, working closely with and housed inside the World Bank Group, and the European Public-Private Partnership Expertise Center, created in 2008 within the European Investment Bank. On topic, Monica Amalia Ratiu, 'The decision made by a public partner to implement a project as a PPP' (2012) Rom. Pub.-Priv. Partnership Law Review 6; Ion Ghizdeanu, 'Public-private partnerships revival: current European approaches' (2015) Rom. Public-Private Partnership Law Review 14; Ion Ghizdeanu, 'PPP's contribution to economic development – a macroeconomic approach' (2012) Rom. Pub.-Priv. Partnership Law Review 42.

fiscal deficit, debt and stock of government contingent liabilities',[61] promoting sensitive analysis of fiscal aspects of a project, thus ensuring protection of public finances.

Also, the same goal of fostering an informed use of public private partnership has been the impetus to develop international guidelines, principles, model contracts, standards of good practice, studies and reports on specific cases, which constitute a normative corpus of extraterritorial applicability, overlapping with domestic norms.[62]

Among the most remarkable examples are the Organization for Economic Cooperation and Development's 'Recommendation of the Council on Principles for Public Governance of Public Private Partnership', the IMF's document entitled 'Public Private Partnerships',[63] the World Bank Group's Reference Guide,[64] and the UNCITRAL Model Legislative Provisions on Privately Financed Infrastructure Projects.[65]

This framework of blended rule making is characterized by a 'soft law' aspect[66]

---

[61]   International Monetary Fund, 'Public-private partnerships fiscal risk assessment model user guide' (Washington DC, 2016) 1.

[62]   Dieter Kerwer, 'Rules that many use: standards and global regulation' (2005) Governance 611. For an historical account of the role of multilateral development banks as regulators of the sector, see Williams-Elegbe, n 38, 9ff.

[63]   International Monetary Fund, n 2.

[64]   International Bank for Reconstruction and Development, The World Bank Group, n 39.

[65]   United Nations Commission on International Trade Law, n 5.

[66]   On the characters of soft regulation, in relation to soft law, see Anna di Robilant, 'Genealogies of soft law' (2006) American Journal of Comparative Law 499; Linda Senden, *Soft law in European Community law* (Hart, 2004); Ulrika Mörth, *Soft law in governance and regulation, an interdisciplinary analysis* (Edward Elgar, 2004); Francis Snyder, 'Soft law and institutional practices in the European Community law' in Stephen Martin (ed.), *The construction of Europe: essays in honour of Emile Noël* (Kluwer Academic Publishers, 1994) 198. Specifically, on soft regulation, see Dimity Kingsford Smith, 'Governing the corporation: the role of soft regulation' (2012) UNSW Law Journal 378, where the author affirms that 'I will use the term "soft regulation" or "SR" to mean standards, codes, guidelines etc, including stock exchange listing rules, issuing from a variety of non-state sources. SR is part of the legal and normative pluralism of corporate regulation and governance, which ranges from statute at one end of the regulatory spectrum to corporate ethics at the other'; Charalampos Koutalakis, Aron Buzogany, and Tanja Börzel, 'When soft regulation is not enough: the integrated pollution prevention and control directive of the European Union' (2010) Regulation and Governance 329, 330: 'Soft regulation refers to a wide range of quasi-legal instruments that differ from hard law as they lack immediate, uniformly binding, direct effects, precision, and clearly delineated monitoring, dispute settlement, and enforcement authorities'; Gregory Shaffer and Mark Pollack, 'Hard vs. soft law: alternatives, complements and antagonists in international governance' (2009) Minnesota Law Review 706: 'Soft regulation refers to a wide range of quasi-legal

and the 'direct and/or indirect participation of non-state actors',[67] which may be firms and non-governmental organizations.[68]

The drafting of such regulations, even in a 'soft' form, could be counter-intuitive, given the fluidity of public private partnership, which, as we noticed, autonomously generated juridical schemes before being disciplined by norms.

However, the self-imposition of standards of rules and practices has the significance of setting transnational standards of conduct that help abate transaction costs and improve efficiency in project design.[69]

---

instruments that differ from hard law as they lack immediate, uniformly binding, direct effects, precision, and clearly delineated monitoring, dispute settlement, and enforcement authorities'; Keith Sisson and Paul Marginson, 'Soft regulation: travesty of the real thing or new dimension?' (Economic and Social Research Council 'One Europe or Several' Programme, Working Paper 32/01, Brighton, 2001). The adoption of practices of soft law in the area of the public contracts regulation has been examined especially by the Italian literature. See, in particular, Sara Valaguzza, 'La regolazione strategica dell'Autorità Nazionale Anticorruzione' (2016) RRM; Sara Valaguzza, *Nudging* pubblico vs. pubblico: nuovi strumenti per una regolazione flessibile di ANAC' (2017) RRM and the related references. Specifically on soft regulation by multilateral development banks, see Sylvia Karlsson-Vinkhuyzen and Antto Vihma, 'Comparing the legitimacy and effectiveness of global hard and soft law: an analytical framework' (2009) Regulation and Governance 400. A more critical approach is taken by Antonio Marques Mendes and Mihaela Meica, 'The quest to justify a long lasting role for multilateral development banks' (SADIF Newsletter and Investment Management Portal, 2005); Koutalakis, Buzogany and Börzel (above).

[67]   Stephen Park, 'Guarding the guardians: the case for regulating state-owned financial entities in global finance' (2014) U. Pa. J. Bus. Law 739. Decentralized government schemes are thoroughly described in Kenneth Abbott and Duncan Snidal, 'Strengthening international regulation through transnational new governance: overcoming the orchestration deficit' (2009) Vand. J. Transnat'l Law 501. For a more critical perspective on the legitimacy of said form of regulation, see Steven Bernstein and Benjamin Cashore, 'Can non-state global governance be legitimate? An analytical framework' (2007) Regulation and Governance 347.

[68]   The juridical literature has described as a 'governance triangle' the process of soft rule making drafted by states, businesses and non-governmental organization. See Kenneth Abbott and Duncan Snidal, 'The governance triangle: regulatory standards institutions and the shadow of the State' in Walter Mattli and Ngaire Woods (eds), *The politics of global regulation* (Princeton University Press, 2009) 63.

[69]   The process mirrors what happened, in general, in the arena of the global market's regulation, which in recent decades 'have witnessed the emergence and growth of market participants of an inherently public, governmental nature ..., as well as multilateral development banks such as the World Bank and International Monetary Fund that are owned and governed by their member states'. Park, n 67. For a comprehensive comment on the participation of private and hybrid organizations to the drafting of transnational regulation, see Victor Ramraj, 'Transnational non-state regulation

Moreover, the lack of a solid national regulatory framework and insufficient governmental experience can undermine the capacity of public private partnership projects to promote growth and generate income.[70]

Therefore, the aim of these documents is to spread successful practices that could reduce specific risks of the project, throughout its lifetime.[71] How to select a private partnership, how to correctly assess the risk allocation of a project and how to evaluate cases of renegotiations of contractual terms are some of the most recurring issues in the international guidelines.

Said rules are 'soft' since the actors that took part in their drafting do not possess the authority to impose binding rules on national governments; their role can thus only be a supportive one. As a consequence, the perspective assumed is that of a public counsellor: said institutions provide administrative authorities with actual procedures, figures and standards that are intended to help them at all the stages of a public private partnership project.

Despite providing an essential reference to international (and even national) public private partnerships, said normative *corpus* is eminently deficient and unbalanced. Indeed, being the product of financial institutions and having the aim of providing concrete advice on correct risk allocation, these instruments overlook some essential problems of public private partnership deriving from the normal dynamic between public and private parties. Therefore, issues such

---

and domestic administrative law' in Susan Rose-Ackerman, Peter Lindseth, and Blake Emerson, *Comparative administrative law* (2nd edition, Edward Elgar, 2017) 582.

[70]   Lee Minsoo et al., 'Hazard analysis on public–private partnership projects in developing Asia' (2018) ADB Economics Working Paper Series 1; Renato Reside and Amado Mendoza, 'Determinants of outcomes of public-private partnerships (PPP) in infrastructure in Asia' (School of Economics, University of the Philippines, Discussion Paper No. 3/2010); Nose Manabu, 'Triggers of contract breach: contract design, shocks, or institutions?' (The World Bank, 2014).

[71]   The relevance of risk assessment is present in numerous documents of the international organizations that are mostly involved in the promotion of public private partnership. The approach taken by the Association of Southwest Asian Nations (ASEAN) is emblematic, affirming in 2014 that: 'The essential differences between a PPP contract and conventional procurement are that PPP contracts are long-term arrangements featuring private capital at risk and the allocation of transactional risk to the private party, including responsibility for lifecycle costs'. Fauziah Zen and Michael Regan (eds), *ASEAN public private partnership guidelines* (Jakarta, 2014). A few years later, the same perspective was taken by the International Bank for Reconstruction and Development – World Bank, which in their Reference Guide of 2017 defined public private partnership as 'a long-term contract between a private party and a government entity, for providing a public asset or service, in which the private party bears significant risk and management responsibility and remuneration is linked to performance'. See International Bank for Reconstruction and Development, The World Bank, n 39. For a comment, see Mokoto Aizawa, 'A scoping study of PPP guidelines' (DESA Working Paper No. 154, January 2018).

as the co-design of the project, how to divide responsibilities in the partner-ship and the measurement of the value brought to the community are often disregarded. This calls for cultural organizations involved with public private partnership to take responsibility in refocusing the attention of those involved to achieving public value rather than on the protection and capitalization of investments.

6   POSSIBLE ISSUES IN INTERNATIONAL PUBLIC PRIVATE PARTNERSHIP: THE NEED FOR A 'PEOPLE FIRST' APPROACH

The described tilt towards a profit-oriented view of the mentioned guidelines is evident by reading the definitions of public private partnership presented therein. Public private partnership is mainly considered as a kind of arrange-ment that can be made for the supply of infrastructure assets and the subse-quent provision of services.

For instance, the IMF describes public private partnerships as 'arrangements where the private sector supplies infrastructure assets and services that tradi-tionally have been provided by the government'.[72] The Asian Development Bank affirms that the expression describes 'a range of possible relationships among public and private entities in the context of infrastructure and other services'.[73] The World Bank Group assumes the more precise following definition: 'A long-term contract between a private party and a government entity, for providing a public asset or service, in which the private party bears significant risk and management responsibility and remuneration is linked to performance.'[74]

All these organizations consider public private partnership as essentially equivalent to concession contracts for the construction of infrastructure. However, also in the international arena, the association between these two-mentioned concepts must be considered problematic. Indeed, the focus on concession contracts fuels the imbalance in partnerships, linked to the need to rely on dominant founders.

The predominance of multilateral development banks over the public private partnership culture during recent years has provoked an international reaction to a strongly economically oriented way of looking at the concept itself.

---

[72] International Monetary Fund, Fiscal Affairs Department, 'Public-Private Partnerships' n 3, 1.
[73] Asian Development Bank, 'Public private partnership handbook' (Manila, 2008) 4.
[74] International Bank for Reconstruction and Development – The World Bank, n 39, 1.

Furthermore, the hegemonic regimes imposed by international financing institutions on concession projects led to the idea that public private partnership feeds a culture of corruption.[75] Specifically, on public private partnership, it has been affirmed that: 'The multilateral development banks have regularly funded infrastructure projects such as dams that displaced local populations and destroyed local communities without adequate consideration or recompense.'[76]

Trying to address a few important criticisms made by scholars and civil service organizations about a financially driven public private partnership model, some international organizations recalled the need to move public private partnership towards a 'people first' approach.

Already after the 2002 Johannesburg Summit of the UN, many stakeholders feared that the preference for public private partnership as a main instrument to achieve sustainable development would push states to avoid governmental commitments on socially and environmentally relevant issues.[77] The involvement of non-state actors to solve crucial global issues was regarded as an abdication of responsibility from public authorities.[78] Moreover, 'there was a concern about inequality of power among parties in partnership'[79] that would favour large governments and companies over smaller and poorer actors.

To address said critiques, a set of principles were drafted at the UN level, calling for partnerships that would be directed towards achieving the sustainable development goals, being 'based on mutual respect and shared responsibility of the partners involved'.[80] In this light, to consider public private partnership as a tool for achieving sustainable development meant to characterize it as a social instrument for growth, aimed at providing opportunities for development to local communities, in a bottom-up logic of governance.

---

[75] Richard Stewart, 'Remedying disregard in global regulatory governance: accountability, participation, and responsiveness' (New York University Public Law and Legal Theory Research Paper Series Working Paper No. 14-30, July 2014). Criticisms regarding the necessity to consider a humanitarian approach in the financing method can be found in Michela Wrong, *In the footsteps of Mr. Kurtz: living on the brink of disaster in Mobutu's Congo* (Harper Collins, 2002); Jessica Evans, 'Abuse-free development: how the World Bank should safeguard against human rights violations' (Proceedings of the Annual Meeting of the American Society of International Law, Vol. 107: International Law in a Multipolar World, July 2013) 298.

[76] Stewart, n 75, 221.

[77] Scherr and Juge Gregg, n 7, 425.

[78] Kenny Bruno and Joshua Karliner, 'The UN's global compact, corporate accountability and the Johannesburg Earth Summit' (2002) Development 33.

[79] Scherr and Juge Gregg, n 7, 440.

[80] United Nations, 'Annex: Guiding principles for partnership for sustainable development' (Bali, Indonesia, 7 June 2002).

This new configuration of public private partnership has been recently embraced and re-proposed by the UN Economic Commission for Europe. Taking a decisive contrasting position towards the way that public private partnership has been mainly applied in previous years, the organization proposed to focus on 'value for people', by fostering 'access to essential public services for all ... and putting people first at the core':[81]

> too often it results in public services that are not targeted to people's needs, assets that are overbuilt or underbuilt, systems that create barriers rather than improve or widen access, services that underserve, etc. Infrastructure and assets that simply do not respond to the people. The obvious solution is for governments and public authorities to improve their listening skills and be more responsive to the needs of the people.[82]

This above-mentioned approach is crucial from a theoretical perspective, as it allows us to reconnect the international dimension of public private partnership to the concept of social participation of all active members of the international community, including non-governmental organizations.

If, as we affirmed, public private partnership has to be intended as a means to achieve sustainable development, then its chief criteria should be to produce value. If, as we said, the reason underpinning the choice to achieve social and environmental benefits through partnerships is to exploit the creativity, skills and resources of the non-state actors dominating the international scene, then the bottom-up initiatives of non-governmental organizations, associations and interest groups should be appreciated if viewed through the lens of how they promote good governance. Finally, if it is true that the strength of public private partnership in the international context is the flexibility of the relationships among members of a goal-oriented network, then guidelines and practices should be directed at providing a cooperative environment in which communication, exchange of views and knowledge take precedence over antagonistic reasoning related to economic gains.

In sum, to produce value for the people, public private partnership should be treated in the international arena as an efficient connector of parties working together to achieve public interests, which temporarily pulls resources together for the goal of reaching economic sustainable growth of a community. Thus intended, international public private partnership would again be valued as an essential engine of democracy, cooperation and development.

---

[81]   United Nations Economic Commission for Europe, 'Revised guiding principles on people-first public-private partnerships for the United Nations sustainable development goals' (New York, 2018).

[82]   Ibid.

With the 'people first' approach, the international dimension embraces, in its entirety, the possible typologies of public private partnership and the multiple political sensitivities standing at the basis of the phenomenon, which can be considered as an instrument of sustainable development only if included in the dimension of personal valorization.

Therefore, the analysis of the international context appears to be essential and rich in insights to be evaluated in the local context, where public private partnership is connected more because of the needs of local governments to legitimate themselves as good administrators than as promoters of a better world.

3. Public private partnership's juridical identity: the local dimension

1   A METHODOLOGICAL PREMISE

With the goal of identifying a juridical definition of public private partnership that could be applied to different circumstances, in the last chapter we looked at the international dimension.

It emerged that public private partnership is suited to cooperation dynamics as a tool for sustainable development goals and as a symbol of participatory democracy in the global arena.

In the international context, this process is driven by the mission of international organizations, both financial institutions and non-governmental organizations, which act – with different interests and attitudes – to implement transnational social and environmental values.

However, given that public private partnership is a phenomenon that belongs to national scenarios as well, the search for a definition cannot disregard a reconstruction of the national level.

Obviously, when we move from the international to the local dimension, the concept of public private partnership acquires new meanings.

A methodological note is required.

In this chapter, the term 'local' will be used to indicate the application of public private partnership in a geographically limited legal framework, belonging either to a national law or to a supranational law as in the case of the European dimension.

The present chapter is the result of an extensive study of national disciplines regarding public private partnership enacted in recent years around the world.

For our purposes, it is worth giving an account of the national disciplines that we considered the most representative of common trends.

Therefore, the present chapter refers to some local legal orders in order to make abstraction understandable through concrete examples. The criteria for the selection of the disciplines was threefold: geographic – to represent Africa, America, Asia, Europe and Oceania – chronological – disciplines enacted in the last ten years – and objective: in the selection, definitions capable of encompassing only concession contracts have been avoided, preferring to appreciate public private partnership in its full extent. The elements drawn from the analysed national disciplines will appear in the dissertation as a part of our theoretical re-elaboration.

2 PUBLIC PRIVATE PARTNERSHIP IN LOCAL CONTEXTS: A CULTURAL AND POLITICAL CHOICE

At a local dimension, public private partnership appears to be a cultural and political choice of the state or of the local government, which become promoters of initiatives that variously involve relationships between individuals, private organizations, markets and institutions. In this scenario, what counts is not the public or private identity of the entity which takes care of the interest of the community but rather the strategic decision to exploit the energies of those who have the interest (even commercial) to embark on an activity for the benefit of the community.

Locally, public private partnership can be primarily considered as a strategic methodology, based on the desire to achieve participation, and to foster inclusion and innovation in providing services to the community, through the presence of private actors in the design and implementation of governance instruments; also in order to react to the spending review policy that can often limit the action of public bodies.

At a local level, public administrations are responsible for looking after specific interests and are thus entrusted by law with specific tasks of public relevance: public lighting, transportation, waste management, environmental protection, promotion of culture, to name a few. The choice on 'how' to perform said tasks belongs to the public bodies, which operate on the basis of their own discretionary powers and organizational structure.

A public authority may decide to perform this task directly using internal resources, both economic and human, to carry out the required activities. On the basis of its organizational structure, it may decide to use one of its branches or a controlled enterprise acting 'in house'.[1] Or, it may decide to externalize the performance of an activity, looking to the market for works, services and goods through outsourcing.[2]

---

[1] For the European dimension, see Article 12 and Recital No. 32 of Directive 2014/24/EU of the European Parliament and of the Council of 26 February 2014.

[2] The perspective of American scholarship is particularly representative of the international academic debate on this theme. In particular, the works of Jody Freeman have significantly contributed to shape and foster the discussion. Among the most interesting works of the author, see Jody Freeman and Martha Minow, 'Introduction: reframing the outsourcing debates' in Jody Freeman and Martha Minow (eds), *Government*

In contracting out and outsourcing, the public task (e.g. to provide public lighting, to clean a railway station, to build a school) is performed by a private operator acting as an executor of the obligations deriving from the public authority's directives as included in the contract. In this scenario, the public authority identifies a public interest *ex ante* and holds the responsibility for the choices and of how the community's interests are pursued by the private contractor, according to the provisions of the awarded contract.[3]

Conversely, whenever a public authority decides to opt for a public private partnership, a more complex and sophisticated juridical relationship is put in place. In these cases, both the identification of the public interest and its concrete satisfaction are the result of a concerted and shared strategy, which requires the contribution of the public and the private sector together.

As we will see in the analysis that will be carried out in more detail in the following pages, we can underline that the most relevant element, in dogmatic terms, is that in a public private partnership there is no delegation – strictly intended – to private actors, since the administrative task is performed by public authorities and private operators together, on the basis of an agreement (contractual public private partnership[4]) or through a newly established co-owned company (institutional partnership[5]).

---

by contract: outsourcing and American democracy (Harvard University Press, 2009) 1; Jody Freeman, 'The private role in public governance' (75) New York University Law Review 543; Jody Freeman, 'Private parties, public functions and the new administrative law' in David Dyzenhaus (ed.), *Recrafting the rule of law: the limits of legal order* (Hart Publishing, 1999) 331; Jody Freeman, 'Collaborative governance in the administrative state' (1997) UCLA Law Review.

   [3]   On this point, see Christopher Pollitt, *Managerialism in the public sector: the Anglo-American experience* (Blackwell, 1990); Jonas Prager, 'Contracting out government services: lessons from the private sector' (1994) PAR 176; Simon Domberg and Paul Jensen, 'Contracting out by the public sector: theory, evidence, prospects' (1997) Oxford Review of Economic Policy 67; Jeffrey Brudney et al., 'Exploring and explaining contracting out: patterns among the American states' (2005) Journal of Public Administration Research and Theory 393.

   [4]   As explained by the European Commission, 'Green Paper on public-private partnerships and Community law on public contracts and concessions' (COM (2004) 327 final), 'The term "purely contractual PPP" refers to a partnership based solely on contractual links between the different players. It covers a variety of set-ups where one or more tasks of a greater or lesser magnitude are assigned to the private partner, and which can include the design, funding, execution, renovation or exploitation of a work or service. In this context, one of the best-known models, often referred to as the "concessive model", is characterized by the direct link that exists between the private partner and the final user: the private partner provides a service to the public, "in place of", though under the control of, the public partner.'

   [5]   Intended as partnerships involving 'involve the establishment of an entity held jointly by the public partner and the private partner'. See European Commission, n

More specifically, it is obvious that, in a public private partnership a portion of responsibility is transferred to the private party; however, the public administration does not limit itself to simply controlling the results of the private party's action. Rather, according to what is agreed in the contract, the public administration remains alongside the private party in a shared activity of co-design and co-management of the project through which the public interest is fulfilled.

This distinctive characteristic of public private partnership allows national governments and local administrations to use it not only as a financing mechanism but, more meaningfully, as an instrument of dialogue with the market and of social inclusion and innovation,[6] for improving public value.

The particular attention to the quality of the service provided through public private partnership is quite evident, for instance, in Russian Federal Law No. 224-fz of 13 July 2015 on public private partnership and municipal-private partnership in the Russian Federation, where it is stated: 'The purpose of this federal law shall be establishing legal background for attraction of investments in the economy of the Russian Federation and increasing the quality of goods, work and services, organisation of provision of which to consumers shall be the responsibility of state and local authorities' (Article 1).[7]

4, where it is further affirmed that: 'The joint entity thus has the task of ensuring the delivery of a work or service for the benefit of the public. In the Member States, public authorities sometimes have recourse to such structures, in particular to administer public services at local level (for example, water supply services or waste collection services)'.

[6]   See Diana MacCallum, *Social innovation and territorial development* (Ashgate, 2011); Alex Nicholls and Alex Murdock, 'The nature of social innovation' (2012) Social Innovation 1; Louis Witters, Revital Marom, and Kurt Steinert, 'The role of public-private partnership in driving innovation' in Soumitra Dutta (ed.), *The Global Innovation Index 2012: stronger innovation linkages for global growth* (INSEAD and World Intellectual Property Organization, 2012) 81; Athena Roumboutsos and Stéphane Saussier, 'Public-private partnerships and investments in innovation: the influence of the contractual arrangement' (2014) Construction Management and Economics 349; Wendy Phillips et al., 'Social innovation and social entrepreneurship: a systematic review' (2014) Group and Organization Management 428; Timothy Besley and Maitreesh Ghatak, 'Public-private partnerships for the provision of public goods: theory and an application to NGOs' (2017) Research in Economics 356; Pedro Marques, Kevin Morgan, and Ranald Richardson, 'Social innovation in question: the theoretical and practical implications of a contested concept' in Environment and Planning C: Politics and Space, July 2017; Giuseppe Tardivo, Gabriele Santoro, and Alberto Ferraris, 'The role of public-private partnerships in developing open social innovation: the case of GoogleGlass4Lis' (2017) World Review of Entrepreneurship, Management and Sustainable Development 580.

[7]   See also the Slovenian public private partnership Act (ZJZP) of 2006, which affirms that 'public-private partnership represents a relationship involving private

In other words, as we will show, public private partnership is increasingly being treated as the leverage for change in the provision of services, based on strategies of evolution and development that are designed alongside the market and the community.[8]

In this direction, as we will see in the next sections, the ability to exploit private creativity allows a public authority to promote innovative ways of taking care of social and environmental issues. In this sense, the construction of smart cities[9] and the development and management of urban spaces[10] depend on a collaborative dynamic between the public and private sectors.

---

investment in public projects and/or public co-financing of private projects that are in the public interest, and such relationship is formed between public and private partners in connection with the construction, maintenance and operation of public infrastructure or other projects that are in the public interest, and in connection with the associated provision of commercial and other public services or activities provided in a way and under the conditions applicable to commercial public services'.

[8]   The strategic approach of collaborations with partners in procurement is evident in the initiative launched in 2018 by the US Agency for International Development of reformation of procurement approaches to achieve self-reliance by establishing a more participatory programme-design process; an orientation to paying partners in relation to the results accomplished and, more generally of establishing collaborative networks with the partners. See USAID policy framework, available at https://www.usaid.gov/policyframework/documents/1870/usaid-policy-framework, accessed 30 June 2019.

[9]   The connection with public private partnership is especially evident in Joop Koppenjan and Bert Enserink, 'Public-private partnerships in urban infrastructures: reconciling private sector participation and sustainability' (2009) Public Administration Review 284; Sam Allwinkle and Peter Cruickshank, 'Creating smart-er cities: an over-view' (2011) Journal of Urban Technology 1; Michael Kort and Erik-Hans Klijn, 'Public-private partnerships in urban regeneration projects: organizational form or managerial capacity?' (2011) Public Administration Review 618; Klaus Kunzmann, 'Smart cities: a new paradigm of urban development' (2014) Crios 9.

[10]   The value of inclusive forms of management of common urban spaces has been studied, in particular, by Michael Carley et al., *Urban regeneration through partnership: a study in nine urban regions in England, Scotland and Wales* (The Policy Press, 2000); John McCarthy, *Partnership, collaborative planning and urban regeneration* (Ashgate, 2007); Jean-Bernard Auby, *Droit de la ville: du fonctionnement juridique des villes au droit à la Ville* (Lexis Nexis, 2013); Mary Dellenbaugh et al. (eds), *Urban commons: moving beyond state and market* (Bau Verlag, 2015); Christian Iaione, 'Governing the urban commons' (2015) Italian Journal of Public Law 170; Marco Bombardelli, *Prendersi cura dei beni comuni per uscire dalla crisi: Nove risorse e nuovi modelli di amministrazione* (Editoriale Scientifica, 2016); Francesca di Lascio and Fabio Giglioni (eds), *La rigenerazione di beni e spazi urbani: Contributo al diritto delle città* (Il Mulino, 2017); Enrico Fontanari and Giuseppe Piperata (eds), *Agenda re-cycle: Proposte per reinventare la città* (Il Mulino, 2017); Katrina Wyman and Danielle Spiegel-Feld, 'The urban environmental renaissance' (2020) California Law Review, forthcoming.

The 'inclusiveness' of public private partnerships allows public authorities to involve the interpreters of social needs – namely members of the community, associations, foundations, committees, businesses and local economic operators – in the shaping and provision of answers to their own social demands.[11]

The variety of spheres of its application – as we have already seen in the analysis of the international arena carried out in Chapter 2 – as well as the numerous forms that the agreements can take make public private partnership an adequate tool to meet potentially any demand.

For these reasons, we believe that it would be limitative to consider, as often happens, the phenomenon of public private partnership as restricted to the realm of concessions for works and services aimed at the construction of infrastructures.

However, considering the national experiences, a tendency frequently emerges to focus the public private partnership discipline on concession-type contracts. This is due to the economic importance of such types of contracts, into which both private loans and public funds of different natures converge. The need to control in detail the spending of public funds justifies the numerous national disciplines on this particular type of public private partnership. The next section is dedicated to this topic.

3   CONCESSIONS: A VERY PECULIAR TYPE OF PARTNERSHIP

The complexity of the instrument and the participation of private parties in the design of the public interest to be satisfied through the partnership requires paying particular attention to the economic and juridical structure of the intended agreement and the social outcomes that the agreement will bring about.

In concession-type contracts, as well as in private financing procedures, this enhanced attention has taken the form of a careful risk allocation aimed at avoiding unsound initial economic assessments and imprecise fiscal classifications that may not adequately represent a project's impact on governmental budgets.[12]

---

[11]   See Harvey Brooks, Lance Liebman, and Corinne Schelling, *Public-private partnerships: new opportunities for meeting social needs* (Ballinger, 1984).

[12]   The element is considered in all the legislations analysed for the present chapter. For a commentary on the point, see Organization for Economic Cooperation and Development, 'Public private partnerships in pursuit of risk sharing and value for money' (OECD Publishing, 2008); Anthony Wall, *Public-private partnerships in the USA: lessons to be learned for the United Kingdom* (Routledge, 2013); Francesco Goisis, 'Il rischio economico quale proprium del concetto di concessione nella diret-

In various forms of public private partnership, including concession-type contracts, particular attention is given to the discipline of the *ex ante* evaluation of the possible outcomes of a partnership.

Albeit different in nature and scope, the two above-mentioned perspectives share a common philosophy, which is to provoke a careful evaluation of proposals that could seem immediately advantageous but that could turn out to affect the administration and community negatively in the long run.

As for risk allocation, the issue is the following: generally, the recording of projects within the government's balance sheet has major consequences as it increases both government deficit and debt. This aspect is emphasized at European level: 'the initial capital expenditure relating to the assets will be recorded as government fixed capital formation, with a negative impact on government deficit/surplus. As a counterpart of this government expenditure, government debt will increase.'[13] Public authorities may opt for public private partnership to avoid such inconveniences, registering projects (even substantial ones) off government balance sheets.

Yet, the recording of a project as off balance sheet may not always adequately represent reality: practice has demonstrated that in the medium- to long-term execution of the agreement, public authorities may be subject to relevant costs which have an impact on the governmental budget. Indeed, unexpected events during the construction or the operational phase may strongly modify the initial economic estimates, requiring renegotiation of the agreements and public outlay. In this regard, it has been affirmed that public private partnership can create an 'affordability illusion (mainly due to the deferral and spreading of public sector payments through time), which tends to be exacerbated when a project is found to be off balance sheet'.[14]

The acquisition of initial (sometimes relevant) monetary availability deriving from the private sector may blur the necessary consideration on the medium- and long-term effects of the project on the government budget. In this regard, to underline the importance of risk transfer in public private partnership can be firstly explained as a reaction to unsound public budgetary policies.

---

tiva 2014/23/UE: approccio economico versus visioni tradizionali' (2015) Diritto Amministrativo 743; Christopher Bovis, *Public-private partnerships in the European Union* (Routledge, 2018) 109ff. For a national perspective, an interesting analysis is the one carried out in Raquel Carvalho, 'As concessionárias dos sistemas multimunicipais' (1997) Revista Direito e Justiça 221.

[13]   Eurostat, 'New decision of Eurostat on deficit and debt: treatment of public-private partnerships' (Decision No. 18 of 11 February 2004) 1.

[14]   European International Bank, European PPP Expertise Centre, 'A guide to the statistical treatment of PPPs' (September, 2016).

In Europe, the elaboration of principles of statistical treatment of public private partnership is due primarily to the work of the statistical office of the European Union (Eurostat). Starting from 2004, Eurostat elaborated principles and rules aimed at tailoring the practice of placing public private partnership projects off balance sheet,[15] basing them on the sequent criteria: 'the assets involved in a public private partnership should be classified as nongovernment assets, and therefore recorded off balance sheet for government, if both of the following conditions are met: (1) the private partner bears the construction risk,[16] and (2) the private partner bears at least one of either availability[17] or demand risk'.[18]

According to the above-mentioned rule, a project should be registered in the government balance sheet, for instance, where the government is obliged to ensure payments to the private partner independently from the level of demand expressed by the users, or apart from the private performance in the provision of a service. The reason being that in such cases, the private partner is not taking any availability or demand risk, leaving the public authority contractually obliged to cover the cost of possible performance faults. In this situation, the operation would be more similar to a traditional public procurement than to a public private partnership, as the public authority would employ and pay a private party for the provision of a service or construction, assuming the risks of the project.

This defining character of the risk element subsequently broke free from the boundaries of the fiscal discipline where it was first elaborated, to be adopted as a general defining element of public private partnership projects in several national legislatures. To give a few examples, in the United Kingdom, one of the pillars of the Private Finance 2 initiative was correct risk allocation, in

---

[15] Eurostat, n 13, 1.

[16] In Eurostat's view, construction risk covers 'events like late delivery, non-respect of specified standards, additional costs, technical deficiency, and external negative effects. Government's obligation to start making regular payments to a partner without taking into account the effective state of the assets would be evidence that government bears the majority of the construction risks'. Ibid.

[17] According to the decision, the private partner 'may not be in a position to deliver the volume that was contractually agreed or to meet safety or public certification standards relating to the provision of services to final users, as specified in the contract. It also applies where the partner does not meet the required quality standards relating to the delivery of the service, as stated in the contract, and resulting from an evident lack of 'performance' of the partner'. Ibid.

[18] Which covers 'variability of demand (higher or lower than expected when the contract was signed) irrespective of the behaviour (management) of the private partner'. Ibid.

order to avoid the 'fiscal illusion'[19] generated by public private partnership. In Italy, Article 3, para 1, point eee) of the Legislative Decree No. 50 of 2016, containing the definition of public private partnership, states that 'the contents of Eurostat decisions apply to the aspects of public finance'.[20]

Risk transfer has thus become a distinctive feature of public private partnership in comparison to public procurement: the idea is that an operation carried out solely at the public administration's expense is not a real 'partnership', since the private sector does not participate in the losses of the operation.

Therefore, the initial assessment of the project risk becomes crucial to correctly assess the commitment of both parties in the agreement and the impact that the partnership may have on the public accounts.

The same reason of *ex ante* control stands at the basis of the legislative requirements of public value evaluation of the partnership proposals. As mentioned, the co-design phase implies a particular attention to the verification of the burdens that the public administration will bear from the agreement and of the effective values that the partnership will likely produce for the community.[21]

---

[19]   UK Office for Budget Responsibility, Fiscal risks report (July 2017) paras 7.65 to 7.67.

[20]   Giving defining relevance to the fiscal rules expressed in the Eurostat decisions, the Italian Court of Auditors, as well as the administrative courts, has considered unlawful projects passed for public private partnership where the substantial construction or availability risks remained on the public authority. See, for example, Corte dei Conti, Sez. Autonomie, Deliberazione No. 15/SEZAUT/2017QMIG; Tar Firenze, sez. I, 28 February 2018, No. 328; Tar Trento, sez. I, 30 November 2016, No. 404.

The above mentioned rigid approach is aimed at reducing abuses of public private partnership application and unsound fiscal practices, which may be covered by an over-optimistic approach towards the injection of private money in the public sector. Nevertheless, the economic literature has underlined the risks of designing dis-balanced projects, where the risk is almost completely upon the shoulders of the private sector. In this optic, other legal frameworks are considered more 'fair', as they provide a balanced portioning of risks among the private and the public sphere. An example can be found in the German legal system, where 'the risk is allocated to the party from which sphere it originates. If a property provided by the public authority cannot be used for the project because of (severe) environmental damage, the risk is, under German law, generally allocated to the public authority (see Section 645 German Civil Code (BGB)). In contrast, if the architect's plan commissioned by the private partner is incorrect and not appropriate for use, this risk is, under German law, generally allocated to the private partner'. Jan Bonhage and Marc Roberts, 'Germany' in Bruno Werneck and Mário Saadi (eds), *The public-private partnership law review* (4th edition, London, 2018) 100, 107.

[21]   This aspect is particularly evident in the case of private unsolicited proposals. For a comment, see Susan Short Jones et al., 'The process of developing a cost-effective public-private partnership: the team approach' (1991) Pub. Cont. Law J. 442; Nolan

Some international organizations like the Organization for Economic Cooperation and Development and the IMF have consistently indicated the need to ground the selection of public private partnerships in value for money.[22] Said expression indicates the need for public administrations to perform an *ex ante* evaluation of the project in order to verify whether a public private partnership 'is likely to offer better value for the public than traditional public procurement – often called value for money analysis'.[23]

The grounds of this analysis can be found in the need to tame the complexity of the public private partnership as an instrument of governance, which requires verification of all the possible outcomes and flows in economic, technical and juridical terms, especially if the proposal comes from the private sector.

Accordingly, a few national legislatures have recently disciplined the need for public administrations willing to undertake a public private partnership project (specifically, ones initiated by private finance) to carry out an *ex ante* evaluation aimed at assessing its 'value for money'.[24]

For instance, in the United Kingdom, private finance initiative projects can now be undertaken only if 'used where it is value for money'.[25] Likewise, Colombian Law No. 1508/2012 states that public private partnership can be used only after a cost-efficiency analysis and a pre-feasibility verification aimed at bringing to the foreground the economic and social utility of the work.[26]

Similarly, the Italian Legislative Decree No. 50/2016 specifies that, in the awarding procedures of public private partnership contracts, the selection of the private partner is preceded by an 'adequate investigation with reference

---

Bederman and Michael Trebilock, 'Unsolicited bids for government functions' (1996) Alta. Law Review 903.

[22] Organization for Economic Cooperation and Development, 'Recommendation of the Council on principles for Public Governance of Public-Private Partnerships' (Paris, 2012); International Monetary Fund, 'Public-private partnership' (Washington DC, 2004).

[23] World Bank, International Bank for Reconstruction and Development, 'Public-private partnership reference guide' (Version 3, Washington DC, 2017) 129.

[24] Jason Fox and Nicholas Tott, *The PFI Handbook* (Jordan Publishing Limited, 1999). See also Teresa de Lemos et al., 'From concessions to project finance and the private finance initiative' (2000) Journal of Project Finance 19; Michael Pitt, Norman Collins, and Andrew Walls, 'The private finance initiative and value for money' (2006) Journal of Property Investment and Finance 363.

[25] HM Treasury, 'PFI and PF2' (Report by the Comptroller and Auditor General, HC 718 Session 2017–2019, 18 January 2018).

[26] Law No. 1508/2012 'Por la cual se establece el regimen jurìdico de las Asociacione Pùbligo Privadas, se dictan normas orgànicas de presupuesto y se dictan otras disposiciones', Articles 15 and 16.

to the analysis of the demand, of the offer, of the economic-financial and social-economic sustainability of the operation, [and] of the nature and intensity of the different risks of the partnership operation'.[27]

The most common method of *ex ante* value-for-money evaluation of public private partnership projects is the 'public sector comparator'. It is a method developed in the United Kingdom that is useful to assess the economic advantages of realizing a project through public private partnership, rather than through traditional forms of public procurement.[28]

Despite often being criticized by the economic literature as unsound, non-transparent and easy to manipulate,[29] the public sector comparator method can be appreciated, along with different instruments of *ex ante* value-for-money evaluations,[30] if seen as a method that requires contracting authorities to critically evaluate and assess the project on the basis of its value for the administered community. Indeed, the comparison between public private partnership proposals and hypothetical alternative methods of procurement requires contracting authorities to reflect on the meaning and effects of a project and to evaluate possible alternatives in order to select the one that achieves the desired result with the optimum quantity of resources.

---

[27]   Legislative Decree No. 50/2016, Article 180, para 3.

[28]   More specifically, it consists in the calculus of the estimate of the hypothetical, whole-of-life and risk-adjusted cost of a public sector project, in case of realization by the public administration. See John Quiggin, 'Risk, PPPs and the public sector comparator' (2004) Australian Accounting Review 14; Robert Bain, 'Public sector comparators for UK PFI roads: inside the black box' (2010) Transportation 447; Carlos Oliveira Cruz and Rui Cunha Marques, *Infrastructure public-private partnerships: decisions, management and development* (Springer, 2013).

[29]   David Heald, 'Value for money test and accounting treatment in PFI schemes' (2003) Accounting, Auditing and Accountability Journal 342; Bain, n 28, 450.

[30]   An interesting example of *ex ante* value for money analysis is provided by the 'public interest test' which in the Australian State of Victoria is mandatory for evaluation of public private partnership. There, projects are evaluated in reference to eight aspects of public relevance: (1) effectiveness: ability of the PPP to meet the public administration's objective; (2) accountability and transparency: whether PPP ensures that the community is informed about the project; (3) affected individuals and communities: whether those affected by the PPP project have been able to contribute to the planning stage; (4) equity: whether disadvantaged groups can effectively benefit from the project; (5) public access: whether mechanisms to ensure public access to the service have been considered; (6) consumer rights: whether and how consumers' rights will be modified by the PPP; (7) safety and security: whether the PPP will provide insurance to the community in terms of health and safety; (8) privacy: whether the project adequately protects the privacy rights of users. See: Department of the Treasury and Finance, State Government of Victoria, Australia, 'Public sector comparator' (Supplementary Technical Note, Melbourne, 2003).

In this way, the project's content and ability to deliver social value are put under scrutiny and evaluated, in comparison with alternative forms of contracting.

Additionally, the attention of the contracting authority necessarily shifts from the entity of private investment to the technical details of the project and juridical allocation of risks, and, ultimately, to the creation of public value of an intended project.

In our research, we noticed that the peculiarity and the importance of concessions in the realm of public contracts shifted the centre of gravity of the juridical discussion on public private partnership and provoked a sort of identification of such contracts with the phenomenon of public private partnership itself. The above-mentioned identification is also corroborated by the tendency of numerous laws to discipline concessions exclusively, or in prevalence, as the most economically important form of public private partnership.[31] This consequently brought the debate on public private partnership to focus on some specific elements – such as the transfer of the operational risk to the private operator, the duration of the contract, the calculation of the returns of the private investment – which, despite being central to the economic framework of concession contracts, in our opinion do not extinguish all the peculiar features of public private partnership as a phenomenon.

What is left out is the description of the modern trends and evolutions of the phenomenon, which, as mentioned, is progressively transforming itself from a financing method to an instrument of market inclusion in public duties and of social innovation based on the valorization of bottom-up initiatives, participation and solidarity.

We believe that this last perspective needs to be correctly evaluated and emphasized, because it represents a modern physiognomy of government, consistent with the current push towards an inclusive, agile, resilient and multilevel governance, able to promote corporate social responsibility.

For this reason, this configuration of partnership will be examined in depth in the following pages, in order to provide a more comprehensive and precise description of public private partnership.

---

[31] See Introduction, section 3.

4   PUBLIC PRIVATE PARTNERSHIP: FROM
        FINANCING METHOD TO INSTRUMENT
        OF MARKET INCLUSION AND SOCIAL
        INNOVATION AT LARGE

For years, public private partnership has been considered as only a method to acquire private capital in order to perform an administrative task, especially when it comes to building infrastructure.[32] This is evident both in the case of infrastructure projects such as urban rail or subway systems, which 'require huge amounts of capital, thus people believe that only funding from the private sector can fill the immense gap between the limited presence of public resources and rapidly growing sustainable urban infrastructure need',[33] and in smaller-scale works which may still be hampered by constraints to the public budget,[34] as is the case for telecommunications,[35] education[36] and health care.[37]

Consequently, especially in developing countries, private investment is a defining (almost all-encompassing) element of the concept of public private partnership.[38]

However, to strongly characterize public private partnership as a financing method would be limiting, as it would not adequately represent the complexity of the instrument as described so far.

---

[32]   See Chapter 1, n 20.
[33]   Martin de Jong et al., 'Introducing public-private partnerships for metropolitan subways in China: what is the evidence?' (2010) Journal of Transport Geography 301.
[34]   On this topic, it is worth recalling the interesting analysis carried out in Kim E Möric, *PPP et SEC 2010: La répartition des risques dans les partenariats public-privé et le déficit public* (Larcier, 2018).
[35]   Dina Jamali, 'Success and failure mechanisms of public private partnerships in developing countries: insights from Lebanon' (2004) Emerald. The International Journal of Public Sector Management 414.
[36]   Felipe Barrera-Osorio et al., 'Expanding educational opportunities in remote parts of the world: evidence from a RCT of a public-private partnership in Pakistan' (The World Bank, 2011); Allah Bakhsh Malik, 'Public-private partnerships in education: lessons learned from the Punjab Education Foundation' (Asian Development Bank, 2010).
[37]   Ken Buse and Andrew Harmer, 'Seven habits of highly effective global public-private health partnerships: practice and potential' (2006) Social Science and Medicine 259.
[38]   In Vietnam, for example, public private partnership is defined as 'a form of investment conducted on the basis of a contract between an authorized State body and the investor (and/or) the project company in order to implement, manage and operate an infrastructure project (or) to provide public services'. Vietnamese Decree on Public-private Partnership Investment Form No. 15/2015/ND-CP.

The operation of co-management of public interests carried out through public private partnership is far more significant from the public law perspective: the private operator is required, first of all, to interpret the needs of the community, to elaborate a solution and to deliver services that belong to the public sphere, in conjunction with the public administration.[39]

Moreover, the juridical schemes that fall within the category of public private partnership may entail different grades of financial involvement from the private side.[40] For instance, the element of private investment is relatively minor – and can also be lacking – in the cases of social partnership agreements for the maintenance of common urban areas, which we will further discuss in the coming sections. In those cases, the distinctive element of the partnership is not the private financing (as it would be in the case of building and operating concessions of public infrastructures) but is the private exercise of an activity in the interest of the community.[41]

In this perspective it is important to underline that some laws have recently started to attribute a wider connotation to public private partnership, departing from the financing and timing elements as the defining elements in order to encompass different and more flexible models of agreement aimed at satis-

---

[39] An interesting example, in this sense, is provided by the experience of the Local Action Groups promoted by the European Commission's LEADER strategy in the context of the agricultural policy of the Union. The initiative calls for civic participation in the revitalization of countryside, as remedy for depopulation and inclusion of rural areas in the wider urban context. See European Network for Rural Development, 'Connecting rural Europe' https://enrd.ec.europa.eu/leader-clld/lag-database_en, accessed 30 June 2019. Another interesting experience is the spread of the so-called 'social impact bonds' in Europe, where the private performance is measured and rewarded in relation to the achievement of public values' objectives.

[40] The wide encompassing character of the concept of public private partnership is mirrored by the flexibility of the juridical schemes adopted to carry out specific activities. This element is particularly evident in the Argentinian normative, where it is affirmed that the shaping of partnership contract shall have the necessary flexibility to adapt its structure to the particular needs of the specific project and its financing, according to the international best practices on the matter. See Reglamentaciòn de la Ley 27.328, Decreto Nacional 118/2017 of 17 February 2017, articulo 1: 'El diseño de los contratos tendrá la flexibilidad necesaria para adaptar su estructura a las exigencias particulares de cada proyecto y a las de su financiamiento, de acuerdo a las mejores prácticas internacionales existentes en la materia'.

[41] In this sense, it is also interesting to note how the Italian administrative case law has recently affirmed that the onerous character of the partnership contract has to be interpreted in a wide sense, in order to comprehend also forms of cooperation with third sector operators that act without the perspective of maximizing their profits. See Cons. Stato, Sez. V, 13 September 2016, No. 3855; Cons. Stato, Sez. III, 17 November 2015, No. 5249; Cons. Stato, Sez. III, 27 July 2015, No. 3685; Cons. Stato, Sez. III, 15 April 2013, No. 2056.

fying the needs of the community[42] and enhancing the social welfare and the productive levels of the country;[43] also, with the intention to implement 'ideas (products, services and models) to meet social needs and create new social relationships or collaborations'.[44]

Public private partnership's inclusive approach opens the doors to active parts of society, such as individuals, organizations, businesses, which are now entitled to propose activities to be managed together with public bodies in the pursuit of the public interest.

For example, the solution to enhance the value of an abandoned historic public building may derive from a local entrepreneur, which may offer sponsorship to turn it into a museum or a theatre, on the basis of the local communities' preferences.

---

[42]   In France, for instance, Ordonnance No. 2004-559 of 17 June 2004 considered public private partnership as an instrument that allowed integral private financing of works and implants, which imposed full private contribution in the project. Clearly, the provision was aimed at satisfying the economic needs of the French contracting authorities, which were thus allowed to answer to the needs of the community without public disbursement. In 2015, Ordonnance No. 2015-899 of 23 July 2015 renovated the concept of public private partnership, repealing the limit of the full private contribution (Article 80) and defining the concept on the basis of its public mission: 'Un marché de partenariat est un marché public qui permet de confier à un opérateur économique ou à un groupement d'opérateurs économiques une mission globale' (Article 67). See in particular Patrick Le Galès, 'Aspects idéologiques et politiques du partenariat public-privé' (1995) Partenariat public-privé et développement territorial 51; Laure Athias and Stéphane Saussier, 'Un partenariat public-privé rigide ou flexible? Théorie et application aux concessions routières à péage' (2007) Revue Économique 565; Laurent Richer and François Lichère, *Droits des contrats administratifs* (LGDJ, 2016) 542. The norms have been thus transferred in the *Code de la commande publique* of Ordonnance No. 2018-1074 of 26 November 2018.

[43]   A clear example is provided by the Mexican Law on Public Private Partnership, which defines public private partnership as projects that enhance social welfare and the levels of investments in the Country. See Ley de Asociaciones Pùblico Privadas of 16 January 2012, as reformed in 2018: 'Los proyectos de asociación público-privada regulados por esta Ley son aquellos ... en los que se utilice infraestructura proporcionada total o parcialmente por el sector privado con objetivos que aumenten el bienestar social y los niveles de inversión en el país'. Similarly, the Congolese normative highlights that public private partnerships should substantially contribute to the economic and/or social development of the Country. See Law No. 13/005 of 11 February 2014 portant regime fiscal, douanier, parafiscal, des recettes non fiscales et de change applicables aux conventions de collaboration et aux projets de cooperation, Article 1: 'Convention conclue entre l'Etat et un groupement d'entreprise, une entreprise ou d'autres institutions portant sur un projet de coopération susceptible de contribuer de façon substantielle au développement économique et/ou social du pays'.

[44]   European Commission, 'Guide to social innovation' (Regional and Urban Policy, February 2013) 6.

Alternatively, a chronic inefficiency in the management of social housing may be resolved thanks to the intervention of a private actor interested in promoting a business close to the site.

Again, a local supermarket may be interested in realizing a roundabout on the public street in front of the market's entrance, in order to lure customers into the shop and, in parallel, ameliorate car circulation.

The issues described above may be efficiently solved by giving voice to the community's actors, which could become protagonists of specific interests of public relevance (such as cultural activities, social housing and safety), according to the perspective of 'participatory democracy' that we outlined in Chapter 1 and to the principle of solidarity, participation and innovation.

4.1   Public Private Partnership as a Means to Foster Solidarity and Participation: Some Examples from Local Legislation

The most recent economic and juridical literature has outlined how the concepts of social innovation are increasingly being used by local governments as an answer to the socio-economic crisis, the administered community detachment from politics, the weakening of the legitimization of certain administrative institutions (even under the pressure of corruption scandals), the enlargement of the economic gap among citizens, the abandonment of peripheral urban areas, and the declining perception of common goods.[45]

Against all that, public private partnership proposes the strengthening of alliances between different parts of society and local government, in order to promote the undertaking of all the members of the community in voluntarily contributing, according to their means, skills and capabilities, in the management of the *res publica*.

In this framework, as a consequence of bottom-up initiatives, individual, businesses and social enterprises put their energy at the service of the community, in a sort of auto-satisfaction of the social needs.[46]

The local community is therefore the primary centre of a mobilization whose aim is to transform individual aspirations into projects of collective interests, through the valorization of the skills of the social forces that compose it.

In this framework, public private partnership facilitates the construction of bridges between public administrations and the wide group of interlocutors

---

[45]   Urban@it. Centro Nazionale di Studi per le Politiche Urbane, *Terzo Rapporto sulle città: Mind the gap: Il distacco tra politiche e città* (Il Mulino, 2018) 203.

[46]   Marisol Garcìa, Santiago Eizaguirre, and Marc Pradel, 'Social innovation and creativity in cities: a socially inclusive governance approach in two peripheral spaces of Barcelona' (2018) City, Culture and Society 363.

that decide, spontaneously, to take on the responsibility of embarking on activities of general interest.

Public private partnership thus becomes the instrument of social inclusion.[47]

A particularly interesting example of public private partnership aimed at the achievement of social inclusion and solidarity can be drawn from the recent Italian legislation on public contracts.

Indeed, Legislative Decree No. 50/2016, which implemented the 2014 European Directives on public contracts, introduced two forms of 'social' public private partnership that encompass a direct involvement of the community's members, as single or as associates, within the management of the *res publica*: the realization of 'works of local interests' by organized groups of citizens (so-called 'interventions of horizontal subsidiarity', Article 189) and operations of cleaning, management or embellishment of local public spaces in exchange for fiscal advantages (so-called 'administrative barter', Article 190).[48]

More specifically, Article 189 of the Legislative Decree allows two kinds of activities. The first makes it possible for public authorities to assign the management of green public spaces and of buildings of rural derivation, dedicated to social and cultural activities to 'citizens',[49] pursuant to the principles of non-discrimination, transparency and equal treatment. The norm is intended to match specific urban needs of re-evaluation and of maintenance of urban spaces with the interests of capable members of the community.[50]

---

[47]   See Joop Koppenjan and Bert Enserink, 'Public-private partnerships in urban infrastructures: reconciling private sector participation and sustainability' (2009) Public Administration Review 284.

[48]   Legislative Decree 18 April 2016, No. 50, Articles 151, 189, 190. In the literature, see Christian Iaione, 'Governing the urban commons' (2015) Italian J. Pub. Law 170; Gianfrancesco Fidone, 'Il partenariato pubblico-privato: una fuga in avanti del legislatore nazionale rispetto al diritto europeo' (2016) Il Diritto dell'Economia 404; Fabio Giglioni, 'Limiti e potenzialità del baratto amministrativo' (2016) Rivista Trimestrale di Scienza dell'Amministrazione 1; Stefano Villamena, '"Baratto amministrativo": prime osservazioni' (2016) Rivista Giuridica dell'Edilizia; Mauro Renna and Valentina Sessa, 'Commento all'art. 190 del Codice dei contratti pubblici (Baratto amministrativo)' in Gianluca Maria Esposito (ed.), *Codice dei contratti pubblici: Commentario di dottrina e giurisprudenza* (Utet Giuridica, 2017) 2226; Roberto Cavallo Perin, 'Proprietà pubblica e uso comune dei beni tra diritti di libertà e doveri di solidarietà' (2018) Diritto Amministrativo 839; Gabriella Crepaldi, 'Il baratto amministrativo: sussidiarietà, collaborazione ed esigenze di risparmio' (2018) Responsabilità Civile e Previdenza 37.

[49]   Here, we use the word 'citizens' as adopted in the mentioned Article 189.

[50]   Giuseppe Piperata, 'Rigenerare I beni e gli spazi della città: attori, regole e azioni' in Enrico Fontanari and Giuseppe Piperata (eds), *Agenda re-cycle: proposte per reinventare la città* (Il Mulino, 2017) 21.

The second type of activity makes it possible for organized groups of 'citizens' to propose works to local authorities on assets to be acquired from the municipality's property. The proposed projects should be in line with the applicable instruments for urban development and ready to realize, with an indication of the costs and the required private financing means.[51] In this sort of project, the local authority only evaluates the proposal involving, if necessary, public and private stakeholders for suggestions and assistance. Fiscal reductions are awarded for the drafting of the proposal and for the completion of the works.

This norm is intended to foster small projects that do not pose particular technical issues, which could be beneficial for some urban areas. It is possible to imagine, for example, the maintenance of a portion of street, the modification of a building's façade, the construction of a waste collection structure or of a park for children. The voluntary realization of works 'of local importance' is repaid – and incentivized – by awarding a tax break.

Article 190 of the Legislative Decree disciplines the way 'citizens'[52] – can present projects concerning the cleaning, the maintenance, the embellishment of green areas, squares or roads, or their valorization through cultural projects.

The private citizens will have to pay the costs of the works, being repaid by reduction or exemptions of local taxes, according to ad hoc regulations drafted by the municipalities.

In this way, the norm recognizes the specific public function carried out by members of the community which voluntarily took on the responsibility of carrying out activities of general interest.

Besides the peculiarities of the national discipline, here it is worth looking at the above-mentioned discipline from a theoretical perspective, as it demonstrates the progressive extension of the role of private partnership in a local dimension.

Notably, the discipline leaves the municipalities free to determine the procedures and the characterization of said social projects, concentrating on their public scope: what is necessary is that these projects are 'useful for the local community, in a view of recouping the social value of citizens' participation in its life'.[53] The stated legislative intention is thus to promote forms of cohesion between the administered community and the administrative authorities, in

---

[51] The local authority gives its opinion on the proposal within two months, with a justified deliberation. After two months without expressed deliberation, the proposal is considered as rejected. Otherwise, in case of approval, the authority will have to regulate the essential phases of the realization process and the execution time. See Legislative Decree 18 April 2016, No. 50, Article 189.

[52] Again, the term 'citizens' is here used as it is in the norm.

[53] See Legislative Decree 18 April 2016, No. 50, Article 190.

a win-win logic: the municipality is enriched as it acquires the private works in its budget or the revitalization of public spaces through private projects and financing. In essence, with this kind of public private partnership, local government easily performs its tasks in cooperation with the private sector and the private sector is repaid through fiscal reduction.

In parallel, individuals, business and organizations can decide to take care of common goods that fall within their area of interest, thus increasing the value of their territory and enhancing the quality of life.

The defining element of this form of public private cooperation is therefore the ability to bring benefits to the local community, by promoting virtuous cycles of the community's participation.[54]

In this sense, it is also interesting to look at the French experience of the '*concierge de cartier*' or 'neighbourhood concierge'.[55] Thanks to a partnership with the Municipality of Paris, in 2015 a private organization instituted a platform of exchange of social demands and answers within the neighbourhood. Registered volunteers with different competences and skills offered their services at a lower price to the neighbours who needed help to solve small everyday problems, from moving, to bricolage, to gardening and baby-sitting. This successful experiment was based on the idea that the community can be empowered to manage its own needs, through the strengthening of the social connections among individuals.

We believe that the French experience is an emblem of the possible benefits that flow from an open cooperation between market, society and government. Whenever the local government moves away from its boundaries, escaping from the ivory tower in which it is sometimes confined, without fear of private initiatives, progress comes in unpredictable forms and content.

Said experiments of social partnership are also an expression of a new way of looking at the way urban spaces are governed. No longer top down, with

---

[54] An interesting example of co-design of local public services is the one carried out in the city of Eger, Hungary. Here, a partnership between the Municipal Government, the local community and the civil organization of the city allowed the design of a more effective and cost-efficient public service provision. The selection of the needed services, the planning and their implementation were all carried out in public private partnership, on the basis of decision conferences at the presence of representatives of the local governments, of the civil organizations and managers of enterprises. For a comment, see Gÿorgy Fenei and Anna Vàri, 'Partnership between local government and the local community in the area of social policy: a Hungarian experience' in Stephen Osborne (ed.), *Public-private partnership: theory and practice in international perspective* (Routledge, 2000) 265.

[55] See Lulu dans ma Rue, https://www.luludansmarue.org, accessed 23 June 2019.

programmes or administrative acts of zoning, but collaboratively, through public private actions of management of the urban space as a commons.[56]

Intended as goods of open access,[57] urban spaces provide individuals with a right to be part of their creation, use and management.

Indeed, through the mentioned co-governance of the common urban space, individuals, businesses and organizations decide to be part of the civic management and renovation, through voluntary initiatives carried out together with the public administration[58] and in the general interest.

In this way, the public private partnership also has a positive socio-political outcome, since it promotes social cohesion and allows an enlargement of the group of interlocutors of the public administration, which in turn becomes more open and more substantially (not only formally) democratic.

Furthermore, the engagement of the private sector and the opening of the dialogue on the framing of the provision of social services is the key to bring innovation to the local context.

4.2   Public Private Partnership as a Means of Fostering Innovation in Smart Cities

In the local arena, public private partnership can also be an engine of innovation.[59]

More generally, we can affirm that the entire concept of smart cities relies on the necessary elaboration of innovative forms of governance through the

---

[56]   Sheila Foster and Christian Iaione, 'The city as a commons' (2016) Yale Law and Policy Review 281.

[57]   Ibid, 281.

[58]   The importance of cooperation with the public administration in said forms of social partnerships, aimed at achieving consistency among different private initiatives, was recently underlined by the Administrative Courthouse of Naples, Italy (TAR Campania, Napoli, sez. I, 9 January 2019, No. 125). In this case, the administrative judges quashed the request of fiscal reduction ex Article 190 of the Legislative Decree No. 50/2016 proposed by a community, which unilaterally instituted a company entrusted with the services of cleaning, waste collection and weeding of the local public streets and squares. It was affirmed that the organization of service of waste management alternative to the one provided by the municipality cannot be the result of a unilateral private initiative but only of an agreement with the local government.

[59]   See Elvira Akhmetshina and Ashkar Mustafin, 'Public-private partnership as a tool for development of innovative economy' (2015) Procedia Economics and Finance 35, 36; Fanny Saruchera and Maxwell Phiri, 'Technological innovations performance and public-private partnerships' (2016) Corporate Ownership and Control 549.

collaboration of local governments with business in the ICT sector.[60] Here, improvements in well-being depend on the stimulation of private ideas and investments, which are put at the citizens' service to improve mobility, connectivity and logistics.

A few examples are e-Mitra, the e-government project launched in 2008 by the Government of the State of Rajasthan in India aimed at providing people with access to information on the government and services (e.g. payment of bills, requests of certificates, emissions of forms and acts) through dedicated kiosks; Smart Village Cairo, an Egyptian technology park inaugurated in 2005 thanks to a partnership between local IT companies, start-ups and the national Ministry of Information and Communication Technology; and the project Estonia Rural Connectivity, aimed at bringing internet connection to rural and scarcely populated areas of the country through an agreement between the government and the national telephone company.[61] Further, in 2017, the City of New York decided to substitute its public pay telephones with more modern infrastructure that allowed internet connection and the creation of a city telecommunications network. Thanks to a public private partnership between the Department of Information and Technology and a consortium of leading companies in the technology sector, 7,500 public phones were replaced with Wi-Fi connected contact points that allow free internet access and free phone calls, thanks to an advertising system that covers the cost of the entire project.[62]

From the cases mentioned above, we can infer that through public private partnership, it is possible to promote a sharing environment, where private actors (widely understood as any member of a community, in single or associated form) and public authorities match the demand and the supply of social needs. In this scenario, innovation of administrative practices and the inclusion

---

[60]   Carlos Oliveira Cruz and Joaquim Miranda Sarmento, 'Reforming traditional PPP models to cope with the challenges of smart cities' (2017) Competition and Regulation in Network Industries 94; Andrea Castelli, 'Smart cities and innovation partnership: a new way of pursuing economic wealth and social welfare' (2018) European Procurement and Public Private Partnership Law Review 207. See also Louis Witters, Revital Marom, and Kurt Steinert, 'The role of public-private partnerships in driving innovation' in Soumitra Dutta, *The global innovation index 2012: stronger innovation linkages for global growth* (INSEAD and World Intellectual Property Organization, 2012) 81. In the report, the authors discuss the cases of three individual cities around the world (namely, Oulu in Finland, Dubuque in the USA, and Beijing in China), which applied public private partnership for urban development.
[61]   'ICT regulation toolkit: public-private partnership in the telecommunications and ICT sector', available at http://www.ictregulationtoolkit.org/practice_note?practice _note_id=3160, accessed 23 June 2019.
[62]   NYCRC, 'LinkNYC Project' available at http://nycrc.com/project.html?id=19, accessed 23 June 2019.

of the private sector in the definition of the methods to meet social needs become essential elements of public private partnership.

5 SPONSORSHIPS AS A FORM OF PUBLIC PRIVATE PARTNERSHIP TO FINANCE ACTIVITIES IN THE PUBLIC INTEREST

The field of sponsorship contracts offers an interesting opportunity for analysis to understand how the private operator is able to shape the public interest in partnership with public authorities.[63]

In so-called passive sponsorship, the public entity is (financially or technically) sponsored by a private party, who provides financial resources and know-how (if not work execution) in exchange for enhancing its image. Said agreement does not entail an expense by the public authority but a profit that can be identified with the economic contribution deposited by the sponsor or with the equivalent of the specific performance which the sponsor offers the administration.

A few examples of this sort of public private partnership are the experiment in the United States called 'Adopt a Highway' we mentioned in our Introduction;[64] the Italian refurbishment of historical and cultural heritage such as the Colosseum and the Trevi Fountain;[65] and the – more controversial – construction of schools in the United Kingdom.[66]

In all the above-mentioned jurisdictions and realms of application, businesses are most attracted by the chance to contribute to the realization of something significant, from a general point of view, included in the institutional tasks of public entities. This is especially true for companies that are able to take advantage, in terms of marketing, of the commitment to aid the

---

[63] On this topic, see Sara Valaguzza, 'Le sponsorizzazioni pubbliche: le insidie della rottura del binomio tra soggetto ed oggetto pubblico e la rilevanza del diritto europeo' (2015) Rivista Italiana di Diritto Pubblico Comunitario 1381.

[64] See Introduction, section 1.

[65] See Claudia Ventura, Giuseppina Cassalia, and Lucia Della Spina, 'New models of public-private partnership in cultural heritage sector: sponsorships between models and traps' (2016) Procedia – Social and Behavioral Sciences 257; Elena Borin, *Public-private partnership in cultural sector: a comparative analysis of European models* (ENCATC, 2017).

[66] Richard Hatcher, 'Getting down to business: schooling in the globalised economy' (2001) Education and Social Justice 45; Richard Hatcher, 'Privatization and sponsorship: the re-agenting of the school system in England' (2006) Journal of Education Policy 599; Paul Henty, 'Chandler v Camden Borough Council; Chandler v Secretary of State for Children, Schools and Families' (2009) Public Procurement Law Review 160.

administration and therefore in favour of their own community, by thereby improving their own 'social' image. In this perspective, it is clear that the leverage of sponsorships depends on the positive image that the administrations are able to convey, an image on which businesses are willing to bet by involving their own brand in order to earn a profit. In this way, the dynamism of the sponsorship is perceived in all those sectors where the economic resources are scarce but the credibility of the administration or of the initiative that will be sponsored is strong.

In this type of public private partnership, the proposal of the sponsor consists in a private initiative of public interest, meaning that the private sector is proposing to the public authority to provide to the community a certain set of public works or services.

The public administration would remain in charge of the '*an*', meaning that it will decide whether or not to accept the proposal and to execute the public works or services. Yet, as with the case of unsolicited infrastructure proposals, if the public authority accepts, the outcome will be an administrative activity carried out on the basis of a private intuition, from which the public interest germinated.

Moreover, in the case of sponsorships, it is even clearer that the association of the image, name and policies of private entities with those of a public administration in the performance of a specific activity results in a blending of the two subjective entities into an objective dimension, related to the provision of a service to the community, such as the transportation service through sponsored bicycles, the sponsored refurbishment of an historic building or a sponsored sporting event.

In all the above-mentioned cases, the private sector contributes to selecting the public interest and manipulates it, in the sense that it shapes it as a part of the agreement with the public administration.

The administrative authority remains in charge of the responsibility to meet the need that it is institutionally mandated to pursue: the evaluation of the proposal is a necessary step to allow the public or public private activity. In this phase, the public authority evaluates whether the private proposal is technologically and financially feasible and if the outcome will fall within its discretionary sphere of action.

In this delicate phase of recollection and evaluation of the involved interests, it is vital that the public authority must strictly adhere to the administrative law principles of transparency, motivation and non-discrimination, in order to avoid biases and senseless choices based on a close-minded short-term perspective.[67] In this sense, normative obligations of thorough evaluation of

---

[67]   The recognition of public private partnership as an instrument of governance and, more specifically, its inclusion in the public contracts market implies the application

the private proposals are pivotal to guarantee that the decision of the public authority is based on technical and objective reasoning and that the proposed project will be ultimately beneficial for the community, in qualitative terms.

At the end of this phase, it is likely that the private proposal will be modified and enriched, in compliance with the requests of the public authority, which in any case has the final word over its execution. At this point, the public authority acts on the basis of its private law capacities, negotiating the clauses of the agreements with the private parties, which may or may not be put in open competition, according to the relevant jurisdiction. The powers of the public authority over the shaping of the public interest are here limited to the economic conditions of the market, in the sense that the solutions elaborated in partnership with the private actor for a specific need of the community will have to be feasible and sustainable, also in economic terms. In this sense, it is possible to say that in a public private partnership, the public interest is shaped through a consensual negotiation between the public authority and the private party.

6   CONCLUSION

Our analysis has led us to highlight the specific characteristics of public private partnership as applied in the modern local arena. We have noticed, in general, how the concept – and, consequently, the laws disciplining its procedural aspects – has undergone a transformation in recent years, from a mere instrument of financing to a complex instrument of social cohesion and innovation.

Public private partnership is, in this new form, a political strategy of co-management of public tasks, based on the active role of the community as interpreter of social needs and participating in the design and implementation of meeting them. This method of community involvement creates a new form of legitimacy for local governments and helps finance projects of public interest.

It is a political strategy, that allows public authorities to present themselves as credible promoters of good administration, innovation, inclusion and substantial democracy.

For these reasons, we believe it is impossible to restrict the notion of public private partnership to one of concession contract. Examples of national disciplines of public private partnership around the world demonstrate a wider and more significant role of this tool, as a form of governance through which it

---

of principles of administrative law both in the selection of the private partner and in the execution of the contract. Sara Valaguzza, *Sustainable development in public contracts: an example of strategic regulation* (Editoriale Scientifica, 2016) 18ff.

is possible to foster social cohesion, solidarity, democratic participation and social innovation.

In order to allow the positive interactions between the public authorities and the local community, public private partnership programmes should be capable of pointing to the achievement of improving public value. Thus, at a local level, flexibility becomes a key-feature of the laws on the matter.

However, procedures and contracts need to be designed keeping in mind that the parties must adequately evaluate risks and benefits, not only for themselves but for the community as direct beneficiary of the project. Consequently, careful evaluation is required to ensure that the agreement is indeed able to produce public value and to enhance the public image.

Thanks to this characterization, public private partnership is now more precisely described in its juridical essence.

The composition of the elements derived from our analysis of the international and local sphere will provide us with a complete profile. Before moving to the *pars construens*, we must differentiate the subject of our study from similar concepts.

4. Clearing up the picture: overcoming common misperceptions

1 INTRODUCTION

The preceding chapters provided us with some elements that we can now use to attempt a juridical definition of public private partnership. However before that, it is necessary to introduce some theoretical specifications which bring us to a sharper level of precision and allow us to overcome the misperceptions that often accompany the use of the term 'public private partnership'.

Firstly, we believe it is relevant to place public private partnership within the broader debate on public intervention in the market, differentiating it from the concepts of 'market failure' and 'horizontal subsidiarity' to which it is usually associated.

Said reasoning will lead us to detect the essential juridical function of the partnership agreement – namely, the cooperation in terms of the private actor's involvement, together with the public authority, in answering the community's need – and to pinpoint a critical feature: the combined presence of private and public parties in the co-management of public tasks. This will consequently bring us to distinguish public private partnership from the similar concepts of privatization, contracting out and the granting of authorizations and permits.

The conceptual work we will carry out in this chapter aims at defining the external boundaries of the topic.

Said deconstructive reasoning will be followed, in the subsequent chapter, by a reconstructive study in which we will try to recollect and unify all the hints emerging during our analysis.

The identity of public private partnership that we will re-define will therefore emerge from a unification of the features emerging from the semantic approach assumed in Chapter 1, the analysis of the international dimension carried out in Chapter 2 and the local dimension dealt with in Chapter 3.

2   COOPERATION VERSUS MARKET FAILURES

In Chapters 2 and 3, we showed how public private partnership allows public authorities, together with a private partner, to directly engage in activities of economic value.

In the economic and juridical literature, it is common to read that public private partnership is justified by 'market failures'.[1] The reason for this association, which we intend to reject here, is linked to the fact that some commentators read the public private partnership phenomenon as a reaction to a negative event, namely the incapacity of the market economy to face the concrete needs of society.

In our opinion, this premise is misleading. Indeed, the concept of market failure is based on a formal dichotomy between a selfish market, where businesses operate only by looking at their own profits, and an altruistic intervention of public authorities, necessary to protect the community's interests when the market economy fails.[2]

---

[1]   See, for instance, Organization for Economic Cooperation and Development, 'Special Issue on public/private partnerships in science and technology' (Science Technology Industry No. 23, 1999); Stephen Martin and John Scott, 'The nature of innovation market failure and the design of public support for private innovation' (2000) Research Policy 437; Bob Jessop, 'The dynamics of partnership and governance failure' in Gerry Stroker (ed.), *The new politics of local governance in Britain* (MacMillan, 2000) 11; Inge Kaul, 'Exploring the policy space between markets and states: global public-private partnerships' in Inge Kaul and Pedro Conceição (eds), *The New public finance: responding to global challenges* (OUP, 2006) 219; Albert Link, *Public/private partnerships: innovation strategies and policy alternatives* (Springer, 2006).

[2]   In extreme synthesis, according to the economic and juridical literature, failures of the market may occur in cases of: (1) dysfunction of the free market economy, which can cause the creation of monopolies or cartels distorting the rules of competition; (2) production of externalities, resulting in costs imposed on society that are not covered by the price of a product or service; (3) those cases in which the price of a product does not reflect costs of production and use imposed on society; (4) inadequacies posed by the fact that the market may not achieve social functions (such as providing a service at an affordable price); (5) information asymmetries between the producer or provider and the consumer; (6) difficulty producing and managing common goods, characterized by 'nonrivalrous consumption (consumption by one person does not create scarcity or preclude consumption by others) and nonexcludability (the good benefits a group of people and no one person or subgroup can easily, or at all, be prevented from enjoying it'. See Alan Randall, 'The problem of market failure' (1983) Natural Resource Journal; Renate Mayntz, 'Common goods and governance' in Adrienne Héritier (ed.), *Common goods: reinventing European and international governance* (Rowman and Littlefield Publishers, 2002) 15. The perspective is especially deepened by Elinor Ostrom and the economists who deepened her intuitions. See Introduction, n 33.

This logic hardly fits with the public private partnership dynamic, where market economy and public sector decide to act together. Rather, public private partnership springs from a government's desire to involve market actors in activities of general interest or from a private initiative's desire to be collaboratively engaged in a value-generating activity.

As we tried to highlight, public private partnership is a cultural and political choice. Said choice is not the reaction to a failure – of the market or the government[3] – but rather it is a cohesive strategy which intends to cross the barriers that traditionally divided the public and the private sector in the past.

For a deeper analysis of the concept, see Francis Bator, 'The anatomy of market failure' (1958) The Quarterly Journal of Economics 351; Harvey Averch, *Private markets and public intervention: a primer for policy designers* (University of Pittsburgh Press, 1990); Tyler Cowen (ed.), *Public goods and market failures: a critical examination* (Transnational Publishers, 1992); Arild Vatn and Daniel Bromley, 'Externalities – a market model failure' (1997) Environmental and Resource Economics 135; Srinivasan Balakrishnan et al., 'Information asymmetry, market failure and joint ventures : theory and evidence' (1999) Journal of Economic Behavior and Organization 99; Joe Wallis and Brian Dollery, *Market failure, government failure, leadership and public policy* (Palgrave Macmillan, 1999); Richard Zerbe Jr and Howard McCurdy, 'The failure of market failure' (1999) Journal of Policy Analysis and Management 558; Stephen Munday, *Markets and market failure* (Heinemann, 2000); Anthony Ogus, *Regulation: legal form and economic theory* (Bloomsbury Publishing, 2004); Clifford Winston, *Government failure versus market failure: microeconomics policy research and government performance* (AEI-Brookings Joint Center Regulatory Studies, 2006); Bronwen Morgan and Karen Yeung, *An introduction to law and regulation: text and materials* (CUP, 2007); Maria Cristina Marcuzzo, *Fighting market failure: collected essays in the Cambridge tradition of economics* (Routledge, 2012); Robert Hetzel, *The great recession: Market failure or policy failure?* (CUP, 2012); Joshua Newman, *Governing public-private partnership* (MQUP, 2017) 40ff.

With special reference to the justification of public intervention in relation to the corrections of dysfunctions of the market, in an optic of allocative efficiency (as is the case of competition laws regulating monopolies and cartels) or to achieve outcomes of public importance (as is the case of public service provisions), see Kieron Walsh, *Public services and market mechanisms: competition, contracting and the new public management* (Macmillan International Higher Education, 1995); James Chivers and Nicholas Flores, 'Market failure in information: the National Flood Insurance Program' (2002) Land Economics 515; Stephen Breyer et al., *Administrative law and regulatory policy: problems, texts and cases* (7th edition, Wolters Kluwer, 2011) 5; Richard Lipsey and Colin Harbury, *First principles of economics* (2nd Edition, OUP, 2004) 169.

[3]   On the concept of government failure and on the differences with the concept of market failure, see Charles Wolf, 'Market and non-market failures: comparison and assessment' (1987) Journal of Public Policy 43; Julian Le Grand, 'The theory of government failure' (1991) British Journal of Political Science 423; Wallis and Dollery, n 2; Mark Bovens, Paul T'Hart, and Brainard Guy Peters (eds), *Success and failure in public governance: a comparative analysis* (Edward Elgar, 2002); Winston, n 2;

Thus, from a legal perspective, at the basis of public private partnership there is neither a market failure nor a market domination; rather, there is a synergic form of aggregation between government and market to meet a community's needs.

In public private partnership, it is the rigid dichotomy between public and private that must be overcome, along with the formalistic distinction between efficiency, profits, economy and freedom of enterprise, on the one side, and absence of market view, public tasks, institutional missions and common interest, on the other.

More than market failure, public private partnership resembles, at least in its spirit, the forms of management of common goods by individuals or communities. These forms of active involvement of private actors in the management of 'commons' are deeply analysed in the studies of Elinor Ostrom and, more recently, in some interesting contributions of the juridical literature.[4]

Said authors have proposed an idea of management of commons that is not based on ownership but on the valorization of the active role of the community in the maintenance and care of said resources, characterized by their function of general interest. Indeed, the most acute elaboration on the governance of commons[5] highlighted that the answer to the so-called 'tragedy of the commons'[6] cannot be found in the national government's control or in the privatization of resources: 'neither the state nor the market is uniformly successful in enabling individuals to sustain long-term, productive use of natural resource systems'.[7] In the described view, the way out of the tragedy is the logic of cooperation in the management of common spaces – so-called 'common pool resources' – where, in extreme synthesis, the management of resources is collectively organized in order to maximize output and conserve resources for future generations.[8]

Being defined by their open fruition and not by their ownership, commons imply, just as public private partnership, the lifting of the dichotomy 'public versus private' and the assumption of responsibility from the community in the

---

Hetzel, n 2; with a specific reference to public private partnership, in Newman, n 2, 38ff.

[4]   See Introduction, n 34.

[5]   Elinor Ostrom, 'Reflections on the commons' in John Baden and Douglas Noonan (eds), *Managing the commons* (Indiana University Press, 1998) 95.

[6]   Garrett Hardin, 'The tragedy of the commons' (1968) Science 1968.

[7]   Ostrom, n 5.

[8]   See, in particular, the guiding principle for collective management of common resources presented in Elinor Ostrom, *Design principles and threats to sustainable organizations that manage commons* (Bloomington, 1999).

general interest. Indeed, it has been affirmed that the value of common goods lies in the empowerment of those who are involved in their care.[9]

The theory of private sector management of common goods shows how it is possible to build social cohesion and relationships aimed at generating virtuous behavioural models educating the sensitivities of individuals and businesses, which will have their own benefits in implementing public value. On this regard, the juridical literature has underlined how the valorization of commons can be an instrument to overcome socio-economic crises, not only because of the intrinsic capacity of said goods to directly satisfy the needs of their users, but also, and more importantly, because their management has a deep social and cultural impact on the construction of a network of relationships based on cooperation.[10]

This virtuous self-absorption of needs of general interest by the community and by its actors, such as businesses and private organizations, has to be read as a success of the market itself. In the private management of common goods what is missed, or risks being missed, is the role of public authorities, which, conversely, is protected while a public private partnership exists.

As seen, what characterizes public private partnership is the vivid pro-activeness of both public authorities and the private sector in sectors of administrative action.

In a partnership, the market does not fail but provides ideas and tools to the public sector.

Through the encounter between a community's needs and public and private resources, public private partnership generates benefits for the community.

The cooperation achieved to perform an activity of public relevance is therefore central to the agreement executed between the public administration and the private operator. In this regard, it is possible to make a few specifications in order to clear the path of misunderstandings and to assess the juridical significance of this last statement.

2.1   Cooperation Does Not Mean Identical Objectives: It Means a Single Aim

When assessing the semantic meaning of the subject of our study in Chapter 1, we affirmed that public private partnership is held by the 'logic of the compromise'. With this expression, we intended to state that public private partnership

---

[9]   Marco Bombardelli, 'La cura dei beni comuni come via di uscita dalla crisi' in Marco Bombardelli (ed.), *Prendersi cura dei beni comuni come via di uscita dalla crisi* (Editoriale Scientifica, 2015) 1, 36.

[10]   Ibid, 33.

is able to bind the public and the private dimension into a new context in which the identities, ambitions and aims of the partners are merged. We also stated that the compromise between the public and the private partner is based on the intention of both parties to achieve a common goal.

It is now possible to clarify this statement in more precise legal terms, in order to avoid possible misunderstandings.

To begin our reasoning, it is necessary to recall that public authorities are bound to pursue a public interest, even when they act with instruments of private law. Since their activity is to be considered bound to the pursuit of the public interest, the final scope of any partnership agreement that they may undertake must also be linked to their public function.

In parallel, we have seen how the private actors who undertake a partnership agreement with public administrations aim to perform an activity of public significance.

On these bases, is it possible to affirm that, in a public private partnership, the public and the private partner share the same objective, as is usually stated in the literature?[11]

In our opinion, contrary to the prevalent belief, the answer to this question should be negative.

In a public private partnership, the parties can surely have different perspectives and aims. Actually, because of the fact that partners may have different objectives, we used the term 'compromise' to characterize their relationship. However, the differences in objectives do not impact on the socio-economic function of the agreement, which is certainly shared.

Indeed, in juridical terms, the objectives of the parties remain external to the agreement if not introduced as specific conditions, terms or otherwise.[12]

Government and businesses may be pushed to stipulate a partnership agreement for many reasons. For example, a local government may decide to adhere to a partnership because it intends to provide a city park with a Wi-Fi system, whereas the private actor may decide to adhere to a partnership to gain a promotion of its corporate image from the same agreement. This does not

---

[11]   The mentioned correlation is made, for instance, in Pamela Bloomfield, 'The challenging business of long-term public-private partnerships: reflections on local experience' (2006) Public Administration Review 400; Carol Jacobson and Sang Ok Choi, 'Success factors: public works and public-private partnerships' (2008) International Journal of Public Sector Management 637; Derick Brinkerhoff and Jennifer Brinkerhoff, 'Public-private partnerships: perspectives on purposes, publicness, and good governance' (2011) Public Administration and Development 2; Malcolm Morley, *The public-private partnership handbook: how to maximize value from joint working* (Kogan Page, 2015) 42.

[12]   Annalisa di Giovanni, *Il contratto di partenariato pubblico privato tra sussidiarietà e solidarietà* (Giappichelli, 2012) 158ff.

mean that there is no shared goal in terms of the socio-economic function of the agreement.

Subjective reasons have no defining juridical relevance in the agreement that provides the regulation of interests between the partners. Furthermore, naturally instincts and motivations are subject to change throughout the life of the agreement, in relation to possible unexpected events: for instance, in case of flooding the concessionaire and the public administration of public works may have very different attitudes and personal motives about their obligations. Yet, they will be bound to the provisions contained in the document that regulates their partnership. For this reason, it is pivotal that the partnership agreement contains a precise and detailed discipline aimed at unravelling possible causes of conflict that could undermine the 'union' between the parties.

In essence, it is therefore evident that the encounter between the public and private dimension has a deeper contractual meaning.

The performance of an activity of public interest is not just an intention or an individual objective of the parties, but rather it is key to the socio-economic function of the agreement (comparable to the financial consideration of the contract).[13] For this reason, different scholars have proposed to consider the public interest as an essential element of the partnership agreement.[14]

As we could observe from the analysis carried out in Chapters 2 and 3, the possible juridical structures of a public private partnership are numerous (e.g. concession, sponsorship, project finance, social barter). Consequently, the goal of a partnership agreement could be the construction of a hospital, providing an educational service, protecting a nature reserve and so on. All these activities, which imply different performances from both parties, are united by the same

---

[13] On the transnational value of cause and consideration in contract law, see Malcolm Mason, 'The utility of consideration – a comparative view: cause and consideration' (1941) Columbia Law Review 825; Lon Fuller, 'Consideration and form' (1941) Columbia Law Review 799; Arthur von Mehren, 'Civil-law analogues to consideration: an exercise in comparative analysis' (1959) Harvard Law Review 1009; Aleck Chloros, 'The doctrine of consideration and the reform of the law of contract: a comparative analysis' (1968) International and Comparative Law Quarterly 137.

[14] See, among others, Akintola Akintoye, Matthias Beck, and Cliff Hardcastle, *Public-private partnerships: managing risks and opportunities* (Wiley-Blackwell, 2003); Michael Essig and Alexander Batran, 'Public-private partnership: development of long-term relationships in public procurement in Germany' (2005) Journal of Purchasing and Supply Management 221; Moira Fischbacher and Phil Beaumont 'PFI, public-private partnerships and the neglected importance of process: stakeholders and the employment dimension' (2010) Public Money and Management 171; Rui Cunha Marques and Sanford Berg, 'Public-private partnership contracts: a tale of two cities with different contractual arrangements' (2011) Public Administration 1585.

social function of the contract, which is to provide an activity that achieves a public interest.

The social function of the partnership is determined and shaped through a process of co-decision and negotiation that precedes the execution of the agreement.[15]

Depending on the jurisdiction, said phase could be carried out in a more or less structured administrative procedure, which could assume the form of a public tender or of a private negotiation (hopefully carried out in light of principles of transparency and non-discrimination).

It is then possible to understand public private partnership as a single 'administrative operation' which is shaped by the private and public parties and may have different contents, all directed at the pursuit of one or more public interests.

This statement helped us identify an essential feature of public private partnership, namely its function of satisfying a specific public interest, and to distinguish it from the subjective inclinations of the parties throughout the contractual relationship.

Nevertheless, said characterization is still not capable enough to distinguish public private partnership from other forms of public private interaction directed at achieving a public interest.

Indeed, as we have already anticipated, public private partnership is also characterized by the common undertaking of both public and private parties in the performance of specific activities. This aspect will clearly emerge, by differentiation, from the discussion of the principle of horizontal subsidiarity, to which public private partnership is usually associated.

3   CO-MANAGEMENT OF PUBLIC TASKS VERSUS HORIZONTAL SUBSIDIARITY

Deepening the reasons and advantages of public private partnership in Chapter 1, we affirmed that one of the main reasons for public officers to approach the private sector is to escape from the isolation of their responsibility.

We intended the concept of 'responsibility' in an organizational sense, to indicate the complex of activities attributed to an administrative apparatus for the performance of a specific function.[16] This acceptance of responsibility

---

[15]   See Chapter 1, n 65.

[16]   For this specific acceptance of the concept of responsibility, see Herman Finer, 'Administrative responsibility in democratic government' (1941) Public Administration Review 335; Arthur Maass and Laurence Radway, 'Gauging administrative responsibility' (1949) Public Administration Review 182; Charles Gilbert, 'The framework of administrative responsibility' (1959) The Journal of Politics 373; Adam Przeworski,

encompasses not only the *ex post* control on the results of a performed activity (closer to the concept of accountability[17]) but also an *ex ante* attribution of the powers to carry out certain tasks in the implementation of public policies.[18] The conferral of administrative responsibility is to be deemed as reconnected to the democratic process of selecting the relevant needs of the community and attributing powers to public authorities for their care.[19]

Nevertheless, if, as we said, the needs of the community can be selected and satisfied through public private partnership, this means that the private sector is allowed to be protagonists in the selection and shaping of the public policies and in the satisfaction of the community's needs. This, in turn, negates the monopoly of government apparatus on the achievement of social outcomes.[20]

Susan Stokes, and Bernard Manin (eds), *Democracy, accountability, and representation* (CUP, 1999). For a more general account of the theoretical foundations and of the different meanings of responsibility, see Anne Elisabeth Auhagen and Hans-Werner Bierhoff (eds), *Responsibility: the many faces of a social phenomenon* (Routledge, 2001); Hans Jonas, *Das prinzip verantwortung: versuch einer ethik für die technologische zivilisation* (1979, Suhrkamp Taschenbuch, 1984).

[17] On accountability as a set of mechanisms for governance improvement, see Richard Mulgan, *Holding power to account: accountability in modern democracies* (Houndmills, 2003) 188ff.; Staffan Lindberg, 'Mapping accountability: core concepts and subtypes' (2013) International Review of Administrative Science 202; Jerry Mashaw, 'Structuring a "dense complexity": accountability and the project of administrative law' (Issues in Legal Scholarship, 5/2005); Richard Stewart, 'Remedying disregard in global regulatory governance: accountability, participation, and responsiveness' (2014) 108 American Journal of International Law 211.

[18] On the difference between the *ex ante* and *ex post* administrative responsibility, see Michael Villey, 'Esquisse historique sur le mot responsable' in Marguerite Boulet-Sautel et al., *La responsabilité á travers les ages* (Sirey, 1989) 75 and, for the Italian literature, Antonio Cassatella, 'La responsabilità funzionale nell'amministrare. Termini e questioni' (2018) Diritto Amministrativo 677.

[19] Gilbert, n 16; Sidney Shapiro, 'A delegation theory of the APA' (1996) Admin. Law J. Am. U. 89; Björn Bartling and Urs Fischbacher, 'Shifting the blame: on delegation and responsibility' (2012) The Review of Economic Studies 67; Ryan Carlin and Shane Singh, 'Executive power and economic accountability' (2015) The Journal of Politics 1031.

[20] As is evident from the reading of the studies on private participation to public policies, among which see: Albert Hirschman and Robert Frank, *Shifting involvements: private interest and public action* (Princeton University Press, 2002); Adam McCann et al. (eds), *When private actors contribute to public interests: a law and governance perspective* (Eleven, 2014); Lez Rayman-Bacchus and Philip Walsh, *Corporate responsibility and sustainable development: exploring the nexus of private and public interests* (Routledge, 2015).

This element has led several scholars to associate public private partnership with the concept of 'horizontal subsidiarity'.[21] The above-mentioned concept expresses the idea that the intervention of the state in the economy is 'undesirable, at least to the extent that there are available alternatives',[22] the justification being the need to preserve deference to the economic freedom of initiative. In order to assess the legal preciseness of the link between public private partnership and this last concept, it is necessary to briefly clarify the derivation and burden of the subsidiarity principle.

In its broadest acceptance, the subsidiarity principle indicates a criterion to attribute legitimacy, stating which logic must be used to understand the relationship of powers between two or more entities.[23] Basically, the principle is used in those cases where different entities have intertwined legitimacy or competence, indicating a scale of priority. The principle indicates: (1) the primarily legitimate entity (namely, the ones that are closer to the beneficiaries of the activity at stake); (2) the secondarily legitimate entities; and (3) the conditions according to which the secondarily legitimate entities are allowed to act in substitution of the primarily legitimate one. Said conditions take place when the primarily legitimate entities are not capable of reaching optimal results or results as good as the ones that could be achieved by the subsidiary entities.

The principle is applied both vertically and horizontally. In its vertical acceptance, the principle indicates a criterion of attribution of power. This is

---

[21]   See, for instance, Jennifer Brinkerhoff, 'Government-nonprofit partnership: a defining framework' (2002) Public Administration and Development 19; Ali Sedhari, 'Public-private partnership as a tool for modernizing public administration' (2004) International Review of Administrative Sciences 291; Ioan Horga, Adrian Ivan, and Iordan Gheorghe Bărbulescu, 'Regional and cohesion policy – insights into the role of the partnership principle in the new policy design' (Regional and Cohesion Policy, 2011, 5); Giorgio Vittadini, 'Subsidiarity: a new partnership between state, market and civil society' in Alberto Brugnoli and Alessandro Colombo (eds), *Government, governance and welfare reform: structural changes and subsidiarity in Italy and Britain* (Edward Elgar, 2012) 17; Giulio Citroni, Andrea Lippi, and Stefania Profeti, 'Local public services in Italy: still fragmentation' in Hellmut Wollmann, Ivan Koprić, and Gérard Marcou (eds), *Public and social services in Europe: from public and municipal to private sector provision* (Springer, 2016) 103.

[22]   Colin Crawford, 'Subsidiarity, local government and privatisation of service' (1997) Holdsworth Law Review 12.

[23]   See Andràs Toth, 'A legal analysis of subsidiarity' in David O'Keeffe and Patrick Twomeny (eds), *Legal issues of the Maastricht treaty* (Chancery, 1994) 39; Robert Vischer, 'Subsidiarity as a principle of governance: beyond devolution' (2001) Ind. Law Review 103; Giuseppe Ugo Rescigno, 'Principio di sussidiarietà orizzontale e diritti sociali' (2002) Diritto Pubblico 5; Paolo Carozza, 'Subsidiarity as a structural principle of international human rights law' (2003) American Journal of International Law 38.

the meaning of the subsidiarity principle implied, for instance, in Article 5 of the EU Treaty, which states the rule according to which: 'Under the principle of subsidiarity, in areas which do not fall within its exclusive competence, the Union shall act only if and in so far as the objectives of the proposed action cannot be sufficiently achieved by the Member States, either at central level or at regional and local level, but can rather, by reason of the scale or effects of the proposed action, be better achieved at Union level.'[24]

The same definition is present in some national constitutions that indicate a criterion for distribution of competences between layers of territorial administrative entities.[25]

In its horizontal definition, the principle lays out a criterion for providing public benefits, establishing whether they belong to the public or private sector. According to the principle of horizontal subsidiarity, the state and the public authorities should preserve the free economic autonomy of the citizens aiming at the satisfaction of a general interest. Consequently, public authorities should preferentially involve interested citizens and organized groups of society and should directly intervene to carry out public tasks only if the private sector is not capable of efficiently reaching the pre-fixed goals.

---

[24] For a comment on the European acceptance of the principle, see, in particular, Paul Spicker, 'The principle of subsidiarity and the social policy of the European Community' (1991) 1 Journal of Social Policy 3; Nicholas Emiliou, 'Subsidiarity: an effective barrier against the "enterprises of ambition?"' (1992) EL Review 383; Andràs Toth, 'The principle of subsidiarity in the Maastricht Treaty' (1992) Common Market Law Review 1079; George Bermann, 'Taking subsidiarity seriously: federalism in the European Community and the United States' (1994) Columbia Law Review 331; Gary Vause, 'The subsidiarity principle in European Union law – American federalism compared' (1995) Case W. Res J. Int'l Law 61; Nicholas Emiliou, 'Subsidiarity: panacea or fig leaf?' in O'Keeffe and Twomeny (eds), n 23, 65; Christian Calliess, *Subsidiaritäs-un Solidaritätsprinzip in der Europäischen Union* (Nomos, 1996); Grainne de Burca, 'The principle of subsidiarity and the Court of Justice as an institutional actor' (1998) JCMS 218; Grainne de Búrca, 'Reappraising subsidiarity's significance after Amsterdam' (Jeanne Monet Working Paper 7/1999); Alessandro Colombo, *The principle of subsidiarity and European citizenship* (Vita e Pensiero, 2004).

[25] For an account of the application in Germany see Johannes Münder and Dieter Kreft (eds), *Subsidiarität heute* (Votum, 1990); Max-Emanuel Geis, *Die öffentliche Förderung sozialer Selbsthilfe* (Sonstiges, 1997); Otfried Höffe, 'Subsidiarität als Staatsphilosophisches Prinzip' in Knut Wolfgang Nörr and Thomas Oppermann (eds), *Subsidiarität: Idee und Wirklichkeit* (Bücher, 1997) 52; Greg Taylor, 'Germany: the subsidiarity principle' (2006) International Journal of Constitutional Law 115. For a Swiss account, see Andreas Ladner, 'Switzerland: subsidiarity, power-sharing, and direct democracy' in Frank Hendriks, Anders Lidström, and John Loughlin (eds), *The Oxford handbook of local and regional democracy in Europe* (OUP, 2011) 201. As for the French jurisdiction, it is possible to quote Charles Millon-Delsol, *L'État subsidiaire* (Paris, 1992).

Rooted in liberal theory that allowed only small windows of intervention of the state in society, where citizens must be kept free to live and interact,[26] as well as in the Catholic conception of the importance of preserving the capacity of individuals to realize themselves in their individual and social life,[27] the principle of horizontal subsidiarity has two sides, one negative and one positive:[28] the negative component is represented by the duty of the state and public powers to abstain from intervention in social life whenever the strengths of the individual are enough to autonomously satisfy his or her needs; the positive component affirms the existence of a duty represented by the duty of the state and public powers to intervene whenever the strengths of the individuals are insufficient to satisfy social needs.

That being said, it is possible to see points of juncture and friction between the described principle and public private partnership.

A shared feature of both concepts is surely the valorization of the private economic initiative, which is regarded as a constitutional value in its capacity to generate value for the community.

The support of the ability of the community to satisfy its own needs is surely something that fits within the juridical concept of public private partnership as we have portrayed it.

Similarly, public private partnership shares with the horizontal subsidiarity principle the idea whereby a task should be primarily attributed to the entities that are closer to the beneficiaries of a specific action.

In this sense, we have affirmed that private operators, individuals, associations and social enterprises, as primary interpreters of the needs of the community, are the best-suited entities to answer to social demands. In this sense, based on a first and generic assessment, it could be affirmed that public private partnership shares a few features with the principle of horizontal subsidiarity.

However, a few specifications have to be made.

Firstly, the horizontal subsidiarity principle is based on an antagonistic conception of the relationship between the state and society; indeed, the primary function of the principle is to determine when public powers should be allowed

---

[26]   The relationship between subsidiarity and liberalism is particularly analysed in Andrew Moravcsik, 'Preferences and power in the European Community: a liberal intergovernmentalist approach' (1993) Common Market Studies 473; Maria Cahill, 'Sovereignty, liberalism and the intelligibility of attraction to subsidiarity' (2016) The American Journal of Jurisprudence 109.

[27]   Höffe, n 25, 53; Simeon Tsetim Iber, *The principle of subsidiarity in Catholic social thought, implications for social justice and civil society in Nigeria* (Peter Lang, 2011).

[28]   The distinction between the two downsides of the same principle is clearly expressed in Alessandra Albanese, 'Il principio di sussidiarietà orizzontale: autonomia sociale e compiti pubblici' (2002) Diritto pubblico 51.

to directly intervene in economic matters. Conversely, in the public private partnership arena, public authorities and private actors are placed on the same level as contributors to producing public value.

Secondly, the above-mentioned principle shows a clear preference for the private sector over the public one, affirming that public authorities should only have a supporting role in promoting private initiative and eventually intervening in case of private failure to deliver benefits.

Yet, in public private partnership there is no express preference for the private subject over the public one. Nor vice versa.

The public intervention is not subordinated to the private one; rather, the two spheres merge, without a pre-fixed criterion of preference of one partner over another.

The coexistence of the public and the private sphere that is generated in a public private partnership is different from the alternative intervention foreseen in the horizontal subsidiarity principle, which, as we affirmed, provides for a criterion of alternative intervention in addressing the needs of the society. It is not the private or, secondarily, the public who address social needs in a public private partnership, but the private and the public together.

Thirdly, as will be more evident from the analysis carried out in the following section, public intervention is not subordinated to a failure of the private side to adequately respond to the needs of the society. Conversely, the recourse to the private sector is justified by the difficulty encountered by public administrations in carrying out one of their tasks.

This need provokes the state to involve the private sector to fulfil its public mission in co-management of public tasks that creates a public private co-responsibility to pursue a specific public purpose.[29]

3.1　Co-management Explained

3.1.1　Differentiation from privatization and 'contracting out'
Public private partnership is often associated with privatization and contracting out, as policies through which public authorities involve private parties to perform public tasks.[30] Yet, in light of the description of public private

---

[29]　The dimension will be discussed in Chapter 7.

[30]　See, for instance, Wendell Lawther, *Privatizing toll roads: a public-private partnership* (Pager, 1946); Daphne Barak-Erez, 'Three questions of privatization' in Susan Rose-Ackerman, Peter Lindseth, and Blake Emerson (eds), *Comparative administrative law* (2nd edition, Edward Elgar, 2017) 533, 534; David McDonald and Greg Ruiters (ed.), *The age of commodity: water privatization in Southern Africa* (Earthscan, 2005); Matthew Flinders, 'Public/private: the boundaries of the state' in Colin Hay, Michael Lister, and David Marsh (eds), *The state: theories and issues* (Macmillan

partnership that we have depicted so far, we are able to make a few distinctions in this matter.

'Privatization' is an expression used to indicate numerous different policies, legislative or administrative measures,[31] that all share the aim 'to reduce government intervention in social and economic life',[32] in favour of the private sector.[33]

Privatization may be carried out in many ways, such as 'the sale by a government of state-owned enterprises (SOEs) or assets to private economic agents',[34] a legislative act of liberalization – meaning the withdrawal of the state from certain areas of the market on the basis of the recognition that free citizens and enterprises would be better served if restrictions and regulations

---

International, 2006) 223; John Forrer et al., 'Public-private partnerships and the public accountability question' (2010) Public Administration Review 475.

[31]   Indeed, privatization lacks an accepted definition, as remarked in Paul Starr, 'The meaning of privatization' (1988) Yale Law and Policy Review 6.

[32]   Barak-Erez, n 30, 534.

[33]   For a broader account, see Martha Minow, *Partners, not rivals: privatization and the public good* (Beacon Press, 2002); Paul Verkuil, 'Public law limitations on privatization of government functions' (2007) North Carolina Law Review 397; Fabienne Péraldi-Leneuf, 'Le recours à l'externalité dans le système administratif communautaire: la délégation de la technicité' in Pascal Mbongo (ed.), *Le phénomène bureaucratique Européen: intégration européenne et 'technophobie'* (Bruyllant, 2009); Martha Minow, 'Outsourcing power: privatizing military efforts and the risks to accountability, professionalism, and democracy' in Jody Freeman and Martha Minow (eds), *Outsourcing and American democracy* (Harvard University Press, 2009) 110; Sharon Dolovich, 'How privatization thinks: the case of prisons', ibid, 128; Alfred Aman, Jr, 'Privatization and democracy. Resources in administrative law', ibid, 261. The topic has been studied by the public law literature in relation to the problem of lack of accountability, *ex multis*, by Mark Freedland, 'Government by contract and public law' (1994) Public Law 86; Jody Freeman 'Extending public accountability through privatization: from public law to publicization' in Michael Dowdle (ed.), *Public accountability: designs, dilemmas and experiences* (CUP, 2006) 83; Jerry Mashaw, 'Accountability and institutional design: some thoughts on the grammar of governance', ibid 115; Jean-Bernard Auby, 'Contracting out and "public values": a theoretical and comparative approach' in Rose-Ackerman, Lindseth, and Emerson (eds), n 30, 552. An interesting study, which well demonstrates the withdrawal of the government as a consequence of privatization, is Amir Paz-Fuchs, Ronen Mandelkern, and Itzhak Galnoor (eds), *The privatization of Israel: the withdrawal of state responsibility* (Palgrave MacMillan, 2018). For a society-based reading of privatization, see also Antenor Hallo de Wolf, *Reconciling Privatization with Human Rights* (Intersentia, 2012).

[34]   William Megginson and Jeffry Netter, 'From state to market: a survey of empirical studies on privatization' (2001) Journal of Economic Literature 321.

were to be repealed or streamlined[35] – or the shift from public to private production of services, through 'contracting out'.

The last-mentioned expression indicates the decision to 'entrust a private entity with a task that remains under public supervision and is not purely left to the market'.[36] In this sense, the concept expresses a privatization that does not imply a total withdrawal of the state from a public function but a practice of government by contract which leaves the ultimate responsibility for the success of the service or good delivery on the contracting public authority. The concept thus overlaps with one of procurement contracts, from which it can only (and hardly) be distinguished on the basis of the closeness of the outsourced duties to the function of an administration.[37]

That being clarified, it is now possible to make some distinctions about public private partnership.

In this regard, we can start by saying that a public private partnership springs from the same ideological ground as the New Public Management theories of the 1970s and 1980s.[38] From the United States[39] to Australia and New Zealand[40] to Great Britain,[41] governments have adopted a policy of externalizing portions of public activities and the reform of public administrations on the basis of business organization models, following the slogan: 'government actors would need to think and behave like entrepreneurs'.[42]

Externalization, outsourcing, privatization and liberalization became the key-words of a governmental revolution that was based on various methods of inclusion of the private sector in the production of goods and services for the administered community.

---

[35] The relationship between public private partnership, privatization and liberalization is addressed in Darrin Grimsey and Mervyn Lewis, *The economics of public private partnerships* (Edward Elgar, 2005); Thomas Krumm, *The politics of public-private partnerships in Western Europe: comparative perspectives* (Edward Elgar, 2016).

[36] See Geoffrey Segal, 'Testimony to the Utah law enforcement and criminal justice interim committee' in Yvonne Fortin and Hugo van Hassel (eds), *Contracting in the new public management: from economics to law and citizenship* (IOS Press, 1994); Simon Domberger and Christine Hall, 'Contracting for public services: a review of Antipodean experiences' (1996) Public Administration 129; Auby, n 33, 552.

[37] Aman, n 33.

[38] See Introduction and Chapter 1.

[39] Jody Freeman, 'The contracting state' (2000) Florida State University Law Review 155.

[40] Domberger and Hall, n 36; Cheryl Saunders and Kevin Yam, 'Government regulation by contract: implications for the rule of law' (2004) Public Law Review 51.

[41] See Chapter 1.

[42] Stephen Linder, 'Coming to terms with the public-private partnership: a grammar of multiple meanings' in Pauline Vaillancourt Rosenau (ed.), *Public-private policy partnerships* (MIT Press, 2000) 19, 20.

These concepts are all unified by the fact that they are techniques of providing goods and services to the public, as a primary mission of public authorities intervening in the market. In this sense, public private partnership could be assimilated to the concepts of privatization and contracting out as techniques of neo-liberal derivation[43] that imply 'reducing the role of government or increasing the role of the private institutions of society in satisfying people's needs'.[44]

Moreover, they can all be considered a reaction to the necessities of public administration to face ever-increasing needs, costs and demands from the community. Said necessity pushes public administrations towards the private sector, which, as we notice, comes in aid of governments in their performance of administrative duties. The same economic or responsibility-allocative reasons could then justify the recourse of a public administration to privatization, contracting out or public private partnership.

However, privatization and contracting out both represent cases in which the state or public authorities retreat from the market,[45] with different grades of intensity: whether the retreat from the market is complete in the case of privatization, contracting out leaves a margin of public intervention and responsibility. This is a first important differentiation between the mentioned concepts and public private partnership. Indeed, the latter implies the active involvement of both public and private parties in carrying out a specific activity. Public private partnership implies a proactive mutual movement towards the market and not a retreat from it.

In a public private partnership, the public authority remains actively involved in the performance of a specific activity, carried out together with the private actor.

It is involved in the decision-making process and in the operational phase, as responsible for portions of implementation of the agreement. The co-management of a specific public task to be performed in favour of the community is a distinctive characteristic of public private partnership, which distinguishes it from both privatization and contracting out. Indeed, in the case of privatization, the public authority 'leaves the scene' to the private sector, which becomes the sole responsible entity and the sole manager of the publicly relevant activity.

---

[43] Privatization is based on the political ideals of individual freedom that were incorporated into the founding of the modern neoliberal movement. On this point, see David Harvey, *A brief history of neoliberalism* (OUP, 2005) 5ff.

[44] Emanuel Savas, *Privatization in the city: successes, failures, lessons* (CQ Press, 2005) 2.

[45] Aman, n 33 uses the expression 'to disembed' from the market. Flinders, n 30, 223, talks about delegation of responsibilities to quasi-autonomous 'para-statal' actors.

In the case of contracting out it is possible to recall what we said in Chapter 2 in relation to public procurement: 'contracting out is characterized by a principal-agent relationship in which the public actor defines the problem and provides the specifications of the solution ... Partnership, on the other hand, is based on joint decision making and production in order to achieve effectiveness for both parties.'[46]

In other terms, contracting out (and public procurement) both imply a pre-definition of the desired output by the public authority, thus leaving the private as a mere executor of the public will. Conversely, as we saw from Chapter 1, partnership implies a co-design of the method through which services, works or goods will be delivered to the community, in a process which grants the private sector an important role as a selector of public interest, co-decision maker and proposer of administrative solutions. In this sense, it is possible to confirm that public private partnership does not imply a principal-agent relational model but rather a horizontal process of co-design and co-management of the public interest.

For these reasons, just as we affirmed for public procurement in Chapter 2:

> contracting out becomes an obsolete arrangement in situations in which neither products nor performance indicators are clear. The number of situations is growing in which the governments involved do not have a clear image of the specifications of the policy, product or project that they want to produce. In such a situation of cooperation between the public and private sector can still be fruitful.[47]

The diversification and widening of the tasks of public authorities in response to the increasing social demands to protect public interests provide a solid ground for the spread of public private partnership as administrative methods for governing complexity.

For this reason, public private partnership can be considered as an evolution of privatization and contracting out:[48] coming from the same ideological conceptions, public private partnership becomes a derivative form of the neo-liberal techniques of government, no longer based on a contrast between the market and the public dimension, but on the synergy between the two worlds, which becomes a necessity especially in complex scenarios that require the invention of new ways of responding to social demands.

---

[46]   Erik-Hans Klijn and Geert Teisman, 'Governing public-private partnerships: analysing and managing the process and institutional characteristics of public-private partnerships' in Stephen Osborne (ed.), *Public-private partnerships: theory and practice in international perspective* (Routledge, 2000) 84, 85.

[47]   Ibid, 86.

[48]   In terms, see Linder, n 42, 20ff.

3.1.2   Differentiation from authorizations and the granting of permits for socially relevant initiatives

The differentiation between public private partnership and privatization or contracting out allowed us more precisely to evaluate the juridical essence of public private partnership as a form of co-management of public interests. In this regard, we came to acknowledge that public private partnership implies an active and direct intervention from public authorities in the matter at stake. This allows us to further distinguish public private partnerships from those public private relationships that are limited solely to the granting of administrative authorization or permits.

As a matter of fact, public administrations constantly come in contact with private actors that, either individually or in associated form, carry out activities in the interest of the community. As already mentioned in Chapter 1, the phenomenon encompasses both 'social entrepreneurship', which represents 'a process involving the innovative use and combination of resources to pursue opportunities to catalyse social change and/or address social needs',[49] and clear forms of private activism for the satisfaction of needs of the community[50] and third sector parties.[51] As seen in the analysis of the national and supranational application of public private partnership, non-profit initiatives and social entrepreneurship play a pivotal role in carrying out publicly relevant activities in important sectors like education, health care, improving environmental conditions, enhancing the value of cultural heritage, scientific research, tourism and protection of human rights.

---

[49]   Johanna Mair and Ignasi Marti, 'Social entrepreneurship research: a source of explanation prediction and delight' (2006) Journal of World Business 36, 44.

[50]   Uncountable private business initiatives may be traced in the most disparate sectors of public interventions (health, culture, environment, social right protection, to name a few). See Roger Martin and Sally Osberg, 'Social entrepreneurship: the case for definition' (2007) Stanford Social Innovation Review 11.

[51]   The relevance of the so-called 'third sector' (as different from the market and the state) in the provision of services of general interest has been recognized in many jurisdictions, even in the form of specific disciplines aimed at supporting the autonomous initiatives of singular or associated citizens in the production of public value. For a discussion of the possible definitions of the concept, see Olaf Corry, 'Defining and theorizing the third sector' in Rupert Taylor (ed.), *Third sector research* (Springer, 2010) 11, where the author affirms that: 'In practice "third sector" is used to refer to widely differing kinds of organization such as charities, nongovernmental organizations (NGOs), self-help groups, social enterprises, networks, and clubs, to name a few that do not fall into the state or market categories'. See also Burton Weisbrod, 'Conceptual perspective on the public interest: an economic analysis' in Burton Weisbrod, Joel Handler, and Neil Komesar (eds), *Public interest law, an economic and institutional analysis* (University of California Press, 1978) 4, 20ff.

Public authorities promote voluntary active participation of society members not only for its intrinsic value of solidarity and social cooperation but also because they largely benefit from the performance of said voluntary social commitment, as it partially removes them from the monopoly over the responsibility of taking care of specific interests. The dynamic is quite similar to the escape from the administrations' responsibility isolation, which, as we addressed in Chapter 1, brings public officials to seek public private partnership. For these reasons, public authorities may find value in promoting non-profit organizations and social enterprises and consequently provide incentives for private participation in social issues.

On the basis of the deeper analysis carried out in the present chapter, we can now specify that not all forms of cooperation of public authorities with social enterprises and non-profit groups can fit into the category of public private partnership, since not all of them imply a co-management of a public task.

For instance, participation in socially important activities may be promoted through regulatory mechanisms such as tax breaks and economic incentives. In these cases, there would not be a co-management of public tasks, but only a regulatory activity aimed at promoting private engagement in socially important activities.

Similarly, it would be impossible to define as a 'partnership' all those cases in which the activity of the public administration is limited to the granting of authorizations or permits, intended as administrative acts that remove a legislatively imposed limit to protect a specific public interest.[52] For example, the opening of a soup kitchen for underprivileged citizens or the construction of social housing will necessarily imply contact between the private operator and the involved municipal authority: authorizations will be required in order to verify the compliance with town planning, fire safety and health regulations.

In such cases, the public authority would act according to the traditional rules and principles of administrative law, exercising a public power. It would come in contact with the private sector only in the procedural phase in order to acquire the necessary data and to provide the necessary participatory right to the interested party. More specifically, it will have to evaluate and verify that the requirements set by law for the performance of a specific activity were

---

[52] A few fundamental and sufficiently encompassing contributions on this point are Mario Pilade Chiti, 'Forms of European administrative action' (2004–2005) Law and Contemporary Problems 37; Sabino Cassese, 'European administrative proceedings' (2004) Law and Contemporary Problems 21; Adrian Vermeule, 'Our Schmittian administrative law' (2008) Harvard Law Review 1095; Herwig Hofmann, Gerhard Rowe, and Alexander Türk, *Administrative law and policy of the European Union* (OUP, 2011) 433ff.; Eric Biber et al., 'The permit power revisited: the theory and practice of regulatory permits in the administrative state' (2014) Duke Law Journal 133.

met, and make sure that the private actor will carry out the economic activity in a balance with the other significant public activities.

However, it would be impossible to assume that in those cases a real cooperation is formed, as the public authority would take no part in the direct performance of the authorized activity. In other words, there would not be any public private partnership.

4   CONCLUSION

The quest to define the exact juridical features of public private partnership has led us to challenge a few common misconceptions on this subject.

Taking a few common beliefs on the topic as a reference, we carried out a line of reasoning that helped us define public private partnership by differentiation from similar figures.

The conceptual operation was useful, in our view, not only to avoid juridical confusion but also to capture some essential characteristics of public private partnerships, as laid out in the analysis in Part I of this book.

The semantic approach attempted in Chapter 1 allowed us to highlight the perspective of cooperation that is intrinsic in a partnership, which implies the mutual presence of public and private actors in the performance of actions in the community's interest as well as the logic of the compromise that dominates the relationships between subjects – public and private actors – with different attitudes, missions and perspectives.

Also, we looked more closely at the logic of the compromise, in a distinction between the partners' goals – which belong to the individuals and generate the need for compromise – and the social function of the agreement, which is shared between all the members of the partnership.

Said social function, as we analysed in Chapters 2 and 3, consists in public and private actors performing activities that are in line with the pursuit of public interest. In the international arena, this function is often evident in the achievement of sustainable development goals, whereas in the national arena the issue of a community's ability to meet its own needs, through initiatives of co-management of public interests, is at the fore.

In Chapters 2 and 3 we analysed how the international and the local spheres offer interesting implementations of public private partnership and why the partnership is so compatible with modern principles of public law such as sustainability, participatory democracy, transparency and cooperation between state and market.

In Chapter 1, we mentioned the need to escape from responsibility isolation, consistency with the principles of participatory democracy and the ability to generate and exploit businesses' social responsibility as the main reasons for and advantages of public private partnership.

We have now clarified that the cooperation allows us to distinguish public private partnership from other forms of providing public services such as privatization, contracting out and the granting of permits and authorizations.

The contour is now clear enough to attempt our definition of public private partnership, on the basis of the features collected from our analysis.

PART II

5. Reconstructing the juridical identity of public private partnership

1   SUMMING UP

The analysis carried out so far brought us to resolve the ambiguity that still dominates the political and juridical debate on public private partnership and to encapsulate the characteristic features of the phenomenon.

In light of the research carried out, we are now able to attempt a definition of the juridical identity of public private partnership. To do that, we need to recollect the outcomes of our studies and summarize their results.

In defining public private partnership, it makes sense to concentrate on its general features, in order to find a concept capable of including all the *species* in the *genus*.

Defining the juridical features of public private partnership means referring to a concept with many different applicative potentialities.

Some of them have been examined in terms of their capacity for generating efficiency and value, whereas some others can be praised as elements of social and economic innovation and instruments to deal with complexity and the increasing demand of governance.

The semantic analysis of the expression allowed us to underline that the concept of public private partnership must be researched outside the traditional adversarial relationships of contractual counterparts, in the contexts of collaboration and synergy. This implies a rational subdivision of the risks and disadvantages connected to a common interest initiative. The success or failure of a project in a public private partnership must be portioned between the members of the alliance.

We affirmed that public private partnership is based on cooperation rather than juxtaposition. Moreover, we stated that public private partnership brings together two entities, at least a public and a private one, which belong to sectors characterized by different logics, tasks and objectives.

For this reason, we have detected as a distinctive element of public private partnership the need to establish a compromise in which the public and the private partners share perspectives and accept the need to mediate their respective positions, looking at the final aim of the process – an aim that, as we clarified in Chapter 4, does not only belong to the single partner's objectives but characterizes the social function of the agreement.[1]

After the semantic analysis, we moved on to an examination of the reasons and advantages of public private partnership, where we detected the need – from the public side – to escape isolated responsibility, through mechanisms of inclusion and participation of the community in governance, and to find new legitimacy for public powers to act in the market; and from the private side to take opportunities in markets traditionally closed to businesses and private persons.

The study into the application of public private partnership in the international dimension (Chapter 2) led us to appreciate the value of flexible networks of state and non-state actors, oriented towards the achievement of public value of global importance, such as sustainable development goals, participatory democracy, social inclusion and cooperation.

The analysis of the local dimension (Chapter 3) led us to emphasize that public private partnership is also a fundamental instrument of co-management of public tasks, carried out together with local communities and businesses, as a consequence of the financial crisis of public funds and in line with the renaissance of policies of social inclusion and innovation.

The political, social and cultural dimension of public private partnership strongly characterize public private partnership both in the international and in the local context.[2] Said dimension promotes forms of cooperation that are capable of generating additional public value, in terms of economic and social growth, through the active role of private parties who contribute to innovation and enhancing the quality of governance.

This aspect, as we concluded in Chapter 4, differentiates public private partnership from privatization, contracting out and authorizations, the granting of permits, and even from public procurement methods.

Lastly, we clarified that the relationship between the public and the private sector in a public private partnership does not reside in any preference between the two, nor is it based on a failure of some sort.

Rather, we assessed that the distinctive feature of public private partnership lies in the breaking of the traditional schemes, through the meeting of interests and wills between parties that otherwise would act separately in their respective domains. This characteristic of public private partnership allows the cre-

---

[1]   Differently, should we discuss public public partnership, or private private partnership there would be an ontological homogeneity between the parties that share a programme of common interest.

[2]   On this point, see also Adam Masters, *Cultural influences on public-private partnerships in global governance* (Palgrave MacMillan, 2018).

ation of value for the community, through the direct involvement of the very same community whose interests are satisfied by the partnership.

2   A SYNTHESIS OF THE OUTCOMES: THE DISTINCTIVE FEATURES OF PUBLIC PRIVATE PARTNERSHIP

The juridical elements of the concept appear now as scattered pieces of a puzzle that must now be recomposed in order to obtain a unitary picture. The identity of public private partnership must now be reconstructed into a general and consistent framework that defines the contours of the profile of public private partnership.

In the section below, we highlight the elements emerging from the various perspectives adopted in the previous chapters. The first four columns of Table 5.1 describe the elements that characterize, in a systematic sense, the notion of public private partnership as derived from: (1) the semantic and agent-oriented approach; (2) the international dimension; (3) the local dimension; and (4) the differentiation from similar concepts. The last column contains the elements for the reconstruction of the juridical notion of public private partnership.

As it is possible to see, the elements proposed in the first chapter as characterizing the concept of public private partnership have been confirmed and specified in all the different perspectives adopted throughout the development of the book. For this reason, it is possible to read the table horizontally as a progressive evolution towards a precise juridical notion of public private partnership.

Starting from the first line, it is clear that the blending of the public and the private dimensions for the performance of one or more activities defines public private partnership across all its dimensions.

Since Chapter 1, we highlighted how public private partnership is based on a necessary compromise between the actors of the agreement. The disruptive force of these partnerships breaks the centuries-old public private dichotomy between the public and the private sector. The partnership binds the parties, who mutually renounce portions of their identity, features and attitudes for the achievement of a common goal.

While in the international dimension the action is driven by global values, in the local dimension public private partnership helps deal with the complexity of the community's needs, providing public bodies with a form of accountability based on inclusion and cooperation with the market.

As we specified in Chapter 4, the compromise required from both the private and the public partners does not imply a unification of their values, interests, motives and objectives. Throughout the design and execution of the partnership, the different attitudes of the partners may still create conflict,

*Table 5.1   Reconstructing the juridical identity of public private
partnership*

Chapter 1 semantic approach, reasons and advantages	Chapter 2 international dimension	Chapter 3 local dimension	Chapter 4 differentiation	Chapter 5 reconstruction
compromise to achieve the same goal	global values	instrument to carry out public tasks	unique aim, different objectives	agreement
cooperation versus juxtaposition	goal-oriented networks	alternative to public procurement	co-management of public tasks	joint management of one or more activities
escape from the isolation of responsibilities	states cannot be left alone	valorisation of bottom-up initiatives	cooperation versus market failure	
participatory democracy	people first approach	political, social and economic dimension of instrument	public interests	satisfaction of a public interest
cooperation	non-state actors as principal protagonists of the achievement of sustainable development goals			

to be solved according to the rules set out in the stipulated agreement. This brings the partnership into the contractual arena, where the single motives and objectives are not relevant if not formalized in contractual clauses. Under this perspective, we could highlight that in a public private partnership, partners do not share their objectives; rather, they come to a compromise in order to achieve the aim of the contractual process, which is the production of public value. In other words, what is shared, what allows the compromise, and what can be defined as the socio-economic function of public private partnership is the performance of an activity of public interest.

The second line of the table focuses on another distinctive characteristic of public private partnership, namely the cooperation requiring the mutual presence and action from the public and the private side.

In the international dimension, we found that the creation of alliances and synergies between agencies, public entities, financing institutions, enterprises, local businesses, citizens, associations and non-governmental organizations was adopted, since the late 1990s, as a method of achieving internationally relevant goals of sustainable development, as an alternative to the formalistic and rigid approach characterizing international relationships in the ambit of environmental and social protection.

The scarcity of public resources and the complication of the economic and social mechanisms brought about the necessity to invent a modern form of governance which could more efficiently and more adequately address impending social needs. In the local dimension, this led to a consideration of public private partnership as a valid alternative to public procurement in all those cases where the complexity of the need to be addressed and the need to acquire private input in the definition of the public response made a stronger involvement of private operators mandatory.

In Chapter 4, we outlined how the above-mentioned mixture of public and private management of public tasks is a defining feature of public private partnership which places it outside the realm of public procurement, privatization, contracting out, delegation of public power, subsidiarity and substitution; where the public authority remains dominant and monopolist of the public needs, both in the selection and execution phases, whereas the private actor remains an executor of the administration's will. Unlike these situations, in a public private partnership we can see a joint action of public and private partners who, together, participate in the selection of which needs to satisfy, the shaping of the adequate answer to said need, and in the execution of the planned activities.

The same dimension dominates the third line of Table 5.1, expressing the relevance of cooperation between public and private partners in co-producing values for the community. Cooperation is the key for public authorities to efficiently meet the demand to satisfy public needs with the involvement of the community itself.[3] In other words, it is the solution to what in Chapter 1 we defined as the need to escape from the responsibility isolation in which public authorities find themselves. Something that in the international dimension was represented as the efficient move to the construction of alliances for the achievement of sustainable development goals and that, in the local dimension, was a pivotal feature of the examples of social partnership, sponsorship and bottom-up initiatives.

As shown in the fourth and fifth lines of Table 5.1, public private partnership modifies the traditional explanations of the public private relationships, inverting the order of governmental action from top down to bottom up.

We see evidence of the capability of participatory democracy both in the international and in the local dimension, albeit with different nuances, reflect-

---

[3]   See Michael Sandel, *Democracy's discontent: America in search of a public philosophy* (Harvard University Press, 1996), where the author affirms that 'self-government ... requires political communities that control their destinies, and citizens who identify sufficiently with those communities to think and act with a view to the common good' 202.

ing the roles of international organizations and central and local governments, respectively.

The central role played by individual, private organizations and economic operators is manifested in a theoretical dimension of public private partnership. The efficiency in producing public value justifies the partnership mission and, specifically, the significant role attributed to the private parties in the performance of activities traditionally reserved for the government.

The guiding parameter for the legitimation of public private partnership can therefore be described as its capacity to achieve efficiently a specific goal consistent with the public interest, on the premise that good governance in complex and modern contexts may derive by stimulating private initiatives and participation.

Therefore, with the elements of our analysis reconstructed, we are now able to define the concept of public private partnership in detail, thus concentrating on a new column in the table, in which all the above-mentioned features will be recomposed in a precise juridical definition that we will propose.

3   RECONSTRUCTING THE JURIDICAL IDENTITY OF PUBLIC PRIVATE PARTNERSHIP

In light of the line of reasoning carried out so far, we possess all the necessary elements to construct a definition of public private partnership:

1. the idea of a compromise between a public and a private actor can be expressed by referring to an 'agreement between at least one public authority and one private entity';
2. the mutual involvement of the public and private partners deriving from the concept of cooperation, as opposed to juxtaposition, can be summarized by affirming that public private partnership requires the 'joint management of one or more activities';
3. the overcoming of the traditional distinction between public and private spheres and the enhancement of participatory democracy, inclusion, social innovation and bottom-up initiatives lead us to affirm that public private partnership is distinguished by the involvement of private actors in the definition and management of 'public interest'.[4]

---

[4]   Shortly we will argue that the private participation in the performance of public tasks brings to the requalification of the notion of public interest itself. Indeed, the concept is posed in subjective terms, in the sense that it expresses the interest belonging to public authorities. Yet, as we could already notice, the interest which is relevant in a public private partnership is not subjectively characterized as it is not derived from the public side. Rather, it is deciphered by the public and private partners together. In

3.1 Elements Left Out of the Definition

The reader will have noticed that some of the most typical elements of the definition of the concept of public private partnership, such as the relevance of private investments, risk and duration of the agreement have been left out of the picture. Some further clarifications on this point are needed, in light of the extensive reference made by legislators and scholars around the world to said elements in the definition of public private partnership.

Analysing the local dimension of public private partnership, we notice some recurring elements that are now left outside our definition of the concept. This is not due to a lack of attention; rather, it is a conscious decision, based on the following reasons.

Indeed, those jurisdictions which placed more stress on the relevance of concession-type contracts indicate private investment as a defining feature of the concept of public private partnership,[5] especially in developing countries, where public private partnership is intended as a form through which the state can acquire funds to realize infrastructure. According to this same perspective, several laws have underlined the element of the risk transfer to private partners as characterizing public private partnership and differentiating it from public procurement. In some jurisdictions, then, public private partnership is seen as existing only if the private partner actually participates in the losses of the operation.

In describing public private partnership, the above-mentioned disciplines also add a third element to these two elements, namely the relatively long duration of the agreement.

These elements certainly characterize concession contracts, but will not be indicated here as essential features of the notion of public private partnership, given that they are present in only some of its *species*.

To give a few examples, the duration of a sponsorship agreement – which we believe represents a form of public private partnership – can be very short, as related to the extent of specific events; in the Italian agreements of 'social barter' the private investment of the private citizens is substituted by specific undertakings that do not require money transfer to the public authority, and the financial lease of public infrastructures present very high risks on the public administration's side.[6] To finance a school with a grant or to organize courses

---

this way, the partnership allows the community (with public and private actors on the same side) to provide itself with an answer to its needs.

[5]   See Chapter 3, section 4.

[6]   The issue is discussed in John Quiggin, 'Risk, PPPs and the public sector compara-tor' (2008) Australian Accounting Review 51; Bernardino Benito, Vicente Montesinos, and Francisco Bastida, 'An example of creative accounting in public sector: the private

by providing skilled teachers does not signify assuming risk. It means contributing to creating value for the public.[7]

This is the reason why we remove the elements of private financing, risk transfer and duration from our proposed definition, to concentrate on those features that, on the basis of the analysis carried out so far, in our opinion more correctly define the *genus* of public private partnership.

3.2   Elements Composing the Definition

That being said, the following elements are the ones that, on the basis of our research, precisely and more extensively describe the essential features of public private partnership: (1) the agreement; (2) the presence of at least a public entity and a private operator; (3) the joint management of one or more activities; and (4) the public interest as aim and social function of public private partnership.

Said elements are broken down and discussed below.

In the following pages, the concept of public private partnership is reconstructed in theoretical terms. However, where possible, we insert references to some national disciplines that offer us insights to compare the results of our research to some real-life experiences.

3.2.1   An agreement ...

The term 'agreement' represents the compromise embedded in a partnership between at least two institutionally different entities, the private, self- and profit-oriented, and the public, per se altruistic and functional to the public interest.

Within the agreement, the parties share a common aim in the interest of the community. The parties willingly find a compromise and accept to take on obligations in order to perform a public task in the interest of the community.

We voluntarily chose not to use the term 'contract' because we intended to depart from the idea that public private partnership necessarily entails an onerous transaction. In a public private partnership, the essence of the agreement is not the exchange between money and works, services or goods. Rather,

---

financing of infrastructures in Spain' (2008) Critical Perspectives on Accounting 963; George Peterson, 'Land leasing and land sale as an infrastructure-financing option' (World Bank, 2006).

[7]   All in all, every contract transfers risks among parties. Which risks and how many risks the parties intend to transfer depend on the regulation of interests that the parties accept and share. And this is valid both for public private partnership and public procurement.

the essence of the agreement lays in the performance of an activity able to generate public value.

For this reason, we deemed it more appropriate to adopt a term ('agreement') that is closer to the public dimension of the aim of the public private relationship.

In some hypotheses of partnership, the agreement will also have an economic content, as for example in the case of sponsorship. At other times, the profit-oriented perspective will not be dominant.

More specifically, the agreement will have a strong economic characterization in those cases in which a private investment is included, as in the case of concessions. On the other hand, in other cases such as a social partnership, the focus will shift to the activities carried out in favour of the community.

At other times, the agreement will give birth to a new juridical entity, as is the case for public private companies entrusted with a specific task of public interest. In other cases, the agreement will only specify the juridical relations between the parties, which will remain separate in their individuality.

Given the complexities of the juridical framework that belongs to the concept of public private partnership, the agreement must be disciplined with particular care, in order to avoid the creation of friction and conflict between the parties, to guarantee mutual loyalty and trust throughout the duration of the agreement, as well as to avoid the logic of profit maximization creating, in time, a deviation from the achievement of the public interest.

The forms of public private partnership all have in common a negotiation between at least a private party and a public authority of the terms of the performance of a specific public task. Since the public authorities are the institutional protagonists and the primary 'managers' of public interests, private actors (citizens, associations, non-governmental organizations, enterprises) may be involved in the management of public interests only in accordance with the public administration responsible for its care.

Unilateral activities carried out by private entities in an ambit of public intervention are not a partnership. Said activities involve public authorizations only in their role as regulators or, at most, authorizing entities. In the mentioned cases, the relationship remains a hierarchical one.

In this regard, we can stress how the term 'agreement' expresses the parallel position that the public authority and the private party hold in a public private partnership as 'co-managers' and enforcers of public interests.

3.2.2   … between at least a public entity and a private operator …
To define public private partnership, it is necessary to detect the presence of at least one public and one private entity, intended as follows.

Using the expression 'private entity' we intend to encompass not only the 'world of business',[8] but more extensively any individual, association or active part of the society at large, willing to interpret social needs and to participate in the shaping of public interest in partnership with a public authority.

We outlined how private enterprises may find it advantageous, for moral or economic reasons, to embark on activities in the interest of the community.

The category of 'private actor' is enlarged to all the possible entities that are not an expression of the power of states. We can include in this group non-governmental organizations, associations, foundations and entities whose primary objective is the pursuit of social and environmental values. This is the case of international organizations such as the Red Cross, Greenpeace and the WWF and, more generally, of international non-governmental organizations.

In light of the various juridical forms that said actors could have, we will use the expression 'private entity' to extensively include the multitude of non-state actors that could be occasionally interested in looking after a public interest, which, in our perspective, includes not only social enterprises but also organizations of the so-called 'third sector' and individuals.

As for the other side of the partnership, we must mention that it is quite difficult to find a shared transnational meaning of 'public administration': an entity can be deemed public for the sole purpose of applying a specific discipline, for example concerning the award of accounting supervision contracts or employment policies.[9] Moreover, it must be taken into consideration that formally private entities can be vested with the task of caring for an interest of the administered community. These subjects are formally private but substantially public.

In order to solve this ambiguity, some laws on public private partnership provided a definition of public subject: in Greece, Law No. 3389/2005 on 'Partnerships between the public and public sectors' states that 'for the purposes of this law, the expression "public entities" shall be understood to mean the following: (a) the State; (b) local government organizations; (c) legal entities under public law; (d) *societies anonymes* whose share capital belongs wholly to Entities included under (a) to (c) above, or to another one or more *societies anonymes* under this clause'.[10]

Conversely, it may be problematic to understand the definitions of the public sector in jurisdictions which identify the public partner by referring

---

[8]   As suggested, for instance, in the 2004 European Commission's Green Paper.

[9]   In the Italian literature, in this regard, they refer to a 'variable geometry administration'. See Sabino Cassese, 'Diritto amministrativo comunitario e diritti amministrativi nazionali' in Mario Pilade Chiti and Guido Greco (eds), *Trattato di diritto amministrativo europeo* (Giuffrè, 1997, I) 9.

[10]   Cf. Law No. 3389/2005, Article 1.

to general categories such as 'public sectors entities' (Brazil), 'government entity' (Puerto Rico) or 'administrative authority' (Egypt), 'public authority' (Burkina Faso).[11]

Here, given our attempt to analyse systematically the phenomenon of public private partnership, besides outlining the possible issues that may derive from a vague reference to public and private partners, we have to clarify the meaning and extension of the term 'public'.

The perspective that we now assume is the one we have adopted from the very first pages of this book, where we affirmed that in the context of public private partnership, public authorities are those bodies which have been formally entrusted with the care of the public interest and with the powers to impact on the individuals' sphere of interest, according to the limits of the rule of law (administrative power). This then excludes from the public side all the entities (social enterprises, associations of citizens, non-governmental organizations, third sector entities) which may occasionally or permanently pursue general interests but do not possess related administrative powers.

3.2.3   ... for the joint management of one or more activities ...

With the expression 'joint management' we indicate the form of co-management of public tasks that defines public private partnership and distinguishes it from the concepts of subsidiarity, privatization and contracting out.

The joint management thus indicates the direct involvement of both the public and the private actors in performing tasks related to the subject of the partnership.

As for the content of said activities, we can point out that public private partnerships are atypical, meaning that they can regard any lawful activity in a legal system.

In some jurisdictions, the scope of application of public private partnership has been limited by the law, in our opinion with an excessively limited perspective. This is the case, for example, in Indonesia, where the Presidential Regulation No. 67 allows the partnership only for transportation, roads, water, potable water distribution, waste water, telecommunication, and provision of electric power, oil and natural gas.

In other countries, such as Singapore and Brazil, public private partnership is applicable only to projects above a certain value threshold.

---

[11]   We are respectively referring to the Brazilian Law No. 12.111 of 9 December 2009, the Puerto Rican Act No. 29 of 8 June 2009 (S.B. 469), the Egyptian Law No. 67/2010, and Law No. 020-2013/AN of Burkina Faso.

To limit the application of public private partnership to specific sectors is a matter of political choice which should not affect its juridical definition. In this regard, it is possible to refer to activities of public interests.

If, as we affirmed, the defining feature of the subject of the partnership agreement is the production of value for the community, then public private partnership can involve any possible activity carried out in the public interest.

3.2.4   ... aiming at satisfying a 'public interest'

Only a few legislative definitions of public private partnership involve the expression 'public interest'. An example is provided by the Brazilian Law No. 12.111/09 of 9 December 2009, which defines public private partnerships as 'agreements entered into between government or public sector entities and private sector entities that establish a legally binding obligation to establish or manage, in whole or in part, services, undertakings and activities in the public interest in which the private sector partner is responsible for the financing, investment and management'.[12]

Similarly, Article 2 of the Slovenian Public Private Partnership Act (ZJZP) states: 'public private partnership represents a relationship involving private investment in public projects and/or public co-financing of private projects that are in the public interest'.[13]

As we have affirmed, public authorities are institutionally entrusted with the care of public interests, whereas private actors may occasionally encounter them. The public interest can therefore be considered as a centripetal force which brings together two otherwise opposed dimensions.

The reference to the public interest as a characterizing element of the partnership is as fundamental as it is obvious: in the nature of relationship, a public administration should refuse to accept a partnership with a private subject when the proposal is not consistent with the interests that the public subject is compelled to meet.

Some jurisdictions impose a preliminary evaluation of the public interest of the private proposal of partnership. For example, the Colombian Law No. 1508/2012 states that public private partnership (as a tool designed for the realization of medium- to large-sized infrastructures aimed at the provision of services) can be used only after a cost-efficiency analysis and a pre-feasibility verification aimed at bringing to the surface the economic and social utility of the work.

---

[12]   Brazilian Law No. 12.111/09 of 9 December 2009, Article 2.

[13]   Slovenian Public Private Partnership Act (ZJZP) No. 310-01/06-8/1 of 23 November 2006.

The tool of the public sector can be intended to serve the same purpose[14] of helping the public administrations assess whether proposals of public private partnerships are in line with the public interest.

These are the reasons why, in our opinion, the concept should have a central role in the definition of public private partnership.

We still have to investigate the meaning of 'public interest' because the element that unifies the two spheres composing the public private partnership is precisely this ill-defined concept.

4   PROPOSED DEFINITION OF PUBLIC PRIVATE PARTNERSHIP

On the basis of the arguments above, we can now provide a precise juridical concept of public private partnership, as:

> the agreement between at least a private entity and a public authority for the joint management of one or more activities in the satisfaction of a public interest.

Our quest has brought us to the identification of a definition that expresses the precise identity of public private partnership as a juridical concept, characterized by distinctive elements that can be found in any *species* of the *genus*.

The elements have been reconstructed on the basis of an analysis of the international legal documents and literature on the topic, which have followed a line of reasoning based on a few perspectives proposed by the semantic study of the terms that compose the expression, and on a reflection on the possible reasons and advantages for entering into such agreements.

As satisfactory as we may find the outcome of the study, we feel that our work is not complete, since a few elements remain implicit in the provided definition, namely 'public interest' and the consequences of the involvement of private parties in its selection and management. The next chapters will deal with these two issues.

---

[14]   See Chapter 3, section 4.2.

6. From public interest to common interests

1 INTRODUCTION: THE REASONS FOR THE NEED TO EXPAND THE CONCEPT OF PUBLIC INTEREST AS A POSSIBLE INHERENT ELEMENT OF PUBLIC PRIVATE PARTNERSHIP

Public private partnership requires, as we have seen in the previous chapters, leaving behind the logic of imperativeness, and adopting one of dialogue; forsaking a model where bureaucracy acts as an unchallenged lord of the administered community; the chance for private operators to associate their image with that of public bodies and public services; the increasing flexibility and meritocracy in public employment; the enhancement of transparency and participation of individuals, businesses and private organizations in administrative activities; the circulation of juridical models; and the introduction of modern techniques of governance.

Mainly, we discovered how the public private mixture altered the traditional binary correspondence between the identification and pursuit of public interest and public authorities.

The previous chapter provided a concept of public private partnership that we believe adequately captures its juridical essence. Now our task is to describe a piece of the reconstructed concept: precisely the meaning of the 'public interest' in reference to a public private partnership.

Indeed, overcoming the dichotomy between public and private and the fact that in a public private partnership, the private operator cooperates in the selection of the needs as well as in the definition and provision of its answer, leads us to question whether the expression 'public interest' is appropriate in the context that we have analysed.

It is necessary to specify, in this regard, that in a public private partnership, both the content of the partnership and its aim are of 'public interest', in the sense that the ambit covered by the public action – even if entangled with the private one – must necessarily pass muster that is in line with the needs of the community, in both its object and aim.

As we are about to see, traditionally the expression 'activity of public interest' indicates the activity assigned to public administrations. Thus, the notion of 'public interests' is characterized in a subjective sense and gives life to an apparently indissoluble pair, in which the subject, i.e. the public administration, and the object, i.e. the activity of public interest, perfectly coincide.

The concept of public interest is wide and ambiguous: in essence, it represents the multiple needs of the community – comprehensively intended as the *ensemble* of all the people physically living in a specific area – as interpreted by public subjects, for example, the refugee emergency, improving the transport system, or the regeneration of peripheral urban areas.

In a public private partnership, those needs do not emerge and are not dealt with through the isolated action of public administrations, but, rather, they are examined, magnified and processed in a pluralistic dynamic in which the private sector earned a role in an area that would traditionally belong to the domain of public powers. As a consequence, portions of public 'territory' are being eroded, as shared with private actors.

In this context, new issues related to the progressive erosion of the boundaries of the public authority and of the traditional conception of sovereignty emerge.[1]

Among these issues, the question must be asked whether the expression 'public interest', as an identified meeting between public interest and public subjects, is still consistent once utilized as a constitutive element of the notion of public private partnership.

On the one side, it is necessary to clarify in precise juridical terms what is intended by 'public interest'; on the other side, we should ponder the appropriateness of said terminology in relation to public private partnership, perhaps finding it more opportune to abandon said traditional expression and leave for new shores.

---

[1]   See Chapter 1, n 8.

2   THE TRADITIONAL IDENTIFICATION OF
         PUBLIC ADMINISTRATION WITH THE PUBLIC
         INTEREST: ORIGIN AND DEVELOPMENT OF THE
         IDENTIFICATION

The concept of public interest has been present since the first theoretical elabo-rations on government,[2] being alternatively identified with the idea of common good,[3] justice,[4] general will,[5] or public reason.[6]

It would be impossible, nor consistent with the subject of our study, to provide a detailed account of the different philosophical theories about the notion of public interest which have been advanced throughout many centuries of studies on governance.[7] However, this does not forbid us from giving at least the essential references to understand the historical reasons for the iden-tification of public interest with public subjectivity. From the very beginning, the concept of public interest was related to the exercise of power by adminis-trations for the benefit of – not individuals or single groups of people – but the

---

[2]   The principle is clearly expressed by Nicola Matteucci, 'Bene comune' in Norberto Bobbio, Nicola Matteucci, and Gianfranco Pasquino (eds), *Dizionario di politica* (UTET, 1990) 74.

[3]   Plato identified the 'public interest' as the 'good', meaning a body of transcend-ent, objective and timeless values that any public policy should aim at, therefore identi-fying it as a guidance for policy makers. See Plato, *Republic*, 506; Plato, *Meno*, 97. For a comment, see Richard Flathman, *The public interest: an essay concerning the norma-tive discourse of politics* (John Wiley, 1966) 53ff.

[4]   See, in particular, John Rawls, *A theory of justice* (Belknap Press, 1971) and, more recently, Joshua Cohen, 'Truth and public reason' (2009) Philosophy and Public Affairs 2.

[5]   The idea of rational will naturally spring from free, rational and equal men gath-ered in the legislative assembly proposed in Jean-Jacques Rousseau, *Du contrat social, ou principes du droit politique* (1762) and has many points in common with the modern theorizations of public interest and democracy. See, in particular, David Estlund et al., 'Democratic theory and the public interest: Condorcet and Rousseau revisited' (1989) American Political Science Association 1317.

[6]   Immanuel Kant's idea of public reason matches the relationship that entan-gles citizens, acting in reciprocal obligation through their practical reason. Claudia Mancina, 'Uso pubblico della ragione e ragione pubblica: da Kant a Rawls' (2008) Diritto e questioni pubbliche 33.

[7]   For interesting summaries of the modern literature on public interest and of their possible classification see: Virginia Held, *The public interest and individual interests* (Basic Books, 1970); Barry Bozeman, *Public values and public interest: counterbal-ancing economic individualism* (Georgetown University Press, 2007) 89ff., and, for the American literature, Stephen King and Bradley Chilton, *Administration in the public interest: principles, policies and practices* (Carolina Academic Press, 2009).

community as a whole. In his *Politics*, Aristotle (384–322 BCE) theorized the 'common good' as the right governmental action.[8]

Thomas Aquinas (1225–1274) subsequently strengthened the link between the government and the common good (*bonum comune*), in contrast with the misbehaviour of rulers who were acting in their own interest (*bonum privatum*).[9]

Throughout the Middle Ages, the idea of public interest was formed as a result of governmental interventions – consisting in regulation and provision of services – to achieve social goals, such as the setting of reasonable prices for necessary utilities, services and occupations such as surgeons, smiths, bakers and ferrymen.[10]

A few centuries later, the English philosopher Thomas Hobbes (1588–1679) theorized that the role of the state is of ensuring the realization of people's interests, in accordance with the maintenance of security and social peace.[11] Again, the elaboration of the satisfaction of the community's needs depended on the action of a public entity.

Despite proposing an alternative conception of governance, John Locke (1632–1704) still identified the 'public good' as the purpose of government in protecting the fundamental rights of the people, such as life, liberty, privacy and property.[12]

The utilitarian philosophy that a century later would be developed by Jeremy Bentham (1748–1832) confirmed the pairing of public interest/public administration, in stating that the standard of governance should be the interest of the many, intended as the sum of the members who compose the society.[13] In this view, the necessity to bring to unity the multitude of interests of the individuals composing a given community[14] justified the identification of

---

[8] See, in particular, *Politics*, Book III.

[9] See Mary Keys and Catherine Godfrey 'Common Good' in Mark Bevir (ed.), *Encyclopedia of political theory* (Sage, 2010) 239.

[10] Jane Johnston, *Public relations and the public interest* (Routledge, 2016) 27. See also Barry Mitnick, *The political economy of regulation* (Columbia University Press, 1980) 245.

[11] Thomas Hobbes, *Leviathan* (1651, OUP, 1996).

[12] John Locke, *Two treatises of government* (1689, McMaster University Archive, 1823). For a modern acceptance, see Michael Sandel, *Democracy's discontent: American in search of a public philosophy* (Harvard University Press, 1996) 166.

[13] James Burns, 'Happiness and utility: Jeremy Bentham's equation' (2005) Utilitas 46.

[14] In the seventeenth century, along with the spread of Jeremy Bentham's utilitarianism, a new concept of public interest took place, as the aggregate of all the individual interests. Considering the community as an aggregate of particular interest and the public interest in abstract terms, as a mass of individual interests, the philosopher paved the way to a nominalistic – and even fictitious – idea of public interest. Jeremy Bentham, 'Introduction to the principles of morals and legislation' in John Bowring, *The collected*

the public interest with the one that the public authorities considered to be of benefit for the community. In this way, it was possible to reach a unification of intentions and vision, through the exercise of power from public bodies.

With the displacement of the *Ancien Régime* by the French Revolution – which gave birth to the concepts of 'administrative power' and 'administrative law'[15] – and the formation of the *Rechtsstaat*, the above-mentioned perspective was reiterated, to become dominant in juridical and socio-economic thinking.

In the wake of above-mentioned theories, in the modern state, public power was justified and legitimized – with different grades of intrusion into the social and economic life of the community – by the fact that public administrations had the duty to maintain social peace, justice and to bring welfare to the community. The assumption of responsibility from public administrations in the execution of public policies had, in this perspective, the sense of ensuring security and justice for the community, which otherwise would live according to the law of nature.[16]

Nowadays, public interest assumes the character of an expression of – and a limit to – the power of the state. Administrative power, which must be enacted according to the rule of law and in the pursuit of the 'public interest', needs to be justified by consistency with the political selection of aims, which depends on the mechanisms of the democratic governance.[17]

---

works of Jeremy Bentham (OUP, 1943) 2. Said revolution created the realization that the public interest could be intended not as a philosophical construct to be imposed by politics through top-down logic, but as the natural result of the actions of the individuals composing the society. Adam Smith famously affirmed that: 'As every individual ... endeavours as much as he can both to employ his capital in the support of domestic industry, and so to direct that industry that its produce may be of the greatest value; every individual necessarily labours to render the annual revenue of the society as great as he can. He generally, indeed, neither intends to promote the public interest, nor knows how much he is promoting it. By preferring the support of domestic to that of foreign industry, he intends only his own security; and by directing that industry in such a manner as its produce may be of the greatest value, he intends only his own gain, and he is in this, as in many other cases, led by an invisible hand to promote an end which was no part of his intention. Nor is it always the worse for the society that it was not part of it. By pursuing his own interest he frequently promotes that of the society more effectually than when he really intends to promote it.' Adam Smith, *The wealth of nations* (1776, Shine Classics, 2014) 242.

[15]   Bernardo Sordi, '*Rèvolution, Rechtsstaat* and the rule of law: historical reflections on the emergence and development of administrative law' in Susan Rose-Ackerman, Peter Lindseth, and Blake Emerson (eds), *Comparative administrative law* (2nd edition, Edward Elgar, 2017) 23.

[16]   Bozeman, n 7, 89.

[17]   See, among the numerous contributions that delve into the above-described relationship, Norton Long, 'Power and administration' (1949) Public Administration Review 260; Luther Gulick, 'Democracy and administration face the future' (1977) Public Administration Review 706; Jürgen Habermas, 'Three normative models of

The state as apparatus is here intended as the only custodian of sovereignty and the only creator of the law,[18] as well as the only entity authorized to set the objective of administrative action. In this dimension, the public interest acquires an aura of sacredness and becomes opposed to the interest of private citizens or businesses as passive recipients of administrative action.[19]

The described binary relation with the state-administration remains solid notwithstanding the significance attributed to the 'public interest'.[20]

---

democracy' (1994) Constellation 1; David Held, *Democracy and the global order: from the modern state to cosmopolitan governance* (Stanford University Press, 1995); John Kirlin, 'The big questions of public administration in a democracy' (1996) Public Administration Review 416; Bent Flyvbjerg, *Rationality and power: democracy in practice* (The University of Chicago Press, 1998); Andreas Schedler, Larry Diamond, and Marc Plattner (eds), *The self-restraining state: power and accountability in new democracies* (Lynne Rienner Publishers, 1999); Arthur Benz and Yannis Papadopoulos (eds), *Governance and democracy: comparing national, European and international experiences* (Routledge, 2006); Brian Cook, *Democracy and administration: Woodrow Wilson's ideas and the challenges of public management* (Johns Hopkins University Press, 2007); Gerardo Munck (ed.), *Regimes and democracy in Latin America* (OUP, 2007); Jerry Mashaw, 'Administration and "The Democracy": administrative law from Jackson to Lincoln, 1829–1861' (2007–2008) Yale Law J. 1928; Eva Etzioni-Halevy, *Bureaucracy and democracy* (Routledge, 2013).

[18] For a discussion on the transformation of the role of the state, see, above all, Dwight Waldo, *The administrative state* (The Ronald Press Company, 1948); Stephen Jacobs, Robert King Jr, and Sabino Rodriguez, 'The act of state doctrine: a history of judicial limitations and exceptions' (1977) Harv Int'l Law 677; Sabino Cassese, 'The rise and decline of the notion of state' (1986) International Political Science Review 120; Jürgen Habermas, *The structural transformation of the public sphere: an inquiry into a category of bourgeois society* (MIT Press, 1991); Giandomenico Majone, 'The rise of the regulatory state in Europe' (1994) West European Politics 77; Rainer Bauböck, 'Political community beyond the sovereign state: supranational federalism and transnational minorities' (Austrian Academy of Sciences Research Unit for Institutional Change and European Integration ICE – Working Paper Series 7/2000); Eric Hobsbawm, 'The future of the state' (1996) Development and Change 267; Sabino Cassese, *La crisi dello Stato* (Laterza, 2002); Colin Scott, 'Regulation in the age of governance: the rise of the post-regulatory state' in Jacint Jordana and David Levi-Faur (eds), *The politics of regulation: institutions and regulatory reforms for the age of governance* (Edward Elgar, 2004).

[19] See Massimo Stipo, 'Itinerari dell'interesse pubblico nell'ordinamento democratico nel quadro generale degli interessi' in Francesco Astone et al. (eds), *Studi in memoria di Antonio Romano Tassone* (Editorial Scientifica, 2017) 2439.

[20] The philosophical elaboration on the concept of public interest is immense, as it goes in parallel with the reasoning on governance and politics. The struggle to identify a precise definition of the concept can be found in almost all the general contributions on the topics, including, *inter alia*, Frank Sorauf, 'The conceptual muddle' in Carl Friedrich (ed.), *Nomos V: The public interest* (Atherton Press, 1962) 183; Glendon Schubert Jr, 'The "Public Interest" in administrative decision-making: theorem, theosophy, or theory?' (1957) The American Political Science Review 346; Frank Sorauf,

Therefore, whether intended as a political strategy of influential groups,[21] a normative interpretation carried out by policy makers of the 'common good',[22] an ethical standard to evaluate public policies,[23] a pre-determined set of values embedded in the shared principles of a determined community at a specific time and place,[24] or as a procedure that reconnects the political or administrative decisions to the democratic circuit according to the majority rule,[25] the concept of public interest remains connected to a public dimension, intended as a set of rules and principles belonging to the state and to its dispensations.

Indeed, the public interest remains determined by a corpus of norms, principles and values that belong to a specific legal framework, directed at curbing and limiting the exercise of administrative power.

In its more developed evolution, the public interest is intended as the justification for a political choice assumed by democratically elected officials: in this perspective, declaring a given statement as of 'public interest' allows and legitimizes the sacrifice of the interests of the minority, in favour of the ones expressed by the majority.[26]

'The public interest reconsidered' (1957) The Journal of Politics 616; Carl Friedrich (ed.), *The public interest* (Atherton Press, 1962); Brian Barry, 'The public interest' (1964) Proceedings of the Aristotelian Society 1; Clarke E Cochran 'Political science and "The Public Interest"' (1974) The Journal of Politics 327; Thomas J Barth, 'The public interest and administrative discretion' (1992) American Review of Public Administration 289; Richard Box, 'Re-describing the public interest' (2007) The Social Science Journal 585.

[21]   Cochran, n 20.

[22]   Charles Cassinelli, 'Some reflections on the concept of the public interest' (1958) Ethics 48.

[23]   Bozeman, n 7.

[24]   See Julius Cohen, 'A lawman's view of the public interest' in Carl Friedrich (ed.), *The public interest*, n 20, 155; Wayne Leys and Charner Perry, 'Philosophy and the public interest' (Committee to Advance Original Work in Philosophy, Chicago, 1959) 31; Sorauf, n 20.

[25]   On the connections between the majority rule and the concept of public interest, see Cassinelli, n 22; Michale James, 'Public interest and majority rule in Bentham's democratic theory' (1981) Political Theory 49.

[26]   Cassinelli, n 22, 60. Accordingly, see Milton Friedman, *Capitalism and freedom* (3rd edition, University of Chicago Press, 2002) 24, where the author emblematically affirms that: 'Unanimity is, of course, an ideal. In practice, we can afford neither the time nor the effort that would be required to achieve complete unanimity on every issue. We must perforce accept something less. We are thus led to accept majority rule in one form or another as an expedient. That majority rule is an expedient rather than itself a basic principle is clearly shown by the fact that our willingness to resort to a majority rule, and the size of the majority we require, themselves depend on the seriousness of the issue involved. If the matter is of little moment and the minority has no strong feelings about being overruled, a bare plurality will suffice. On the other hand, if the minority feels strongly about the issue involved, even a bare majority will not do.'

In this sense, the public interest allows for the connection between politics, choices of public officers and administrative function. Public officials (and more generally public entities) must direct their actions not on the basis of their personal inclinations and beliefs, but on the basis of an external interest, imposed on them by their mandate.[27] Therefore, the public interest is a justification for administrative actions that has the role of legitimizing them in the eyes of the community.

This perspective captures the prevalence of politics over administration and claims a supremacy role for democratically elected bodies on the selection of public interests,[28] which is consistent with the fact that, as we have already highlighted, there are political reasons of social organizations at the basis of the conjunction between public interest and the actions of public administrations.

3   EVIDENCE OF THE CONTRAST WITH PUBLIC PRIVATE PARTNERSHIP

The above-presented excursus delivers a precise relation between administrative activity and the public interest.

According to administrative law, administrative action, to be legitimate, must be consistent with and finalized towards the pursuit of a public interest.[29]

---

[27]   The perspective was deepened, in particular, by Flathman, n 3. In the optic of the author, the public interest does not belong to the acting official but is the one resulting from the portion of sovereignty embedded with the authority of the governmental body to which the official belongs: 'government is expected to justify its decisions and actions in terms of a standard appropriate to the position which requires those decisions, its position as a public agent', 8.

[28]   As Bozeman summarised, 'Richard Flathman (1966) argues that the public interest is a normative standard, one used to express commendation and to provide justifications'. Bozeman, n 7, 91.

[29]   The above-mentioned axiom runs across all jurisdictions of administrative law, being intrinsically linked with the essential role of public bodies and rules of governance, as shaped in modern Western states. For the French manualistic literature, see in particular, Maurice Hauriou, *Précis de droit administratif et de droit public géneral* (Larose et Forcel, 1933) 5; Guy Braibant and Bernard Stirn, *Le droit administratif français* (4th edition, Presses de Sciences Po et Dalloz, 1984) 13; Yves Gaudemet, *Droit administratif* (LGDJ, 2018). Some classical German studies on administrative law that mostly underline the discussed profile are Michael Stolleis, *Geschichte des öffentlichen Rechts in Deutschland* (CH Beck Verlag, 1999); Christoph Möllers, 'Braucht das öffentliche Recht einen neuen Methoden-und Richtungsstreit?' (1999) Verwaltungsarchiv 187. For a modern commentary, see Matthias Ruffert, 'The transformation of administrative law as a transnational methodological project' in Matthias Ruffert (ed.), *The Transformation of Administrative law in Europe* (Sellier, 2007); Andreas Voßkuhle and Thomas Wischmeyer, 'The "*Neue Verwaltungsrechtswissenschaft*" against the backdrop of traditional administrative law scholarship in Germany' in Rose-Ackerman, Lindseth, and Emerson, n 15, 85. For Spain, see Manuel Colmeiro, *Derecho administrativo Español* (Eduardo Martinez,

When it does not happen, administrative action is to be considered unlawful. When, conversely, the administration moves within the boundaries of the public interest, its determinations are 'sovereign', to the extent that even the judicial authority must defer to the exercise of the administrative power in pursuit of the public interest. The matters related to the exercise of power cannot thus be reviewed with a substitution of the judicial power for the administrative one.[30]

The interpretation and application of the public interest in the specific case can be considered as the main clarification of the administrative action,[31] but

---

1876) 3. As for the Italian manual, the analysed dynamic is particularly evident in Alberto Romano, 'Il ruolo e le funzioni dell'Amministrazione' in Leopoldo Mazzarolli et al., *Diritto Amministrativo, I, Parte Generale* (4th edition, Monduzzi Editore, 2005) 1. For a European account, see Mario Pilade Chiti, 'Forms of European administrative action' (2004–2005) Law and Contemporary Problems 37. For Argentina, see Agustin Gordillo, *Tratado de derecho administrativo* (Macchi, 1974, III) 9. For Chile, see Luis Cosculluela Montaner, *Manual de Derecho administrativo* (2nd edition, Editorial Civitas, 1991) I, 122.

The above-described relation between administrative power and limits is not just limited to the administrative law systems. In the United Kingdom, the manual by William Wade and Christopher Forsyth, *Administrative law* (11th edition, 2010, OUP) clearly describes the same connection, at 27 and 177. The American elaboration on the boundaries of administrative action is particularly vast. See, in particular, Woodrow Wilson, 'The study of administration' (1887) Political Science Quarterly 2; William Willoughby, *The government of modern states* (The Century Company, 1919); Ernst Freund, *Administrative powers over persons and property – a comparative survey* (The University of Chicago Press, 1928); Emmette Redford, 'The protection of the public interest with special reference to administrative regulation' (1954) The American Political Science Review 1103; Jerry Mashaw, *Creating the administrative constitution: the lost one hundred years of American administrative law* (Yale University Press, 2012).

[30] The American acceptance of the deference doctrine – and, more importantly, of its limits – has been clearly expressed in a recent ruling of the Supreme Court of the United States: *Kisor v. Wilkie*, 588 US __ (2019). Here it was recalled that under the 'Auer' deference doctrine, courts should defer to an agency's reasonable reading of its own genuinely ambiguous regulations. See *Auer v. Robbins*, 519 US 452; *Bowles v. Seminole* Rock and Sand Co., 325 US 410. As affirmed by the Supreme Court, the deference doctrine 'is rooted in a presumption that Congress intended for courts to defer to agencies when they interpret their own ambiguous rules. The Court adopts that presumption for a set of reasons related to the comparative attributes of courts and agencies in answering interpretive questions. But when the reasons for the presumption do not hold up, or when countervailing reasons outweigh them, courts should not give deference to an agency's reading.'

[31] Glendon Schubert, '"The Public Interest" in administrative decision-making: theorem, theosophy or theory?' (1957) American Political Science Review 346; Pierre Moor, 'Définir l'intérêt public: une mission impossible?' in Jean Ruegg, Stéphane Decoutère, and Nicolas Mettan (eds), *Le partenariat public-privé: Un atout pour l'aménagement du territorie et la protection de l'environement?* (Presses polytechniques et universitaires romandes, 1994) 218, 219.

officials should be rational and transparent, giving reasons to justify their decisions in accordance with public law principles *ex ante* and not *ex post*.

The overlapping between public interest and administrative action excludes the private sector from taking on a role in the public interest. Here lies the contrast between this notion of public interest, in which the interest of the community takes form in public bodies, and public private partnership as we have described it so far: in the latter case, there is no space for private participation in the genetic phase of the need to be satisfied.

The above-mentioned conflict can no longer adequately represent the current relationship between the public and the private sector in serving the interests of the community. The role that the private sector and the market covers in this regard depends on many factors, and mostly on the balancing that the legal frameworks make between the two – equally compelling – needs to favour the expansion of businesses' creativity[32] and to maintain the govern-

---

[32]   The issue is particularly discussed in Friedman, n 26. In the second chapter of this book, the author analyses the role of government in a free society, elaborating the liberal thought of John Stuart Mill in modern times and proposing a limitation of the government's role to a specific set of limited functions, related to those situations where absolute freedom is impossible and where the market would be not able to act on its own, for instance in the determination, arbitration and enforcing of rules. As the author affirms: 'These then are the basic roles of government in a free society: to provide a means whereby we can modify the rules, to mediate differences among us on the meaning of the rules, and to enforce compliance with the rules on the part of those few who would otherwise not play the game', 25.

The modern tendency of economic studies is quite different from the one that inspired Milton Friedman, who emphasized the freedom of enterprise to protect it from political, legislative or administrative invasive interventions. Nowadays, in a context where the freedom of enterprise is undeniable, the issue that worries the economist is the opposite one of how businesses can increase the value of a community through social actions. In this regard, public private partnership is a precious instrument of the legal framework, since, as we noticed in Chapter 1, it recognizes and promotes social behaviours from enterprises, pushing them to take care of the common good.

A more 'social' approach towards the discussion on the relationship between governmental intervention and businesses is the one taken by Michael Sandel, *Justice: what's the right thing to do?* (Ferrar, Straus and Firoux, 2009); Michael Sandel, *Liberalism and the limits of justice* (2nd edition, CUP, 2010); Michael Sandel, *What money can't buy: the moral limits of markets* (Penguin, 2013). In his reasoning – which could be considered opposite to Milton Friedman's – the author acknowledges that the market is not something that should be protected by public policies. On the contrary, the market is something that nowadays is able to dominate any possible aspect of social life. Anything can be bought, from privileged access to medical care, to a better prison cell, to a position in line at the post office, to the killing of an endangered species animal.

In this dynamic, the risk is to lose track of what should be sold and what should be rather excluded from the dynamic of supply and demand, as characterized by a specific morality, or intrinsic value. In this view, there are some spaces in which the market

ment's directing role as 'architects of choices'.[33]

---

does not belong and should not be consequently authorized to guide social relation-ships. The theory is interesting for our reasoning because it poses the issue of the need to expand social considerations in the market. Something that, as we affirmed, is con-sistent with the positive role of public private partnership. However, if brought to its extreme consequences, the demarcation posed in some specific ambit of the social and economic life between the market space and the social space could bring to limit the expansion of virtuous public and private initiatives that require a blending of the two dimensions.

[33]   The expression is taken by Richard Thaler and Cass Sunstein, *Nudge: improving decisions about health, wealth, and happiness* (New Haven, 2008). Drawing from the research on behavioural economics, the authors applied the theories on pre-dictability of human choices on public regulation, proposing a model of flexible regulation. The crucial point of these studies is embedded in the concept of 'liber-tarian paternalism': in order for a public institution to be efficient, it is necessary to bring to unity two opposite concepts: the one of paternalism and the one of liberal-ism. In this concept, people should be left free to do what they want, if they want to do it (liberalism); however, it is legitimate for governance as architect of the choices to try to influence the behaviour of people, in order to achieve their goods (pater-nalism). Therefore, individuals should be guided gently towards a specific objec-tive detected and interpreted by the government, through a soft method of regulation based on the concept of 'nudging'. Among the most recent contributions of the authors, see Cass Sunstein, 'Nudges vs. shoves' (2014) Harvard Law Review Forum 210; Cass Sunstein, 'Do people like nudges?' (2015) Administrative Law Review 1; Richard Thaler, *Misbehaving: the making of behavioural economics* (Penguin, 2015); Cass Sunstein, *The ethics of influence: government in the age of behavioral science* (CUP, 2016); Cass Sunstein, 'Nudges that fail' (2017) Notre Dame Journal of Law, Ethics and Public Policy 4; Cass Sunstein and Lucia Reisch (eds), *The economics of nudge* (Routledge, 2017). This setting has provoked a debate in the American litera-ture on the role of government in a society. In particular, it is interesting to read the debate between Cass Sunstein and Robert Sugden. See Robert Sugden, 'Do people really want to be nudged towards healthy lifestyles?' (2017) International Review of Economics 113; Cass Sunstein, '"Better off, as judged by themselves": a comment on evaluating nudges' (2017) International Review of Economics 1; Robert Sugden, '"Better off, as judged by themselves": a reply to Cass Sunstein' (2017) International Review of Economics 9. The reasoning on libertarian paternalism is yet another inter-esting ambit of discussion for the subject of our study, as it underlines the strong correlation between individuals, governments and businesses, whose actions and behaviours are mutually influenced in a dynamic that can no longer be represented as dominated by an opposition of two separate spheres (the public and the private one) but by the continuous search of both governments and individuals or economic oper-ators for ways and instruments of value generation for the community. For a broader debate on this topic, see David Dyzenhaus, 'Emergency, liberalism and the state' (2011) Perspectives on Politics 69; Karen Yeung, 'Nudge as fudge' (2012) The Modern Law Review 122; Riccardo Rebonato, *Taking liberties: a critical examination of libertarian paternalism* (Palgrave MacMillan, 2012); Pelle Hansen and Andreas Jespersen, 'Nudge and manipulation of choice: a framework for the responsible use of the nudge approach to behaviour change in public policy' (2013) The European

Besides the different ideological conceptions of the relationship between the state and the market and between states and individuals, the above-mentioned traditional view conflicts with reality for at least two reasons.

Firstly, the complexity of social needs implies a sophistication of governance that makes it difficult for the public administration to deal with every possible need.[34] The involvement of the private sector as protagonist and primary interpreter of social demands is thus fundamental in the perspective of achieving responsiveness.

Secondly, if – as is the case for modern governments – the tasks of public administrations – and especially of the local ones – grow and detach from the typical ones of the public administration, such as security, defence and health care, to include the provision of welfare,[35] it therefore becomes inefficient to keep these tasks reserved to public bodies. Governments are globally evaluated and ranked on the basis of welfare provision,[36] to the extent that the expression 'gross national happiness' was coined to describe the index used

---

Journal of Risk Regulation 3; Ryan Calo, 'Code, nudge, or notice?' (2014) Iowa Law Review 773; George Wright, 'Legal paternalism and the eclipse of principle' (2016) Miami Law Review 194.

[34] For the characters of modern society in evolution, it is possible to refer to Niklas Luhmann, *Theory of society* (1997, translation by Rhodes Barrett, Stanford University Press, 2013).

[35] On the expansion of the tasks of the government, see Felix Frankfurter, 'The tasks of administrative law' (1926–1927) U. Pa. Law Review 614; Waldo, n 18; Stephen Skowronek, *Building a new American State: the expansion of national administrative capacities 1877–1920* (CUP, 1982); Paul Pierson, 'The new politics of the welfare state' (1996) World Politics 143; Gøsta Esping-Andersen, *Social foundations of postindustrial economies* (OUP, 1999); Walter Kickert, 'Expansion and diversification of public administration in the postwar welfare state: the case of the Netherlands' (1996) Public Administration Review 88; Anna Grzymala-Busse, *Rebuilding the Leviathan: party competition and state exploitation in post-communist democracies* (CUP, 2007); Majone, n 18; Nicholas Barr, *Economics of the welfare state* (6th edition OUP, 2012); David Levi-Faur, 'The welfare state: a regulatory perspective' (2014) Public Administration 599.

[36] See Carrie Exton and Michal Shinwell, 'Policy use of well-being metrics: describing countries' experiences' (OECD Statistics and Data Directorate, SDD Working Paper No. 94, SDD/DOC(2018)7, 6 November 2018) and the studies by Ángel Álvarez-Díaz, Lucas González, and Benjamin Radcliff, 'The politics of happiness: on the political determinants of quality of life in the American states' 72 The Journal of Politics (2010) 894; Richard Easterlin, 'Happiness, growth, and public policy' (IZA Discussion Paper No. 7234, 2013).

to measure the collective happiness and well-being of some populations of the world.[37]

In the modern world, then, administrations are entities acting in competition to attract communities to their territories, offering them services and better life conditions, in an attractive economic and social context. To do so, the traditional conceptual paradigm of the administration acting in isolation as sole holder of the power-duty to take care of the public interest is not suitable; instead, cooperation among enterprises, individuals and private organizations is essential.

In this regard, it is particularly interesting to refer to the theories of public governance that have more strongly acknowledged the importance of the role of the private sector in the production of value for the community and in the provision of services of general interest. Said elaborations give a modern account of administrative law dynamics, in which the traditional characterization of the public and of the private entities fade away, to give relevance to the production of benefit for the administered community.

If, in public private partnerships, private actors are allowed to participate in the interpretation of a community's needs and in the joint activity necessary to meet social demands, then the activity performed in favour of the community, by the public and the private sectors together, acquires an objective dimension, as it is detached from the public or private nature of its protagonists.

4   HINTS OF EVOLUTION: TOWARDS AN OBJECTIVE VIEW OF GOVERNANCE

In what we have already referred to as the '*crise de la modernité juridique*'[38] the state can no longer be considered as supreme ruler, sole creator of the law and monopolist in satisfying community needs.

On the one side, the globalization of governance forces us to consider the values, the challenges and the issues of human society as a

---

[37]   See Centre for Bhutan Studies and GNH, 'A compass towards a just and harmonious society' (2015 GNH Survey Report, 2016).
[38]   See Introduction, n 23.

whole.[39] Problems such as climate change, clean air, terrorism, human migrations, and the fight against corruption cannot be solved with a national perspective of state sovereignty, but require thinking about administrative action in the interconnected world of international cooperation.[40]

On the other side, the mutation of communities – which, as we affirmed, can no longer be seen as limited to formalistic concepts of citizenship – as well as the mutation of the expectations of the community towards the actions of public institutions and the exponential multiplication of possibilities provided by technological evolution, impose a more direct relationship between those who express needs and those who meet them.[41] More and more often, initiatives derive from the grassroots level, and not from a political decision or from an administrative activity of programming. The bottom-up process is not completely neutral from a theoretical point of view. As a consequence of dealing with the continuous process of demand and response together with private sector, the government loses the monopoly over the process of policy making.

---

[39] The issue is studied, in particular, by the scholars who elaborated and deepened the concept of 'global administrative law' since the publication of the paper by Benedict Kingsbury, Nico Krisch, and Richard B Stewart, 'The emergence of global administrative law' (2005) Law and Contemp. Problems 15. See, among the vast literature on the topic Sabino Cassese et al. (eds), *Global administrative law: the casebook* (IRPA-IILJ, 2012); Sabino Cassese, 'Global administrative law: the state of the art' (2015) International Journal of Constitutional Law 465; Sabino Cassese, *The global polity: global dimensions of democracy and the rule of law* (Global Law Press, 2012); Eyal Benvenisti, 'The future of sovereignty: the nation state in the global governance space' in Sabino Cassese (ed.), *Research handbook on global administrative law* (Edward Elgar, 2016) 483.

[40] See Chapter 1, n 8.

[41] The process is described and examined in David Levinson, Reinaldo Garcia, and Kathy Carlson, 'A framework for assessing public-private partnerships' in Piet Rietveld and Roger Stough (eds), *Institutions and sustainable transport: regulatory reform in advanced economies* (Edward Elgar, 2007) 285; Deirdre Oakley, 'The American welfare state decoded: uncovering the neglected history of public-private partnership' (2006) City and Community 243; Thimothy Dixon, Gaye Pottinger, and Alan Jordan 'Lessons from the private finance initiative in the UK' (2005) Journal of Property Investment and Finance 412; Mark Carl Rom, 'From welfare state to opportunity, Inc. public-private partnerships in welfare reform' in Pauline Vaillancourt Rosenau (ed.), *Public-private policy partnerships* (MIT Press, 2000) 161.

Horizontal contractual relations[42] – or '*consensualisme*',[43] as it is referred to in the French literature – becomes extremely valuable to overcome the difficulties and the flaws of a traditional and hierarchical way of addressing social needs.[44] In doing so, states and public administrations give up portions of their authority, as they enter into the market as operators, and not as regulators. This places them in the same position as the private sector.[45]

Further, the need to be responsive to social demands pushes public authorities to find new paradigms of administrative organization, which involve the structure of a network composed by the active parts of the society. This allows direct engagement and a more active participation of citizens in governance.[46]

---

[42]   See, above all, Jody Freeman, 'The private role in public governance' (2000) NYULR 543, where the author emblematically affirms that the public administration can be seen as a 'set of negotiated relationships. Specifically, public and private actors negotiate over policy making, implementation, and enforcement. This evokes a decentralized image of decision making, one that depends on combinations of public and private actors linked by implicit or explicit agreements. One might describe this conception by using the term "shared governance," but "governance" implies a hierarchy of control in which there is one thing – or a set of things – to be governed, and a centre of control that does the governing. In my conception, however, there are only problems to confront and decisions to make. There is nothing to govern', 548. See also, for a French account, Maryvonne Hécquard-Théron, 'La contractualisation des actions et des moyens publics d'intervention' (1993) AJDA 451.

[43]   Consensualism represents the technique of governance which tends to the elaboration of a common will between parties that hold different (or even opposite) interests, in an environment of concertation and cooperation. Gérard Cornu, *Vocabulaire juridique* (11th edition, PUF, 2016). M Amilhat, 'Contractualisation, négociation, consensualisme: nouvelles approches du droit public' (2018) Revue française de droit administratif 1. The above-mentioned concept is different from the one of 'negotiation', which only describes the action necessary to reach an agreement, to encompass the execution of a certain program or project, through the agreement with private actors. See also Jan Wouters, 'Government by negotiation' in Cassese (ed.), *Research handbook*, n 39, 196 and Pascal Lokiec, 'Contractualisation et recherche d'une légitimité procédurale', Actes du colloque 11, 12 and 13 October 2007 'La contractualisation de la production normative') 95.

[44]   Amilhat, n 43, 5.

[45]   As actors of the market, public administrations are 'contraint de composer avec les pouvoirs économiques privés, en s'efforçant d'obtenir leur collaboration pour la réalisation des objectifs de politique économique'. See Jacques Chevallier, 'Contractualisation et régulation' in Sandrine Chassagnard-Pinet and David Hiez (eds), *La contractualisation de la production normative* (Dalloz, 2008) 87.

[46]   'The emergence of new patterns of networked community governance reflects and implies new patterns of networked community governance away from the state and towards civil society, and some consequent loss of control by government policymakers and managers'. John Benington, 'From private choice to public value?' in

Scholars from Harvard's Kennedy School of Government[47] highlighted the opportunity of posing the individuals making up the community as 'the most important arbiters of value'[48] and affirmed that 'citizens could debate the role of government in society, and contribute to deciding which individual circumstances and social conditions they wanted to treat as a collective public responsibility to be managed by government'.[49]

The perspective is similar to the one that has led some Italian scholars to abandon the subjective view of public services, to embrace an objective definition of the concept that may be more suitable to representing the 'institutional pluralism' characterized by the coexistence of public administrations and other organisms that are equally oriented toward satisfying irrepressible social needs.[50]

John Benington and Mark Moore (eds), *Public value: theory and practice* (Palgrave MacMillan, 2011) 31, 36.

[47] Mark Moore, *Creating public value: strategic management in government* (Harvard University Press, 1995); Mark Moore, *Recognising public value* (Harvard University Press, 2013); Benington and Moore (eds), n 46. In summary, the theory holds that 'ground-level regulatory decision-making processes are accessible primarily to well-organized groups seeking regulatory rents, that those process generate information primarily about those groups' regulatory demands and how they can be met, that regulatory decision-makers operate in an environment free from oversight that interferes with agency supply of regulatory goods, and finally that only a few parties typically participate in the development of a regulatory policy'. Steven Croley, *Regulation and public interests: the possibility of good regulatory government* (Princeton University Press, 2008) 25.

[48] John Benington and Mark Moore, 'Public value in complex and changing times' in Benington and Moore (eds), n 46, 8.

[49] Ibid, 9.

[50] Umberto Pototschnig, *I pubblici servizi* (Cedam, 1964) 143–44. The objective notion of 'public services' elaborated by the Italian literature offers some useful suggestions to re-interpret the concept of 'public interest' in an objective sense. The line of reasoning on public services is particularly complex and subject to numerous and important scientific studies. In particular, the concept has been thoroughly studied by the French literature, of which it is possible to quote the fundamental contributions of Marie Josè Guedon, *Sur les services publics* (Paris, 1982); Jean-François Auby, *Les services publics locaux* (Berger-Levrault, 1982); Jean-François Auby, *Les services publics en Europe* (PUF, 1998); Didier Linotte and Raphaël Romi, *Services publics et droit public economique* (Paris, 1992); and Jacques Fialaire, *Le droit des services publics locaux* (Litec, 1998). Here, we concentrate on the arguments of who tried to understand the concept as part of the framework of a wider and more general idea of administrative action. The issue that the Italian literature tried to solve was: how is it possible to identify the notion of public services, in light of the absence of a legal definition? Which activity carried out in the interest of the community could be qualified as 'public service'?

This theory appears to be particularly modern, as it is consistent with the necessity, clearly emerging with public private partnership, to find a neutral concept of 'public interest'.

Despite the actual application of the theory,[51] what is important to stress here is that the objectification of the notion of public service was a necessary conceptual step to overcome the criticisms posed by a monolithic and all-encompassing conception of the public authority.

As also demonstrated by these last theories, the revolution that we have described here triggers the need to abandon the juridical concepts that belong to the old era of the sovereign state. Words like 'public interest', 'public authority', 'imperativeness', 'public principle' may become inadequate to describe the new reality as they all reflect the identification of the public dimension with the public bodies.

Enhancing the overlap between the public interest and the interest represented and interpreted by an entity entrusted with public power, part of the scholarship embraced a subjective notion of public subject, understood as any service that could be reconnected to a public body. The most recent and comprehensive contribution on the topic is Riccardo Villata, *Pubblici servizi: discussioni e problemi* (5th Edition, Giappichelli, 2008).

Other authors elaborated a new perspective, known as the objective notion of public services. In particular, in a pivotal work of 1964, Pototschnig challenged the traditional subjective view, on the basis of an innovative interpretation of the Italian Constitution. The objective theory elaborated an objective notion of public service, connected to the contents of the action and to their relevance for the administered community, rather than to the entities entrusted with their provision. The author's reasoning was influenced in particular by the French juridical literature on the concept of *service publique* and, in particular, Gaston Jèze, 'Le service public' (1926) Revista de drept public 161; Gaston Jèze, *Les principes généraux du droit administratif: Tome II: La notion de service public, les individus au service public, le statut des agents publics* (1925, Dalloz, 2003); Maurice Hauriou, *Précis de droit administrative et de droit public general* (Larose et Forcel, 1933). According to the author, the subjective notion of public service could be criticized, above all, because it was not adequately able to distinguish the public services from the ones provided by private subjects in favour of the community and it led, *in extremis*, to the identification of the notion of public interest as a formalistic criterion, depending on arbitrary legislative discretion (see Pototschnig, 139–40). More specifically, the subjective concept was consistent, in the author's view, with an outdated and all-encompassing notion of the state, which, already in the 1960s, had been substituted by the already-mentioned 'institutional pluralism'. Through an articulated reasoning on the Italian constitutional norms, the author came to the conclusion that: (1) to have a public service it is not necessary that the service 'belongs' to the state or to a public entity; (2) not any activity of the state or of a public entity which is not a public function is necessarily a public service (ibid, 417).

[51]   As discussed in Villata, n 50.

Public private partnership thus imposes the need to adopt a new juridical vocabulary, composed of 'neutral' words, which represent the objective dimension in which public and private entities together cooperate to generate value for the community.

Indeed, in a situation of complexity, public administrations are pushed to find new strategies and patterns of work if they want to improve their responsiveness to the highly complex needs of society:

> These include attempts to move beyond the mass-production of separate policies and standardized services by different professions and organizations, and to develop more 'joined-up' strategies and 'people-centred' approaches, in which different levels of government work together in closer partnership with other public, private, voluntary and informal community organizations, in trying to promote 'community wellbeing' and satisfaction'.[52]

The described governmental action moves into a stretched idea of 'public sphere', which encompasses values, ideas, places, organizations, rules and resources belonging to public authorities, individuals and organizations and characterizing a community 'with a sense of belonging, meaning, purpose and continuity'.[53]

This new-dimensioned community enhances partnership, which provokes a fracture in the wall traditionally dividing the public and the private sector: models of public and private law are mixed and used interchangeably; private actors voluntarily decide to embark on activities of public interest or are formally entrusted to carry out public tasks together with the public sector; public authorities find allies in the private sector and test new models of governance, either to face the challenges coming from new needs or to deliver an efficient and modern administration.

As described in the previous chapters, the partnership substitutes the adversarial relation between public and private subjects for the logic of cooperation. The cooperation becomes the alternative to the responsibility isolation of public bodies in identifying social needs and replying to them.[54]

In a partnership, what emerges as 'public interest' is not the public interest in the sense that emerged in the previous section: it is not the result of an isolated evaluation by the public authority of the community's needs. Conversely, in this complex and multi-faceted scenario, where public and private inputs are

---

[52] Benington, n 46, 33.

[53] Ibid, 43. See also Richard Sennett, *The fall of public man* (CUP, 1977); David Marquand, *Decline of the public: the hollowing out of citizenship* (Polity, 2004).

[54] See Geoff Mulgan, 'Supply and demand and measurement of value' in John Benington and Mark Moore (eds), *Public value: theory and practice* (Palgrave MacMillan, 2011) 212, 217.

almost indistinguishable, the 'public interest' changes physiognomy because it loses the characteristic of being representative of a holistic and self-referential perspective of the public administration.

It appears clearly that the traditional notion of public interest is not suffi-ciently able to describe the object and the aim of public private partnership.

In public private partnership, there is space for the co-creation of public value, 'through closer linking of users and producers in creative joint develop-ment of products and services tailor-made to meet unmet human need'.[55]

The focus then shifts from the public authorities as sole controllers of the communities' interests to the cooperation between public and private sectors as a tool of modern governance. In parallel, the attention moves from the tradi-tional 'public interest' concept to a new conceptualization, concentrated on the importance of a cooperative management of social needs.

In this dimension where public private partnership has led us, the interest that the public policies should pursue is not a transcendent value imposed by the law on public administrations. Rather, it is something that naturally springs from the society and that can be addressed both by public authorities and private actors. The conciliation of different individual wills can be carried out not only through administrative procedures, but also through negotiation and *consensualisme*. Therefore, there is no single 'public interest' to pursue as an interest that is subjectively indicated by the administration, but rather many interests exist, which are produced in everyday social dynamics.

In this context, public private partnership is the exemplary expression of the multiplicity of interests that implies the need to cease identifying the public administration with the public interest,[56] to adopt a more objective and neutral view, which focuses the community as a recipient of the admin-istrative action, rather than on the subjective features of the promoter of said activity.[57]

---

[55]   Benington, n 46, 45.

[56]   See in particular Hiraku Yamamoto, 'Multi-level governance and public private partnership: theoretical basis of public management' (2007) Interdisciplinary Information Sciences 65; Geert Dewulf, Anneloes Blanken, and Mirjam Bult-Spiering, *Strategic issues in public-private partnership* (2nd edition, Wiley-Blackwell, 2011).

[57]   An example of this vocabulary is provided by the French concept of 'intérêt général', which is more suitable to describe the interest pursued by public and private organizations acting through horizontal relationships. According to the French litera-ture, the general interest is not something externally imposed by the law but, rather, dynamically generated from the interactions between public authorities and active members of the society. Due to the adoption of contractual methods of governance, the general interest is transformed from transcendent into something that is strictly related with the individual wills that helping shaping it. See, in particular, Didier Truchet, *Les fonctions de la notion d'intérêt général dans la jurisprudence du Conseil d'État* (LGDJ,

When the public interest loses its sacred aura, to come within the reach of the community, it returns to being interpreted by the individuals and communities to which it ultimately belongs. It becomes plural and closer to the changeable flow of public private relations and a community's sensitivities.

5 CONCLUSION: THE NEED FOR A CHANGE IN THE CONCEPT – FROM PUBLIC INTEREST TO COMMON INTERESTS

In the present chapter, we intended to specify our definition of public private partnership that we provided in Chapter 5 by concentrating on a specific aspect: the public interest as an inherent element for the concept of public private partnership.

We felt the need to look more closely at the issue because referring to the concept of public interest as a defining element of the subject of our study was leading us to the past, at a time when the identification between the public interest and public subjectivity was indissoluble.

To examine the possibility of an alternative definition, we asked ourselves what could be intended as public interest and in what ways the concept could be accepted, before moving to a proposal of interpretative solution.

We started from the traditional correlation of administrative action with the pursuit of public interests, to question whether we could find a concept of public interest that could conform with public private partnership as a form of co-management of public tasks. In our excursus, we found that the concept of public interest, even in its more flexible acceptance, does not adequately represent the dimension of governance that public private partnership can generate.

For this reason, we turned to theories of public governance that embed the need to recognize the critical role of private players in the shaping of administrative interests and types of action. Said theorizations led us to embrace a wider and more objectified vision of administrative action, aimed at the production of benefits for the community.

In this new and modern scenario, detached from the authoritative view of public administration, the notion of public interest is transformed and objecti-

---

1977) 125ff.; Jean Rivero, *Droit public et droit privé: conquête ou* status quo*?* (Dalloz, 1947) 69; Jacques Chevallier, 'L'intérêt général dans l'administration française' (1975) Revue internationale des sciences administratives 325; Francois Rangeon, *L'idéologie de l'interet general* (Vedel, 19869; Julien Damon (ed.), *Intérêt Géneral: Que peut l'entreprise?* (Institut Montaigne, Paris, 2013); Pierre Crètois and Stéphanie Roza, *De l'intérêt général: introduction* (Asterion, Dossier 17/2017); Lokiec, n 43; Amilhat, n 43, 12.

fied, as it is freed from its subjective connotation. Here we find a new profile, which merges private creativity and innovation with the authority of the entity which represents the community as a whole.

We can define this new profile as 'common interests', in plural, to indicate the composite nature of the concept, which embeds at least two subjective visions belonging to the public and private partners and enhances the value of the partnership for the recipient, namely the community.

The use of the term 'common' demonstrates the intention to depart from that cultural heritage that considers the public entity as the undiscussed lord of the public interest and signifies a radical change in the process of selection and manipulation of the communities' interest.

The term indicates that the interest at the centre of a public private partnership belongs neither to the public nor to the private parties that contributed to their definition. It is not a matter of ownership, in the sense that no one can claim their sole right over it. It is, rather, qualified by its scope, meaning its social relevance: just as 'commons' can be defined on the basis of their relevance and function for society, 'common interest' is identified on the basis of social relevance.

We intended not to characterize them as collective, in order to avoid confusion with those widespread rights whose violation may be invoked in legal proceedings by organized groups of citizens such as consumers' associations or environmental protection committees. The term that we used to describe the aim of public private partnership is wider, as it encompasses interests that are not confined in a private sphere but that are shared among portions of organized groups of people, named communities.[58]

Said expression is capable of merging the public and the private spheres in the objective dimension of administrative action that we have previously described as the theoretical framework of public private partnership, into a realm in which the subjective figures that contribute to the definition of administrative action and policies are blurred.

In the vocabulary of public private partnership, the expression 'common interests' signifies, then, both the interests of the community and the ones of the partners, whose juridical relationships are characterized by coordination more than antithesis. In this regard, the expression 'governing common interests' thus represents a synthesis of the complexities and synergic differences that emerge in a public private partnership, as an instrument of governance that is able to bend the ordinary praxes of both private and public action. It signifies

---

[58]   The word willingly echoes the perspectives assumed in Peter Haas, *Epistemic communities, constructivism, and international environmental politics* (Routledge, 2015).

the need for both partners to come to a compromise, in order to find a shared ground of values and objectives, to use as guidelines for carrying out the joint administrative activity.

On the one side, the private actor will have to set aside the rule of freedom of will in those cases in which this is in conflict with the common interests set forth in the partnership agreement. On the other side, the public authority will necessarily lose portions of authority and accountability, since its activity must be carried out along with a private actor: its action will not be functional to a public interest but to common interests.

We can consequently further specify the definition elaborated in the previous chapter as follows:

> an agreement between at least a private entity and a public authority for the joint management of one or more activities aiming at governing common interests.

7. Conclusion

The consequences of the transition: governing common interests from the bottom up

---

1   GOVERNING COMMON INTERESTS FROM
     THE BOTTOM UP: A NEW PARADIGM FOR
     ADMINISTRATIVE ACTION

The analysis that we have carried out thus far has led us to affirm that through public private partnership, public administration changes in shape, procedures and contents.

Public private partnership is, at the same time, cause and consequence of a transformation that has its roots in a line of reasoning regarding the relationship between *government* and *governance* carried out in the 1990s,[1] which suggestively put at the centre of public action the participation of individuals, enterprises and community.

In a condition of the public administration's scarce capacity to respond timely and efficiently to the needs of the community, and faced with flourishing and promising business activity, the loss of accountability of public operators inevitably created a shift towards private action. First it triggered an opening of dialogue with the private sector and a call for businesses to be entrusted with activities of common interest through outsourcing and contracting out; and secondly, a search for consensus through the direct involvement

---

[1]   The reference is to Elinor Ostrom, *Governing the commons: the evolution of institutions for collective action* (Political Economy of Institutions and Decisions, 1990); Elinor Ostrom, Roy Gardner, and James Walker, *Rules, games and common-pool resources* (The University of Michigan Press, 1994); Elinor Ostrom, 'Reflections on the commons' in John Baden and Douglas Noonan (eds), *Managing the commons* (Indiana University Press, 1998) 95; Elinor Ostrom, *Design principles and threats to sustainable organizations that manage commons* (Bloomington, 1999); Elinor Ostrom et al., *The future of the commons: beyond market failure and government regulation* (The Institute of Economic Affairs, 2012).

of individuals and economic operators in taking charge of specific tasks of general interest.

Obviously, the phenomenon is much wider than the spread of public private partnership and includes diversified tools of particular interest. An example of other tools for the promotion of a dialogue between the public and private sector is provided by the spread of the forms of public consultation to win preliminary consent for the realization of public works such as the French public debate, described in detail, also in its relation to the concept of participatory democracy.[2]

Indeed, the spread of public private partnership's schemes of action had the consequence of introducing a new form of governance, deeply different from the traditional one, which was based on the formal sovereignty of public powers and on the clear separation between those who take care of the public interest (public bodies) and those who deal with individual or business profit (the private sector). The new form of governance which has emerged because of the influence of public private partnership logic is inspired by a form of co-administration – in the sense of co-management of common interests – similar to governance networks. Through public private partnership, governance ends up becoming a dynamic that sees public bodies and the private sector working side by side towards the satisfaction of common interests. Public and private actors are, together, the interpreters and providers of the community's needs.

This explains the title of this book: 'Public private partnership: governing common interests'. With this expression, we intend to affirm that, while partnering, the act of governing belongs both to the public and private sectors taking care of common interests together. In essence, the formal conception of governance, as an exclusive affair of a public body, leaves the floor to a subjectively neutral one.

Public private partnership challenges the traditional identification of public bodies with the recipients of the mission of public interest. A new, shared governance activity arrives in its place: the administered community – who traditionally relied on the holders of public functions – shifts from the side of the government.

We named this scenario: governance of the common interests.

This formula expresses a collaborative exercise of sovereignty. In this context of dialogue, the administration does not identify the (public) interests to pursue in abstract and ideological terms; rather, it dialogues with those to

---

[2]   See Martine Revel et al., *Le débat public: une expérience française de démocratie participative* (La Découverte, 2007).

whom its actions are destined, in order to select and pursue, precisely, common interests.

In systematic terms, this also means that public private partnership turns the focus of governance from the authoritative power of public administration[3] to participative governance, where the irreconcilable elements between public and private[4] fade away and a continuous contamination of instruments, stakeholders, ideas, disciplines, principles and logics takes place.

To clarify this statement we can use an image. In a public private partnership, the relationship between public bodies and private actors – individually or collectively intended – puts all of them in the same boat; the public administration, instead of rowing, steers, choosing the direction.

While steering, public administration should trace the route towards the interest that must be pursued and guide the partnership without letting the private objectives alter or diminish the consistency of the mixed – public and private – action, compared to the needs of the administered community.

Through public private partnership, the mutual participation of market actors in performing the public task, together with the institutions, blends the initial identities and forces them to use a common vocabulary representing a set of shared and transversal principles which is different from the languages of both the public and private worlds.

In this view, public private partnership is the cause of a genetic mutation of administrative action; but it is also the consequence of the phenomenon, because where the logical framework of the imperative of public action is weakened because of political, ideological, economic, social or financial reasons, it is physiological to allow and indulge private sector projects, including in the sectors that are traditionally reserved to the public sphere.

Whenever the traditional approach of administrative action, self-determined and self-performed, is not considered sufficient to guarantee a good performance in favour of the community, efficacy and efficiency are enhanced; so, the involvement of enterprises is inevitable and decisively positive because it brings added value in both social and economic terms. Social added value comes from the involvement of the community – i.e. individuals and private entities and non-profit organizations – in administrative action; economic added value comes from the ability of enterprises to act efficiently and profitably.

---

[3]   See Gregorio Arena, 'Introduzione all'amministrazione condivisa' (1997) Studi parlamentari e di politica costituzionale 29.
[4]   Norberto Bobbio, *Stato, governo, società: Per una teoria generale della politica* (Einaudi, 1985).

Moreover, with public private partnership the paradigm of administrative action changes: the traditional public principles are subject to a twisting, get decomposed and recomposed to be adapted not only to the public action sphere and principles but also to the private one.

Therefore, for example, the legality principle, if inserted in the context of public private partnership, cannot be understood in its strictest sense – as necessity of a norm authorizing a specific action – because this would contrast with the enhancement of the freedom of economic initiative required by public private partnership; consequently, it will be necessary to understand how to decompose and re-elaborate it to adapt it to the subject of our study. Also, it would be possible to question how the right to access information in light of the transparency principle could be exercised in public private partnership without hindering the necessary confidentiality inherent to the business logic of private partners.

Observing public private partnership from the angle of public administration, not only does the public interest change, becoming common interest, but also the principles of public action assume new connotations. Which leads us to embark on a new specific analysis that will lead us to build a theory of partnership activity (neither entirely public nor entirely private).

To verify how public private partnership creates a general and global transformation of general principles and rules of public action at large, including outside the area in which partnership operates, it is necessary first to clarify the essential features of the subject of the transformation.

It is easily understood that the analysis of this topic will inevitably remain on a generic level, considering the global dimension of the work. We thus will look at the defining characters of the general physiognomy of administrative action without penetrating into a specific analysis of one jurisdiction or another. Otherwise, we would lose the wide-ranging value of the research.

Subsequently, we will move on to the second aspect which we have previously identified, namely the attempt to study the consequences of the spread of public private partnership on the character of administrative action.

2   FROM TRADITIONAL ADMINISTRATIVE LAW TO GOVERNING FROM THE BOTTOM UP

We begin our investigation of the mutations of administrative action by finding the elements characterizing the basic, universal and necessarily generic notion of public administration.

In civil law countries, the origin of the 'juridification' of public power is identified in the modern state of French derivation. Government and its operative branches, no longer intended as *legibus soluti*, become powers regulated by the law, subject to the general will and limited by the warranties attributed to private people, with consequent subjection to judicial review.

Progressively then, the legality principle comes to represent not only the limit to the exercise of public power, but also its source of legitimation.

From this point on, almost everywhere a special legal framework and discipline arose to regulate public authorities, aimed at elaborating a particular *status* for the entities entrusted with imperative powers and to discipline the – also special – acts that were the expression of said public power.

We can easily agree on the fact that, depending on the historical period, public power, exercised in a more or less incisive way against private people, has always been – and still currently is – characterized by the presence of bodies instituted by the law or by an act for a specific purpose. Said bodies act according to a precise mission (attributed by the law or by the institutive act) that is related to the organization and the development of interests that remain external to them – often defined as 'public' by induction, as belonging to public bodies – and belonging to the community that said bodies must administer in a rational and ordered manner.

Historically, administrative law and public bodies have been entrusted with the task of being a force (i.e. a power) of order and social cohesion.

In the passage from the absolute state to the so-called 'State of Rights', some of the ancient characteristics were not abandoned but – even though re-elaborated within the theories of the liberal state – transited into the new form of administrative action. Therefore, for instance, the imperativeness of an administrative act is a reflection of the imperativeness of the act of the Prince.[5] After all, public administration is entrusted with a particularly delicate task, beyond imperativeness and warranties, which is one of realizing the balance between the interest of the state and individual liberties.

The literature demonstrates how, at least in continental Europe,[6] there are significant commonalities, largely shared and then practised in the different jurisdictions: it is possible to think about the principle of legality of public administration, the rule of law, the possibility of promoting judicial review to contest the acts enacted by the representatives of the public power, the capacity of the administrative acts to impact on private peoples' juridical sphere – even in reference to property rights – without their consent, the regulation of business activity, and administrative discretion.[7]

---

[5]   Giuseppe Morbidelli, *Il diritto amministrativo tra particolarismo e universalismo* (Editoriale Scientifica, 2012).

[6]   Ibid, 16.

[7]   It is well known that the Anglo-Saxon theories arrived at the construction of an administrative state through a different path. Albert Venn Dicey, *Introduction to the study of the law of the constitution* (1885, Liberty Fund, 1982) first opposed the systems

We are now going to concentrate our analysis on these elements, without delving into single national systems of administrative law, including in light of the global dimension of administrative law's transformation that has taken place since the 1990s.[8]

In particular: unilaterality and imperativeness, as features of traditional administrative law, coexist, today and almost everywhere, with ever more extended forms of consensual relationships and participation; the differences between administrative law and private law progressively fade away and the instruments of private law – such as the contract – also become common instruments in administrative action. A responsibility of the public administration for torts in case of illegitimate wrongdoings is affirmed, according to the rules and principles of private law. The legality principle is enriched by new content, to discipline ever stricter and more specific boundaries of administrative action.

These genetic mutations have a universal character. Or, at least, a 'quasi-universal' character, noticing that, at the moment, it is not possible to detect a unique global legal framework with institutionalized law making bodies. Consequently, we will prefer to reconstruct tendencies and to conjecture upon perspectives.

Table 7.1 summarizes the universal mutations public private partnership brings about, which will be discussed in the following sections.

---

of administrative law to the system of the rule of the law, dominated by the subjection of the administrative activity to the common law, valid for any other individual. Yet, in the nineteenth century, England saw the evolution of an administrative state, 'prompted by the demands and problems that exploded with the Industrial Revolution'. Bernardo Sordi, '*Rèvolution, Rechtsstaat* and the rule of law: historical reflections on the emergence and development of administrative law' in Susan Rose-Ackerman, Peter Lindseth, Blake Emerson (eds), *Comparative administrative law* (2nd edition, Edward Elgar, 2017) 23, 29. To the end that Dicey himself 'acknowledged the emergence of a distinct legal regime' (Ibid, 31) in his essay 'The development of environmental law in England' (1915) Law Quarterly Review 31. In parallel, the American literature has acknowledged the existence of an administrative state long before Roosevelt's New Deal. See, in particular, Jerry Mashaw, 'Administration and "The Democracy": administrative law from Jackson to Lincoln, 1829–1861' (2007–2008) Yale Law J. 1928. In both these systems, the administrative state was characterized by the imperativeness of determined acts, the rule of law as a limit to public power, the challengeability of the administrative acts enacted *ultra vires*, and the subordination of administrative power to the democratic circuit.

8 Sabino Cassese, 'Crisi dell'amministrazione e riforme amministrative' (1996) Giornale Dir. Amm. 869; Eberhard Schmidt-Aßmann, *Verwaltungsrechtliche Dogmatik: Eine Zwischenbilanz zu Entwicklung, Reform und künftigen Aufgaben* (Mohr Siebeck, 2013).

Table 7.1   Mutations of the traditional administrative action provoked by public private partnership

Mutations of the principles of administrative action
A new principle of non-discrimination
From good administration to sustainable development
From bureaucratic administration to building a public image for the market. From the principle of competition to the principle of consistency: integrity, awareness and flexibility
From the reason-giving duty to the reinforced motivation
Mutations of the modalities of administrative action
From direct intervention to public private co-administration: from unilaterality to mutual trust and 'alliancing'
From the rigidity of public procurement to innovative and flexible awarding procedures
From pursuing the public interest to governing common interests
Mutations of the expected results
From compliance to a better response to social needs
From the economy principle to value for money
Mutations of the public administration's liabilities
From administrative liability to common law shared liability: From liability for an unlawful act to liability for fact

3   MUTATIONS OF THE PRINCIPLES OF ADMINISTRATIVE ACTION

3.1   The Enlarged Dimension of the Non-discrimination Principle: A New Integrity for Public Administrations

In the previous chapters it emerged that public private partnership allows public administration to exit the isolation it was confined to while acting in imperative and unilateral ways. The isolation is, indeed, a feature of administrative action that is related to the supremacy attributed to public bodies.

Whenever a space is opened for public private partnership and the public administration is not the only entity entrusted with pursuing the community's interests and vested with the correlative responsibilities, one of the first consequences is a twisting of the principle of non-discrimination.

If the administrative action is exercised in a traditional way – unilateral and imperative or through the logic of the juxtaposition between public and private – the principle of non-discrimination tends to observe public administration from within, to verify that similar situations are not treated in a different way and to avoid that individual interest may affect the impartial evaluations that the public administration must carry out.[9]

From the field of public private partnership, the non-discrimination principle acquires an additional, interesting meaning. Non-discrimination means access to all the subjects interested in offering their cooperation to the administration for the care of common interests.

Everybody should have the same chance to play its game.

In addition, if interpreted in the sense we are reconstructing, non-discrimination also means that in order not to discriminate against potential operators, public administration should be prepared, at any time, to discuss private proposals about common interests.

Therefore, non-discrimination means that the administration must be capable of evaluating the proposal of cooperation in partnership with sufficiently equal distance and without overlapping interests – political, institutional, of public image or other.

Thus, for example, when faced with a proposal of public private partnership capable of responding to the needs of the community with a project that would bring advantages to the community, the public administration, to be non-discriminatory, should evaluate and verify the quality of the proposal, without denying a dialogue with the private partner on the basis of its supremacy in the matters of public interest.

The juridical reflections about public private partnership show that non-discrimination acquires a more complex dimension: to be non-discriminatory it is not sufficient for public administration to treat the same situations with the same rule. Rather, it is necessary to abandon administrative solipsism, which was once indissolubly linked with the exercise of imperative power – *ius imperii*.

Conversely, once public private partnership, even by fostering corporate social responsibility, has broken the barriers that for centuries divided the exercise of public powers and the fulfilment of general interests, on the one side, and private activity, considered only egoistic and profit-oriented, on the other, the principle of non-discrimination also implies a duty of loyal cooperation of public bodies with civil society and businesses. The aim of the principle, so intended, is to verify, without ideological approaches, the feasibility of solu-

---

[9]   In the sense intended, *ex multis*, in Christopher McCrudden, 'Equality and non-discrimination' in David Feldman (ed.), *English public law* (OUP, 2004) 499. For a reasoned discussion on the different perspectives of equal treatment, non-discrimination and impartiality in public administration, an interesting comment can be found in Bo Rothstein and Jan Teorell, 'What is quality of government? A theory of impartial government institutions' (2008) Governance 165.

tions that could enrich the response to the needs of the community, towards the pursuit of common interests and the creation of additional value.

The principle of non-discrimination also acquires, in this way, a substantial outline, as it gives value to the dialogue and, in procedural terms, in the investigation during which all proposals of cooperation converge, whose advantages and possible externalities must all be evaluated and weighed.

In the reconstructive and systematic perspective we are presenting, non-discrimination and participatory democracy are strictly linked.

Indeed, we recall that public private partnership allows public authorities to overcome their limits by establishing fruitful relationships between institutions, economic operators and civil society, thus enabling them to respond to the increasingly complex needs of modern communities. Further, that public private partnership's ability to involve private operators in the selection of the relevant needs to be satisfied through administrative action implements a more direct approach to the principle of democratic participation.

This denotes, clearly, that there must be a moment in which the various proposals of cooperation are discussed. In this moment, the public administration should approach the market and civil society without a self-referencing attitude. Otherwise, the theorized change in sovereignty simply will not happen.

The above-described mutation builds a new public consciousness and a new version of public administration's integrity, which, from public private partnership, exceeds the limit of this sector to embrace one of administrative activity in general.

3.2   From Good Administration to Sustainable Development

According to the general theory of administrative law, administrative action is evaluated – as well as by compliance to the applicable norms, in terms of legitimacy – by its capability of reaching determined objectives – namely efficacy – and from the relationship between the obtained results and the means implied to achieve them, namely efficiency.

On the other hand, both in the international and local dimension, public private partnership is justified for its capacity to deliver social and environmental benefits and, more generally, sustainable development, intended as inclusive of participatory democracy targets.

The relevance of the principle of sustainable development gains, in this context, a prominent position, as it indicates, in a decidedly modern way, an administration capable of responding quickly, democratically and flexibly to the needs of society and, simultaneously, of respecting the globally shared values, from which the unwinding line of development policies derives. Such policies enable economic progress to improve individual and businesses satisfaction, the environment and the health of the communities, through actions characterized by a rational and dynamic planning, in respect of human rights.

As leverage of the spread of the most recent forms of public private partnership, the principle of sustainable development, a synthetic principle leading in the direction of a rational and human-centred progress,[10] provides a new key for re-reading the traditional principles of administrative law. As a consequence, the principle of economy of public expenditure now faces new needs.

Public private partnership induces sustainable development and the latter, in turn, enhances its application.

Sustainable development means, for example, rationalizing urbanization, renewing urban peripheries, using technologies enabling the spread of information for free, using contractors' selection criteria that enhance the quality and not merely the economic element during a public tender, thus enhancing public private partnerships. In light of sustainable development goals, the goodness of administrative action should be measured not only in the view of the principles of efficacy and efficiency. Public private partnership promotes a new hierarchy, based on the pivotal role of sustainable development, as a

---

[10]   On this matter, the literature is vast, given the global relevance of the perspective. For a comprehensive and insightful comment, see Jeffrey Sachs, *The age of sustainable development* (Columbia University Press, 2015). On this same topic, see: Beate Sjåfjell and Anja Wiesbrock (eds), *Sustainable public procurement under EU law: new perspectives on the state as stakeholder* (CUP, 2016), which quotes the Communications of the European Commission, 'Europe 2020; a strategy for smart, sustainable and inclusive growth', COM (2010) 2010 final and 'A global partnership for poverty eradication and sustainable development after 2015', COM (2015) 44 final. For the application of the principle in the sector of public procurement, see UN Environment, '2017 global review of sustainable public procurement' (New York, 2017); Anna Beckers, 'Using contracts to further sustainability? A contract law perspective on sustainable public procurement' in Sjåfjell and Wiesbrock (eds), above, 206. Commission, 'Buying social: a guide to taking account of social considerations in public procurement' (European Union, 2010); Commission, 'Buying green! A handbook on green public procurement' (3rd edition, 2016). To further underline the global relevance of the phenomenon, it is worth mentioning a few political initiatives: Organization for Economic Cooperation and Development, 'Recommendation of the Council on Improving the Environmental Performance of Government' (20 February 1996, C(96)39/final); Organization for Economic Cooperation and Development, 'Environmental strategy for the first decade of the 21st century' (16 May 2001); Organization for Economic Cooperation and Development, 'Recommendation of the Council on Improving the Environmental Performance of Public Procurement' (23 January 2002, C(2002)3); UNEP 'Capacity building for sustainable public procurement in developing countries' (December 2009) and, lastly, the UN Convention of Sustainable Development, '*Rio +20*'. For a more detailed bibliography, see Sara Valaguzza, *Sustainable development in public contracts: an example of strategic regulation* (Editoriale Scientifica, 2016).

'strategic' principle reflecting the current socio-economical-political sensitivities coming from the global community.

The adaptation that results from the merging between the private and the public sector implies the twisting of the principles of administrative action, which are reshaped in a twofold manner: firstly, they lose the strictly subjective connotation of imperative administrative action; secondly, they look at the goals and at the global values that can be generalized beyond national borders, thus losing the unique and isolated cultural and conceptual references related to their national character.[11]

Therefore, as a consequence of the growth of the phenomenon, the criteria of good administration become deeply substantial. New sensitivities arise to interpret already-existing principles, or to create new ones capable of adapting to the new economic and social demands.[12]

Now, if the phenomenon that we are describing is intrinsically linked to the spread of public private partnership, it is true that it tends to expand well beyond the borders of the principles governing public private partnership.

In administrative law, it frequently happens that general principles are enriched through time by sectorial sensitivities, arising with reference to specific ambits or sectors of administrative action; which subsequently produces general rules applicable to all administrative actions. For instance, the proportionality principle,[13] born to defend private property against the

---

[11]   On the transnational features of administrative law, see Nicoletta Marzona, 'Il potere normativo delle autorità indipendenti' in Sabino Cassese, Claudio Franchini (eds), *I garanti delle regole* (Il Mulino, 1996); Maria Rosaria Ferrarese, *Diritto sconfinato: Inventiva giuridica e spazi nel mondo globale* (Laterza, 2006); Sabino Cassese, *Chi governa il mondo?* (Il Mulino, Bologna, 2013). As mentioned in the previous chapters, some scholars have interpreted the transversal presence of essential principles of administrative law in standards, guides and rules implemented by international actors and national bodies with international relevance, capable of impacting choices and behaviours of operators of a determined sector of the market. See in particular, Benedict Kingsbury, Nico Krisch, and Richard B Stewart, 'The emergence of global administrative law' (2005) Law and Contemp. Problems 15 and, more recently, Sabino Cassese (ed.), *Research handbook on global administrative law* (Edward Elgar, 2016).

[12]   'Sustainable development is a way to understand the world as a complex interaction of economic, social, environmental, and political systems: Yet it is also a normative or ethical view of the world, a way to define the objectives of a well-functioning society, one that delivers wellbeing for its citizens today and for future generations'. Sachs, n 10, 11.

[13]   On the international dimension of the proportionality principle see Grainne de Búrca, 'The principle of proportionality and its application in EC law' (1993) Yearbook of European Law 105; Takis Tridimas, 'Proportionality in Community law: searching for the appropriate standard of scrutiny' in Evelyn Ellis (ed.), *The principle of proportionality in the laws of Europe* (Hart Publishing, 1999) 65; Matthias Klatt and Moritz Meister, *The constitutional structure of proportionality* (OUP, 2012); Cohen-Eliya

imperative intrusions of public administrations, passed from a crucial principle of urban law to a general rule applicable to all expressions of public power. Alternatively, the precautionary principle, born in environmental issues, now pervades all administrative law. The European case law has indeed clarified that 'the precautionary principle can be defined as a general principle of Community law requiring the competent authorities to take appropriate measures to prevent specific potential risks to public health, safety and the environment, by giving precedence to the requirements related to the protection of those interests over economic interests'.[14]

Therefore, in these dynamics, the principle of sustainable development, in its multi-faceted and slippery content, becomes, from the international dimension of public private partnership, the guiding principle of administrative action.

3.3 From Bureaucratic Administration to Building a Public Image for the Market. From the Principle of Competition to the Principle of Consistency: Integrity, Awareness and Flexibility

Thanks to public private partnership, in administrative procedure the acquisition and balancing of all the relevant interests is not carried out in an antagonistic form. There is instead a continual exchange of views between the different

---

Porat, *Proportionality and constitutional culture* (CUP, 2013); Cheng-Yi Huang and David Law, 'Proportionality review of administrative action in Japan, Korea, Taiwan, and China' in Francesca Bignami and David Zaring (eds), *Research handbook in comparative law and regulation* (Edward Elgar, 2014); Jude Mathews, 'Searching for proportionality in American administrative law' in Sofia Ranchordàs and Boudewijn de Waard (eds), *The judge and the proportionate use of discretion: a comparative study* (Routledge, 2016) 160; Sanchez Yoan, 'Proportionality in French administrative law', Sofia Ranchordàs and Boudewijn De Waard (eds), *The judge and the proportionate use of discretion: a comparative study* (Routledge, 2016) 43. Paul Craig, 'Proportionality and judicial review: a UK historical perspective' in Stefan Vogenauer (ed.), *General principles of law: European and comparative perspectives* (Hart Publishing, 2017) 145; Jud Mathews, 'Proportionality review in administrative law' in Rose-Ackerman, Lindseth, and Emerson (eds), n 7, 40.

[14] Case T-74/00, *Artegodan v. Commission* ECLI:EU:T:2002:283 (2000) ECR II-2583. On the development of the application of the principle by the European Court of Justice, see, in particular, Alberto Alemanno, 'The shaping of the precautionary principle by European courts: from scientific uncertainty to legal certainty' in Lorenzo Cuoccolo and Luca Luparia (eds), *Valori Costituzionali e Nuove Politiche del Diritto* (Bocconi Legal Studies Research Paper No.1007404, 2007). For the institutional European perspective, see European Commission, 'Science for environment policy: future brief: the precautionary principle: decision-making under uncertainty' (September 2017, Issue 18) and the cases therein cited.

stakeholders, which are authorized to present their views on the possible achievement of specific goals.

With public private partnership, the relationship between administration and private actors is built according to consensual frameworks. Public private partnership generates agreements, contracts and conventions in which the activity of common interest is disciplined.

If we look at the subject of our analysis in a purely economic way, public private partnership opens the door to new markets which match the sectors traditionally reserved for public powers. The public private partnership operation can be attractive under numerous points of view for enterprises, which can associate their name and their image with a programme of public interest and an institutional reality, thus benefiting in commercial and reputational terms.

The possibility of contributing to the realization of something significant in terms of the general interest, in an area encompassed by the institutional missions of public bodies, is something that is very attractive to private operators. This is true especially for the enterprises that can exploit, in terms of marketing, the project alongside the public administration and in favour of the community, thus consolidating a social image. The above-mentioned perspective has been examined closely, especially in Chapter 1, in relation to the concept of corporate social responsibility.

In this perspective, the ability to resort to public private partnership depends on public administration's ability to project a positive image. It is on this public image that private operators decide to bet, associating their image with it to acquire a benefit in return.

Yet, since the public image is particularly sensitive in political terms, the choice of the partner must also be adequately and carefully evaluated. The selection of the private partner should not be motivated only by economic evaluations, but also by political and institutional motivations, pursuant to the principles of *par condicio* and competition. This is obvious, even though not easy to disentangle.

We can look at the following example: an entrepreneur, willing to run as a candidate in political elections, offers his business activity to the benefit of the community. He does so for personal reasons. How could the public administration evaluate the sincerity of this proposal? How could the administration protect itself from a rash initiative that could turn detrimental for the common good?

Alternatively, it is possible to look at a different case: an enterprise with a turbulent past in fiscal terms – because it was obliged to pay burdensome sanctions for tax evasion – proposes itself for a programme of partnership with a local administration, in order to 'clean up' its public image. Could the public administration agree to associate its image with such a troubled past?

Another scenario could be the following: a multinational company could put itself forward to a public administration for social initiatives in the health care field, not because of a genuine interest in the partnership, but rather to bring advantage to an affiliated company that provides medical products.

In synthesis, what we want to stress, with these few examples, is that it is not banal at all to identify criteria that are adequate for the selection procedures of the partner, in a dialogical framework such as the one of public private partnership. It would be wrong to think that the same criteria of public procurement apply.

The equation that is used among procedures of selection for concessions and public procurement does not hit the mark. It is true that concession is the most similar situation, in technical and juridical terms, to traditional public procurement. However, even in this case the identification of the concessionaire with the provider of public function, in a long-lasting merger, suggests a higher propensity to choose the valorization of the *intuitus personae*.

In the cases that we have laid out, the consistency between the image of the private actor and that of the public body is a parameter that cannot be overlooked. The value of consistency, in our perspective, cannot be sacrificed in the name of competition.

In light of the very special features of public private partnership, it should not scandalize anyone to affirm that consistency between the public image and ethics and the goals – meaning the aim of the contract – at the basis of the partnership to be undertaken is the primary good to preserve.

What is to be considered as consistency with the public image and ethics is easier to understand if the term is broken down into the elements that constitute the expression: a choice based on consistency is the result of the public administration's integrity, awareness – as capacity to weigh the partner in reference to its subjective characteristics before the ones of its proposal – and flexibility. Indeed, the rigidity of procedures, in light of the maximization of the principles of competition and *par condicio*, ends up clipping the wings of a rational and strategic administrative action.

In addition to what we have already pointed out, it is therefore necessary to keep in mind that, in a public private partnership, the partner is not really a counterpart, rather, it is a member of an alliance. In a public private partnership, the partner shares with the administration a role of impulse and responsibility.

This means that in the procedures for selection of the partner, in a public private partnership the criterion of the lowest price is to be excluded if, as we said, it is necessary to carry out verifications of consistency.

It is, in relation to public private partnership, an inevitable landing point.

However, taking inspiration from the world of public private partnership, a wider line of reasoning, in our view, is necessary for the whole area of selective procedures for the awarding of public contracts: the image of public administration must always be preserved.

3.4   From the Reason-giving Duty to the Reinforced Motivation

The examination of public private partnership's implications for the general theory of administrative law leads us to clarify another important aspect, related to the need for adequate and reinforced motivation to support critical administrative decisions.

Provided that, according to what we have discussed in the previous chapters, public private partnership implies a loss – even if partial – of sovereignty from the public side, in favour of a co-administration that increases the importance of the private role even in defining what is to be intended as 'common interests', public private partnership must be accompanied by a reinforced motivation to provide detailed reasons for the choices that brought the holder of public power to share it with the private side.

Indeed, in public private partnerships the private actor is not involved as in a form of outsourcing. Rather, the private partner is involved in a dynamic of cooperation, certainly more delicate in terms of control of the substantial pursuit of the interests of the administered community.

As we noted in the preceding chapters, public private partnership is supported by what we defined as the 'logic of the compromise', to underline that in public private partnership, public and private entities both lose a portion of their individual identity, to converge in a neutral territory – partially private and partially public – in which they act in tandem to pursue the interests of the community. These interests lose the connotation of 'public' because they are not defined, identified and pursued only through the action of a public body; conversely, they are pursued thanks to a joined action in which the contamination of the identities – public and private – is an essential element.

Thus, public action sets aside a part of its special character and public principles simmer down to encounter private ones, in a zone of mutual exchange that necessarily cannot conserve the traces of the imperativeness of public power.

As we affirmed, public private partnership also modifies the concepts of sovereignty and accountability for public action. This shift to forms of cooperation with private actors does not necessary mean that public bodies are not able to respond to society's needs. Indeed, as we outlined in the previous sections, partnering is, first of all, a political choice. But this political choice is not neutral from the side of the consequences for the role of government in a society.

While the administration is, by law, bound to pursue missions of public interest – and for this reason is inserted in the democratic circuit – the private operator, on the contrary, must adhere to the decisions assumed by the public body and, as external to the democratic circuit, cannot assume decisions or take actions that require consistency with the majority of the constituents. Public private partnership derogates from this principle, allowing private operators to enter the 'control room'; also, public private partnership requires respect for a delicate equilibrium between pursuit of the common interest, whose control belongs to the administration, and the dialogical schema of the alliance constituting the partnership.

Here – given the mutation of the character of administrative action – the necessity arises for adopting a reinforced motivation to resort to the instruments of public private partnership, in order to make visible and transparent the reason for opening the exercise of typically public tasks to one or more private actors.

This last statement is closely related to a fundamental question arising from public private partnership tools: does the proposal deriving from an economic operator to promote activities in the general interest alongside the public administration generate the duty for the latter to proceed? In other words, are the private proposals undeniable?

In our perspective, the answer is strongly negative.

The proposal of an economic operator willing to become a partner is not sufficient at all to loosen the knot of administrative discretional choice on the '*an*' – namely the 'if' – of the partnership; not even in the presence of considerable private funds.

Indeed, it must be considered that the framework of public private partnership, albeit being an opportunity that increases the possibilities to answer the needs of the community, implies an effort of management and a considerable use of resources including from the side of public bodies, which must be adequately used.

The administration could have an interest in using those resources and energies in different ambits. Consequently, it is not correct to expect an automatic link between the private proposal of partnership and the public interest in realizing it.

The schemes of public private partnership imply different and complex evaluations, of economic, institutional and political character, which must be adequately dealt with at a preliminary phase and which cannot be renounced by the administration.

Besides, the reinforced motivation will make it possible to verify whether the administration effectively faced the new dimension of non-discrimination that we have discussed above, or whether it preferred to fall back to its auto-referential isolation, which as we affirmed can no longer be justified in the context of cooperation which public private partnership implies.

Therefore, a modern focus on the function and structure of the motivation for the administrative decisions is promoted by public private partnership to administrative action as a whole.

An administration willing to be ready to interact with the social community must necessarily follow the path of dialogue and open data.

4   MUTATIONS OF THE MODALITIES OF ADMINISTRATIVE ACTION

4.1   From Direct Intervention to Public Private Co-administration: From Unilaterality to Mutual Trust and 'Alliancing'

In the general context of public law, we can trace a tendency of administrative action to lose its authoritative content,[15] toward a more modern consensual

---

[15]   It is widely acknowledged by scholarship that administrative law is in continuous evolution. Not being autonomous from the legal system, it changes according to the legal, social and economic modification of its legal framework. The above-mentioned crisis of the national dimension of administrative law, the emergence of global values to pursue, of actors that are able to enact transnationally valid regulations, the spread of instruments of administrative action based on consent rather than the traditional expression of power are only a few examples of the change of the rules and principles applicable to the exercise of administrative action. See Donald Kettl, *The transformation of governance: public administration for the twenty-first century* (Johns Hopkins University Press, 2002). In particular, the loss of the authoritative character of administrative action can be seen in: the spread of negotiating schemes of governance (Jody Freeman, 'The private role in public governance' (2000) NYULR 543); the value attributed to public contracts as strategic elements of public policy – See Valaguzza, n 10; the digitalization of the public administrations – See Sergey Kamolov, 'Digital public governance: trends and risks' (2017) Giornale di Storia Costituzionale 33; the publicity of public data and information – See Ig Snellen and Wim van de Donk (eds), *Public administration in an information age: a handbook* (IOS Press, 1998); the increased flexibilities of administrative procedures (Richard Stewart, 'Vermont Yankee and the evolution of administrative procedure' (1977–1978) Harvard Law Review 1805; Carol Harlow and Richard Rawlings, *Process and procedure in EU administration* (Hart Publishing, 2014); the enlargement of the instruments of participation in administrative decision (Catherine Donnelly, 'Participation and expertise: judicial attitudes in comparative perspective' in Rose-Ackerman, Lindseth, and Emerson (eds), n 7, 370); the fragmentation of the subjective situations of the recipients of the administrative act (Sara Valaguzza, *La frammentazione della fattispecie nel diritto amministrativo a conformazione europea* (Giuffrè, 2008); sometimes of the administrations themselves (Oswald Jansen and Bettina Schöndorf-Haubold (eds), *The European composite administration* (Intersentia, 2011); the increasing importance of the timeliness of administrative action and the consequent demise of the dogma of its inexhaustibility (Michele Trimarchi, *L'inesauribilità del potere amministrativo: Profili critici* (Editoriale Scientifica, 2018).

research on administrative action, in which administrative decisions are not imposed and passively suffered, but are the result of a path characterized by dialogue and cooperation, which involves the community toward which the administrative action is directed.

Moreover, the logical and juridical structures that currently characterize the procedures for awarding public contracts, as regulated by the applicable norms and according to the interpretation provided in the administrative, criminal and civil courts, do not favour the creation of a harmonic and collaborative environment between the public and private parties. Said parties are not even reciprocally selected on the basis of reciprocal trust but happen to work together as a consequence of the procurement procedure.

The passage from the antagonistic contractual modes to more collaborative ones is a Copernican revolution that, from public private partnership, opens the way to a refocusing of attention on the contract as the place for a careful regulation of interest aiming at the creation of additional value through cooperation.

From public private partnership to public contracts at large, it is pivotal to avoid conflict between the parties. Public administration and private operators must speak the same language. If the juridical structure of the contractual relationship is typically adversarial, clashes and frictions are favoured.

It is precisely this antagonistic structure that created the lacerations, contradictions, conflicts, claims, additional costs, design errors, and inertia which relentlessly afflict public contracts.

Conversely, by regulating the contractual relationship with cooperative schemes, the focus shifts.

The concept of collaboration is quite wide. In psychology, it has been analysed to understand how group dynamics influence individual behaviours. The so-called 'hidden profile'[16] is a paradigm that occurs in the process of group decision making when a part of information is not shared. According to these studies, unshared information creates fear in individuals and is the main cause for failure in interaction. In a group, when people are not fully informed, collaboration is a tool for pooling unshared information aimed at identifying the optimal decision choice.

In economic theories, those scholars who contributed to the evolution of game theory by focusing on relational dynamics[17] outline the differences

---

[16] For example, see Garold Stasser and William Titus, 'Hidden profiles: a brief history' (2003) Psychological Inquiry 304.

[17] See Joseph Farrell, 'Cheap talk, coordination, and entry' (1987) Rand J. Econ. 34; Joseph Farrell, 'Communication, coordination and Nash equilibrium' (1988) Econ. Lett. 209; Joseph Farrell and Matthew Rabin, 'Cheap talk' (1996) J. Econ. Persp. 103; Elchanan Ben-Porath, 'Rationality, Nash Equilibrium and backward induction in

between individualistic behaviour and cooperative attitudes. The latter, since it avoids centrifugal forces, is better able to achieve the agreed purposes of the group.

In relation to contract theory, the most modern techniques of collaborative contracting are explored in a very recent book by David Mosey on collaboration construction procurement.[18] In the book, 'collaborative contracting' is defined as a set of processes and relationships, with legal discipline and effects, through which a team can develop, share and apply information in ways that improve value in unpredictable terms.

Cooperation techniques, also named 'alliancing', have been defined in different – sometimes a-technical,[19] at least for jurists[20] – ways. Indeed, the term does not indicate a precise archetypical concept.

To indicate the same concept, the literature has used the expressions 'collaborative contracting', 'alliancing' and 'collaborative behaviours'.[21]

For instance, it was affirmed that: the expression 'alliancing' encompasses those agreements that bring together two or more actors – national or international – to share objectives and common economic interests;[22] collaborative contracting means agreements in which enterprises create an added value in favour of the progress of society and the final client;[23] there are contracts dealing with cooperation among different members aiming at creating a syner-

---

perfect information games' (1997) Review of Economic Studies 23; Charles Holt and Monica Capra, 'Classroom games: a prisoner's dilemma' (2002) The Journal of Economic Education 229.

[18]   David Mosey (ed.), *Collaborative construction procurement and improved value* (Wiley, 2019).

[19]   The definitions can be found in different manuals and monographic studies. It is possible to consult, for instance, Denny McGeorge and Angela Palmer, *Construction management new directions* (2nd edition, Blackwell Science, 2002).

[20]   We should point out that the definitions are included mostly in technical books; which naturally creates an approach that is not always precise in its references to juridical conceptual categories.

[21]   The book by David Mosey, n 18, inventor of the most adopted standard model of collaborative contract, contains a global analysis of the alliancing techniques. For the Italian part, see Sara Valguzza, 'How do collaborative procurement operate in Italy?' in Mosey (ed.), n 18, 445.

[22]   'A relationship between two entities, large or small, domestic or foreign, with shared goals and economic interests'. See United States Trade Center, 1998 http://ustradecenter.com/alliance.html#introduction, accessed 28 June 2019.

[23]   'Organisations with capabilities and needs come together to do business and add value to the other partner, at the same time working to provide a product which enhances society and the capability of the ultimate client'. See G Nicholson, 'Choosing the right partner for your joint venture, Fletcher construction' (Proceedings of Joint Venture and Strategic Alliance Conference, Sydney, Australia, 1996).

gic strategy that contributes to ameliorating the expected results from a shared project.[24]

The definition that seems more consistent with the actual configuration of the instrument, even though still quite generic, was elaborated by Love and Gunasekaran. According to the authors, in 'alliancing' it is possible to include those agreements that constitute an organizational network aimed at disciplining the behaviour of members, for the achievement of specific common goals.[25]

Given the difficulty of distinguishing a specific and detailed category to associate with the juridical notion of collaboration, some interesting studies[26] proposed elaborating on the concept of alliancing using the theory of family resemblance by Wittgenstein.[27] Through this path, the authors suggest a wide and flexible notion, capable of adequately representing the phenomenon and the different articulations present in different jurisdictions and in global law, without losing its complex character.

According to the German philosopher, faced with a complex and articulated concept, the defining approach is one of resemblance: just like within a family, there are somatic and character resemblances among relatives, linking not any

---

[24] 'A cooperative arrangement between two or more organisations that forms part of their overall strategy, and contributions to achieving their major goals and objectives for a particular project', Tommy Kwok and Keith Hampson, 'Building strategic alliances in construction' (Queensland University of Technology, AIPM Special Publication, 1996). Similarly, collaborative contract is defined as the contract in which 'the client and associated firms will join forces for a specific project, but will remain legally independent organisations. Ownership and management of the cooperating firms will not be fully integrated although the risk of the project is shared by all participants', Alexander Gerybadze, 'Strategic alliances and process redesign' (Walter de Gruyter, 1995).

[25] It is stated that alliancing aims to 'establish inter-organisational relations and to engage in collaborative behaviour for a specific purpose' in Peter Love and Angappa Gunasekaran, 'Learning alliances: a customer–supplier focus for continuous improvement in manufacturing' (1999) Industrial and Commercial Training 88. Similarly, alliancing was defined as a strategic alliance in which 'an inter-organisational arrangement which usually exists between two companies that extends beyond a specific project and the parties would expect ongoing, mutually beneficial business' in Renaye Peters et al., 'Case study of the Acton Peninsula Development: research and case study of the construction of the National Museum of Australia and the Australian Institute of Aboriginal and Torres Strait Islander Studies. School of Construction Management and Property' (Queensland University of Technology, Australia, 2001).

[26] See in particular, John Yeung, Albert Chan, and Daniel Chan, 'The definition of alliancing in construction as a Wittgenstein family-resemblance concept' (2007) International Journal of Project Management 219.

[27] Ludwig Wittgenstein, *Philosophical investigations* (1953, Wiley, 2009).

member but only a few of them; complex concepts aggregate different exemplars, characterized by belonging to a specific family.

Proceeding with the recalled method, 'collaborative contracting', 'alliancing' and 'collaborative behaviours' would be characterized by some hard elements as well as by soft ones, defined by considering the modalities in which the contractual relationship is developed and studied in light of the behavioural sciences. In the first group are: the written form of the contract and a precise regulation of responsibilities and revenues for the parties. In the second: trust, long duration of the relationship, common goals, advantages for any component of the collaboration, flexibility, equilibrium in the division of tasks and earnings, alternative dispute resolution systems, agile forms of communication among the parties, periodical meetings, and involvement of the contractor in an early stage of the project.[28]

When discussing alliancing, we do not refer to a specific contractual type. Rather, we refer to a non-standardized regulation between two or more parties which regards the discipline of the interaction among more contracts.[29]

To organize a collaborative platform is a very complex activity. In addition to the activities assigned with the main contract, precisely defined, the collaborative procurement introduces a second level discipline, inspired by flexibility, in which the individuals act not only in pursuing their own profits but also considering they are members of a larger alliance.

Each alliance member is committed to bringing added value to the group, facing unforeseen events and seeking to improve the shared objectives.

In achieving added values with alliancing, a contractual framework based on agreed targets is required.

Alliance contracts are the appropriate instrument to regulate collaborative behaviours.

Flexibility and agreed targets push alliance members to use their creativity and individual efforts in promoting collaboration ends.

---

[28]   Yeung, Chan, and Chan., n 26, 219.

[29]   An exception is the model of collaborative contract named 'Framework Alliance Contract FAC-1' drafted in the UK by David Mosey of the King's College of London and the Association of Consultant Architects of London. The model is standardized and belongs to the best practices of good public clients. In general, on the English experience, it is possible to obtain continuously updated information on the practices of alliancing and on the new model contracts at http://www.allianceforms.co.uk/about-fac-1/, accessed 28 June 2019. On the contents of the FAC_1, see the Briefing Paper available at https://www.kcl.ac.uk/law/research/centres/construction/FAC-1-Briefing-Paper.pdf, accessed 28 June 2019.

From a purely legal perspective, alliance contracts build bridges between different parties and different contracts, with the aim of creating added value though collaboration.

A collaborative contract should be built starting from an analysis of the network of contractors involved in the client's project, considering both juridical and factual elements of possible interaction.

The more collaborative contracts are able to include the supply chain and professional collaborators, the more likely is the success of the alliance.

Observing the context in which a determined contract is set highlights a wider dimension in which acts and facts deriving from different causes are entangled.

In synthesis, the theory of collaborative contracts reveals the logical fiction that contracting continues to indulge. It is simply not true that the single contract is isolated and that its vicissitudes only affect the interactions of its parties.

The single contract is a unitary element, which is inserted in a wider network of relations, also juridical, of extreme relevance, composed by different relationships and contracts. The breach of contract of one contractor can be the consequence of the mistake of a supplier; the incapacity of an administration to respect the delivery of certain areas can depend on third parties which, in turn, are influenced by other contexts, and so on.

In Figure 7.1, the logical and juridical system of collaborative contracts in their operative context is schematically represented.

The construction of the network has a particularly deep meaning for the sector that we are analysing: to design with precision the map of the protagonists of a determined public project, the relationship among the parties and the relative flows brings transparency, including for the benefit of the controlling authorities. The cooperation and the network dynamic, if observed in light of the problems of public contracts, offer an important possibility to the public client that, through the collaborative contract, can build a precise framework and have a direct perception of the entire structure of the juridical relationship linked to the contract awarded to a single economic operator. Rebuilding the network, the administration acquires consciousness of all the relationships of its contractor with the entire supply chain.

Thus, the issue of supply chain is not only observed by the client in formal terms, related to the verification of the existence of determined criteria on the sub-contractor but also becomes substantial. Through collaborative contracts it is possible to perceive what happens in the supply chain and therefore take any necessary steps to correct or reward behaviours in light of the achievement of specific objectives. Moreover, it is possible to acknowledge and control the moral and professional qualities of those who directly or indirectly participate in the realization of programmes of public interest.

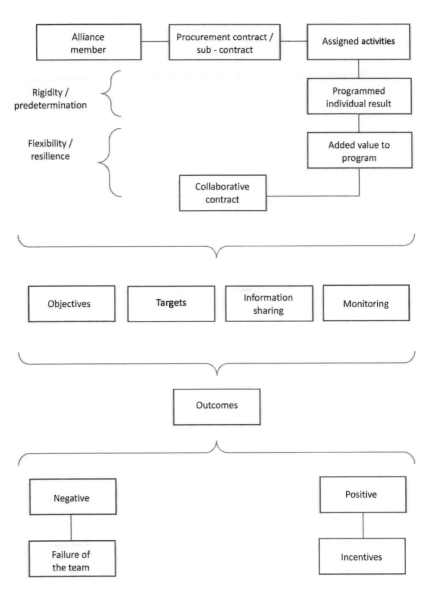

Figure 7.1 Collaborative contracts in operation

In sum, once a collaborative network is composed and strengthened, through the design of ad hoc contractual rules, the single contractors, even if parties in different contracts, take part in defining a bigger plan in which the initiative of every member ameliorates or negatively affects the performance of others.

Each member of the alliance is committed to bringing added value to the group, facing unforeseen events and looking to improve the shared objectives.

The 'juridical elements' that create interference between two different juridical relationships could be, for instance, the one generated whenever a contract qualifies an event as 'action of a third party', which cannot be attributed to the contractor. Said event usually depends on the activity of a different actor, which is in turn subject to the action of other parties. The discipline of the network should regulate said interference, realizing a favourable environment for cooperation between the contractor, the client and third parties, on the basis of the shared interest of all the parties to create value through the realization of a programme of public interest.

'Factual elements' creating interferences can be any unexpected event that can alter the timetable of the programmed activities, also belonging to the responsibility of different parties; in this case, the collaboration framework can channel the strengths and energies of alliance members to deal with the unexpected event, in order to elicit the effort of the group in avoiding possible additional costs or increased times.

The collaborative contract, by identifying the network, creates an alliance in which the economic operators and the client know each other, accept being united to pursue a common objective, and channel the energies of all the members to capture the opportunities emerging in the execution phase of the different contractual relationships.

From that, the advantages shown in Table 7.2 are reached.[30]

Public private partnership is clearly an experience of collaboration and, more precisely, of cooperation. While to have collaboration, it is sufficient that two actors coordinate their own action to achieve a common interest, in public private partnership the relationship assumes a more specific organizational form in which undertakings and responsibilities are divided in a shared programme.

In any case, in our opinion, public private partnership should be completed with the above-described new forms of contract, of the kind of alliancing and collaborative behaviour. Said techniques would complete public private partnership because, as we have seen, it lives in a dimension that is not one of juxtaposition but of cooperation. Therefore, it needs to develop through con-

---

[30] The presented perspectives are more deeply discussed in Sara Valaguzza, *Governare per contratto: Come creare valore attraverso i contratti pubblici* (Editoriale Scientifica, 2018) and Sara Valaguzza, *Collaborare nell'interesse pubblico: Perché passare dai modelli antagonisti agli accordi collaborativi* (Editoriale Scientifica, 2019).

Table 7.2   Advantages of collaborative contracts

Advantages of the alliance for the client
Formalization of bodies of the network with control and monitoring tasks on the daily development of the programme
Escape from the typical isolation of being responsible for the works
Acknowledgment of the network relationship and creation of a direct relationship with possibly all members of the supply chain
Transparency and sharing of the programme's data and relevant information
Identification of the additional substantial objectives creating added public value
Optimization of the management of unexpected events
Incentive to 'do more and better' for the contractors
'Black ship' syndrome for the member that does not cooperate
Advantages for economic operators
Abandonment of selfish behaviours in favour of co-responsibility
Involvement of sub-contractors
Economic, contractual and reputational incentives
Possibility to demonstrate and valorize competences and quality
Sharing of issues and unexpected events with the client
Adhesion to a win-win logic
Introduction of substantial evaluation criteria and logics 'of result'
Possibility of dialogue with the client
Advantages for the community
Participation
Added public value
Timely delivery
Public money savings and optimization

tractual instruments in which there is more room for the flexibility of activities useful for the achievement of shared goals than pre-defined duties laid upon the parties.

Cooperation, from public private partnering to public contract and administrative action, generally speaking is the correct tool to build a juridical relationship for improving public value.

4.2   From the Rigidity of Public Procurement to Innovative and Flexible Awarding Procedures

The modification of the relational scheme from an adversarial to cooperative one also leads to a transformation in tender procedures.

Considering that public private partnership is based on the initiative and creativity of the partner, which contributes to selecting the instruments and the innovative modalities to satisfy common interests, the selection procedure must include the discussion of ideas and perspectives with candidates. The different scenarios offered by bidders must be examined and compared with competing solutions.

We noticed in the previous chapters that, in the local dimension, the spread of public private partnership is often connected to the need to provide services to the community, characterized by an elevated technical and technological content, which the administration can hardly execute without the cooperation – from the start of the creative phase – of specialized and qualified economic operators as holders of the due know-how and technologies.

Therefore, it is absolutely necessary to consider procedures for the award of contracts of public private partnership that are able to enhance the confrontation of the competitors, on the one hand, and the dialogue with the public client, on the other.

In general, it is worth using competitive procedures, competitive dialogue and any other selective procedure with moments of exchange of ideas in favour of the best definition of the public interest.

The European Directive on concession contracts offers some interesting examples. As for the principles on the procedures, the one of free administration by public authorities – disciplined by Article 2 of Directive 2014/23/EU – provides a noteworthy elasticity in stating that national, regional and local authorities should decide the best way 'to manage the execution of works or the provision of services, to ensure in particular a high level of quality, safety and affordability, equal treatment and the promotion of universal access and of user rights in public services'. This principle concerns firstly the choices of the administration related to the selection and organization of the tender procedure and secondly the choice between auto-production and externalization.

In the same way, Title II of the cited Directive, related to the rules on the award of concessions, repeats the freedom that the contracting authority holds in the organization of the procedure leading to the choice of concessionaire subject to compliance with the Directive itself (Article 30). More specifically, the cited Directive establishes the possibility to conduct free negotiations with the candidates of the tender, provided that the awarding criteria and the minimum requirements are not changed during the course of the negotiations (Article 37, para 6).

Further, Article 41, para 1 allows for modification of the ranking of importance of the awarding criteria in case the contracting authority receives an innovative solution 'with an exceptional level of functional performance which could not have been foreseen by a diligent contracting authority or contracting entity'. Thus, this is an awarding procedure that is able to adapt to the specific needs of the case.[31]

The line of reasoning on public private partnership shows that flexibility and substantiality of tender procedures is an interesting opportunity for any phenomenon of awarding public contracts.

4.3   From Pursuing the Public Interest to Governing Common Interests

In light of what was discussed above, it should now be clear why we used the expression 'governing common interests' in the title of our book, instead of the more traditional 'pursuing the common interest'.

When the private sector associates with the public to provide performances aiming at governing common interests, it is not a mere executor: rather, just like the public entity, it is an interpreter and a creator of a mission of general interest.

We highlighted many times throughout this book that it is impossible to define public private partnership in terms of pursuit of public interest belonging to a public body and entrusted to the care of a private entity. Rather, a special form of co-administration is created, as well as a form of governance in which the pursued interests cannot be defined as 'public'. We have already clarified why we prefer to use the expression 'common interests' to carry within the definition of public private partnership, which implies the adoption of a neutral perspective, detached from the 'totally public' or the 'totally private'.

Governing common interests means to exercise a form of government from the bottom up, by means of cooperation as a tool to regulate a complex interac-

---

[31]   The literature on concession procedures is quite extensive. Here it is possible to quote, for their comprehensive view, Roberto Caranta, 'The changes to the public contract directives and the story they tell about how EU law works' (2015) CML Review 391; Martin Farley and Nicholas Pourbaix, 'The EU Concessions Directive: building (toll) bridges between competition law and public procurement' (2015) Journal of European Competition Law and Practice 15; Steven van Garsse, 'Concessions and public procurement' in Christopher Bovis (ed.), *Research handbook on EU public procurement law* (Edward Elgar, 2016) 593. A more international perspective is assumed in Caroline Nicholas, 'Devising transparent and efficient concession award procedures' (2012) Uniform Law Review 97. With a more critical approach, see Sue Arrowsmith, 'Revisiting the case against a separate concessions regime in the light of the concessions directive: a specific directive without specificities?' in Fabian Amtenbrink et al. (eds), *The internal market and the future of European Integration: essays in honour of Laurence W. Gormley* (CUP, 2019) 370; Albert Sanchez-Graells, 'What need and logic for a new directive on concessions, particularly regarding the issue of their economic balance?' (2012) EPPPL, 94.

tion to the benefit of the administered community. Governing from the bottom up also means that the community is less enslaved to changes coming from the political agenda. Individuals, markets and private operators are able to pursue their objectives and submit their proposals to any government. Sometimes, in certain unstable or conservative political contexts, initiatives coming from the bottom are the only answer to continue working to meet global values.

The fact that the interest does not belong to administrations, closed in their ivory towers, but is rather the outcome of different sensitivities – both social and belonging to the market – does not mean that the public body loses its institutional prerogative.

For this reason, we deemed it necessary to maintain the term 'governing' in the title. The aim was to underline that the role of guarantor –in a democratic sense – of the interests of the community does not cease when the administration decides to embark on a partnership. Rather, its task is changed in a partnership agreement, since control and surveillance must be exercised in a way that forbids the private party from deviating from the shared direction to follow its own personal gains.

With public private partnership, not only the public is charged with the act of governing, also the private party contributes, in a virtuous exchange, to the selection and to the eventual re-adaptation of the strategy to respond effectively to the needs at the base of the shared programme.

As in a personal relationship, there will be fights, uncertainties and divergences which will require, from both sides, patience, dialogue, confrontation and new enthusiasm.

Conversely, if public private partnership is approached as outsourcing, or as a public procurement, in the logic of the relationship between client and contractor the model of governing common interest is disregarded, and the partnership is destined to become something else.

The phenomenon that we are describing regarding public private partnership is far wider than one would expect. Some dynamics discussed in Chapter 4 to differentiate public private partnership from analogous profiles could be included.

For example, the granting of permits and authorizations, volunteering, and contracts of public services are all juridical instruments that could – with the necessary specifications – be framed within the logic of governing common interests, whose dimension would progressively expand to erode the ambits characterized exclusively by an authoritarian and imperative view of public administration, isolated and differentiated from the market.

5   MUTATIONS OF THE EXPECTED RESULTS

5.1   From Compliance to a Better Response to Social Needs

We have already argued that compliance with formal rules is not sufficient to qualify an administrative activity as 'good administration'.

In the complexity of modern society, the relationship between law, rules and principles must be virtuously connected to the expected results. What is expected from the public administration is not mere compliance to the rules. This was the objective of the administrative law of warranties, aimed at limiting the arbitrary use of sovereign powers. It is not the main purpose of the administrative law of cooperation and social welfare.

Said perspective is clear in public private partnership, which places a substantial evolution at the centre of a public decision, in terms of social usefulness, of an initiative deemed of common interest.

Therefore, public private partnership forces policy makers to come to terms with the failure of a public action excessively suffocated by pervasive regulations, and pushes them to regulate in a soft manner, without excessively limiting the creativeness of public and private actors.

According to the traditional logic of administrative isolation, now overcome thanks to public private partnership, the failure of the public organization is accepted as far as it is kept remote from the sphere of individuals entrusted with the exercise of an administrative function. Those who pursue a public career are often inspired by a desire to impact, at a personal level, the policies of governance and the welfare of the administered communities, more than by the performance of the organization to which they belong.[32]

The detachment which sometimes is possible to notice between public officials and administrations also has a meaning in this perspective: it permits us to distinguish the successes and failures of the public official separately from the ones of the organizational reality to which he or she belongs.

So, a Nobel prize-winning professor can teach in a public university where merit is not rewarded, without being identified with the eventual poor administration of the academic organization.

This condition – namely the scarce identification between people and organizations in the public dimension – is deeply pathological, as it leads to the

---

[32]   Valaguzza, *Governare per contratto*, n 30, 46–47. On this point, see also the comprehensive study of Filomena Maggino (ed.), *A New Research Agenda for Improvements in Quality of Life* (Springer, 2015). The consequences of the shift from formalism to results in administrative decision making are analysed in Anna Romeo, 'Dalla forma al risultato: profili dogmatici ed evolutivi della decisione amministrativa' (2018) Diritto Amministrativo 551.

acceptance of governmental wrongdoings, as if they were something external to the personal dimension.

In contrast, public private partnership pushes towards a different configuration of the administrative organization, whose image and perspective must be populated by excellent professionals and presented in a good way, in order to maintain attractiveness towards the private sector.

Reasoning in terms of abstract rationality, the failure of the partnership would also be the failure of the private party that decided to associate with the administration – not with the single representative of the administrative body.

In public private partnership, the success of both partners is crucial as organizational realities.

The partnership does not involve a single human being but displays the logic of efficiency in the administrative organization, therefore helping transform the battle of the brave public officials from a failure of Don Quixote to the success of D'Artagnan.

In public private partnership, the tension deriving from the political system and from the organisms of mass communication aims precisely at the performance.

The partnership and the sharing of information and sovereignty that it requires, as well as the implied compromise which impacts the role of the state institutions, is justified by reason of the capacity to ameliorate the expected results in terms of answers to the community's needs.

This awareness marks a relevant change in the system of administrative law. While the traditional administrative activity was justified per se as compliance with the tasks assigned by the law to the holders of public powers, the dialogical framework of the partnership is to be pursued only in light of the capacity to organize an adequate answer to the needs of the complex world of our social coexistence. On the contrary, if there is no improvement of public value, the partnership, being a choice of efficiency and efficacy, is not justified at all and must be abandoned. In this sense, public private partnership is also the emblem of a new approach to the norms of administrative law. The compliance to said norms is not for its own sake but is instrumental to the achievement of programmed substantial goals.

5.2   From the Economy Principle to Value for Money

We can now highlight another mutation that, from public private partnership, influences the entire administrative field of action.

Public private partnership introduces, as a principle for the sound and prudent management of public money, the virtuous use of economic resources, according to the principle of value for money.[33]

Faced with the change of perspective that we have so far described, which implies the shift from a strict and formal compliance with the rules to a focus on the satisfaction of the needs of the community as the primary mission for public administration, the criteria for the management of public funds is also transformed, turning from a mere principle of saving to a more complex verification of the effects produced by the use of determined resources.

With public private partnership, the administration is obliged to focus on the substance of the project and on its effects in social and environmental terms. As we have already clarified, an administration could not accept a proposal merely on the basis of its economic advantages – for instance because it guarantees considerable savings in providing a determined service. Rather, the decision to embark on a public private partnership initiative must be justified on the basis of a more substantial and qualitative criterion: the proposal must be the one that delivers the best value for money. This precisely expresses the idea that public administrations should not only act in a way that is economically advantageous in terms of gains and losses deriving from an intended

---

[33]   The concept of the value for money was firstly developed in the 1980s by the British conservative government of Margaret Thatcher, along with the idea that private commercial instruments, methods of evaluation and organizational structures should be applied in the public sector. Sue Arrowsmith, *The law of public and utilities procurement* (Sweet and Maxwell, 2014) 19. The concept was defined as the need for public administrations to reach the so-called '3 Es': economy, efficiency and effectiveness, and it was especially referred to local authorities in the provision of public services. See: Audit Commission for Local Authorities and the National Health Service in England and Wales, 'Improving value for money in local government: a compendium of good practice from audit commission value for money report' (London, 1995); Stephen Cirell and John Bennett, *Best value: law and practice, for an international overview* (Sweet and Maxwell, 1999); an interesting insight on the British policies and legislations aiming at the provision of economic, efficient and effective services for the local communities is embedded in Penny Badcoe, 'Best value – an overview of the United Kingdom government's policy for the provision and procurement of local authority services' (2010) Public Procurement Law Review 92 and in James Segan, 'Exploring the "Best Value" duty' (2013) Judicial Review 93; for a more international perspective, see: Organization for Economic Cooperation and Development, 'Value for money and international development: deconstructing myths to promote a more constructive discussion' (2012). In the public procurement sector, to achieve the best value for money means to obtain the best quality of services, goods or works with the available resources, in strict relation with the most economically advantageous tender as a selection criteria. Marc Frilet and Florent Lager, 'Public procurement issues in the European Union' (2010) Eur. Bus. Law Review 21.

transaction, but in order to maximize the benefits for the community[34] or, in other terms, the 'public value'.[35]

This principle puts the community rather than the administration at the centre of administrative action:[36] financial management should be inspired, according to value for money, by the best allocation of resources in the interest of value production, rather than by the lowest expenditure for the sake of the economy principle.

In other words, administrations should base their actions not solely on the basis of price, but through a more complicated calculus that is able to assess the 'optimal combination of quantity, quality, features and price (i.e. cost), expected over the whole of the project's lifetime'.[37]

This requires administrations to adopt specific methods of evaluation that enable them to correctly assess whether or not public private partnership is able to deliver the best possible outcome, also in comparison to alternative public policies. Examples of said methods are the public sector comparator, the cost-benefit analysis and the multi-criteria decision making discussed in Chapter 3.

It is important to underline, for the systematic purpose of our analysis, that the described principle does not only apply to the design of the project and the selection of the partner. Rather, it is a criterion that should be kept as a parameter for the assessment of the performances throughout the entire execution of

---

[34] See, for instance, European Commission, 'Green paper on public-private partnership and community law on public contracts and concessions', COM (2004) 327 final, 55; World Bank, International Bank for Reconstruction and Development, 'Public-private partnership reference guide' (Version 3, Washington DC, 2017) 129.

[35] British Department of Transport, *Value for money framework: moving Britain ahead,* (London, 2015) 8

[36] For this reason, this rule is present in many public procurement regulations and acts of soft law. See Directive 2014/24/EU of the European Parliament and of the Council of 26 February 2014 on public procurement, Recital No. 91; European Commission, 'Public procurement guidance for practitioners' (Brussels, 2018); Organization for Economic Cooperation and Development, 'Recommendation on public procurement' (Paris, 2015). In the context of public contracts regulation, 'value for money' is intended as 'the best mix of quality and effectiveness for the least outlay over the period of use of the goods or services bought'. The concept expresses the idea that contracting authorities should not buy the cheapest products, services or works, as this could negatively affect quality of performance, costs of maintenance and increase externalities. Differently, contracting authorities should select the offer which provides 'the optimum combination of whole life costs and quality'. See HM Treasury, 'Managing public money' (2013, A.4.6.3).

[37] See Organization for Economic Cooperation and Development, 'Getting infrastructure right: a framework for better governance' (Paris, 2017) 29; Organization for Economic Cooperation and Development, 'Multi-dimensional review of Uruguay. Volume 2. In-depth analysis and recommendations' (Paris, 2016) 92.

the contract.[38] In this context, the principle, as incentivized by public private partnership, acquires the broader sense of closely controlling that the resources used actually correspond to the production of value.

In general, it can be affirmed that, to evaluate the performance of administrative action, it is not sufficient to avoid waste in the use of public resources. Rather, it is necessary to ensure that the implied resources are able to generate value in terms of benefits in favour of the community and according to the typical economic criteria of measurement.

6   MUTATIONS OF THE PUBLIC ADMINISTRATION'S LIABILITY

6.1   From Administrative Liability to Common Law Shared Liability: From Liability for an Unlawful Act to Liability for Fact

Especially in those systems (e.g. France, Germany, Italy, Spain), where there are special bodies entrusted with the control of public civil servants – and in some cases private operators acting as concessionaires[39] – who, by violating their service obligations, caused financial or economic damage to public administration, public private partnership creates the need for further specifications, while still of universal character.

---

[38]   See John Rehfuss, 'Contracting out and accountability in state and local governments: the importance of contract monitoring' (1990) State and Local Government Review 44; Martin Kestenbaum and Roland Straight, 'Procurement performance: measuring quality, effectiveness, and efficiency' (1995) Procuring Productivity and Management Review 200; John Cibinic Jr et al., *Administration of government contracts* (5th edition, Wolters Kluwer, 2006); Peter Trepte, *Public procurement in the EU: a practitioner's guide* (OUP, 2007); Trevor Brown, Matthew Potoski, and David Slyke, 'Managing public service contracts: aligning values, institutions, and markets' (2006) Public Administration Review 323; Hong-guang Peng and Jian-hu Cai, 'Measuring performance of public procurement for innovation' (IEEE, 2008); Silvia Appelt and Fernando Galindo-Rueda, 'Measuring the link between public procurement and innovation' (OECD Science, Technology and Industry Working Papers, No. 2016/03, OECD Publishing, Paris, 2016); Ralph Nash et al., *The government contracts reference book: a comprehensive guide to the language of procurement* (4th edition, Wolters Kluwer, 2013).

[39]   See, for instance, the case law of the Italian Court of Auditors, considering the administrative liability for damage to public finances as extended to the concessionaires of public works. To quote some of the most recent ones, see Corte dei Conti, Sez. Giur. Lazio, 1 August 2018 No. 426; Id., 14 October 2013, No. 683; Cassazione, Sez. Un, 2 February 2018, No. 2584.

If the activity of public private partnership is developed in a context of cooperation, then, at least in logical terms, it is necessary to distinguish between liabilities that certainly belong to one of the two spheres of action and liabilities that result from the interaction.

In the latter case, it is difficult to continue reasoning within the parameters of administrative law. Indeed, while public administration is, as a legal entity, capable of being holder of rights and duties, the private party – despite being entrusted with the exercise of specific public *munera* – cannot change its nature in a partnership, assuming *tout court* the features and the powers that define the public body.

This implies that, in reference to the liability deriving from the above-mentioned dimension of interaction in which the private party has an active and fragmented role, we would assert the need for a new common law liability, similar to the shared responsibility that in countries of civil law is known as joint and several liability. In this kind of liability, more actors are called on to answer, with the same grade of liability, for facts caused by one or the other.

It will be a liability similar to the one affecting the members of a temporary association of enterprises with different titles and competences, getting together for a limited period of time to carry out an activity in common.

It will be a liability connected to a fact, more than a liability for an unlawful act, because in a public private partnership the public administration is transformed in providing a different kind of performance in favour of the community.

And it could be not only a liability for tort but also a liability for failure to perform a contractual obligation.

In this sense, if, on the one hand, with public private partnership the public administration, as said, is freed from its isolation, on the other hand, it could be directly involved in a liability – civil or with the character of political accountability – in those cases in which it is co-protagonist of an illicit action, a poor performance or of a failure to achieve the result, even if it did not directly provoke it.

The focus on goals that the public private partnership requires, from the moment of its creation, is an incredibly powerful driver to determine the success of a project and an incentive to get out of the quagmire of formalism and to enlighten a new form of bureaucracy.

It will hardly ever be a liability to discuss in a judicial review. Rather, it will be a liability for torts, to be claimed in a civil court, or a political accountability that could give birth to complaints about the accuracy of the choices made in overseeing how the interests of the community are met.

Substantially, public private partnership expands the genre of the combination that can lead to configure a liability for the administration. However, the speciality of said liability fades away, also being channelled to a more neutral area that can overlap with a regime of substantial co-administration in the management of activities of common interest.

The highest grade of liability that the administration and the private person could assume is one of embarking on a partnership project that could lead to a failure to satisfy the demands of the community. All in all, as Michael Sandel affirmed in his *Democracy's Discontent*, 'at its best, political deliberation is not only about competing policies but also about competing interpretations of the character of a community, of its purposes and ends'.[40]

7   A NEW INTEGRITY FOR THE PUBLIC BODY

The outcome of public private partnership is not a 'leader-follower relationship'[41] but a cooperative environment which reduces the distance between public authorities and private parties and improves the organizational relationship.

Sharing, co-responsibility, bottom-up approach, and common interests are the routes of a new integrity of public administration, which is measured by its capacity to recognize a space for the community, intended in its general meaning as the set of individual and collective components that populate territories.[42]

Through communities, 'bureaucracy' (in the positive sense) can again play a leading role in our global future, but in a new dimension: collaborative and dialogical, in which the energy can flow from the bottom up and where politics supports the force that comes from the grassroots, without compressing it with an adversarial approach. This leads to overcoming the ideological limits that for years predicated the irreconcilability between public and private.

---

[40]   Michael Sandel, *Democracy's discontent: America in search of a public philosophy* (Harvard University Press, 1996) 350.

[41]   Peter Schaeffer and Scott Loveridge, 'Toward an understanding of types of public-private cooperation' (2002) Public Performance and Management Review 169.

[42]   On the meaning of 'community', see Henry Maine, *Village-communities in East and West* (Murray, 1871); Andrew William Lind, *An island community, ecological succession in Hawaii* (University of Chicago Press, 1938); Conrad Arensberg, 'The community study method' (1954) American Journal of Sociology 109; Adriano Olivetti, *L'ordine politico della comunità* (Nuove Edizioni, 1945); Conrad Arensberg, 'American communities' (1955) American Anthropologist 241; George Hillery, 'Definitions of community: areas of engagement' (1955) Rural Sociology 20; Roger Bastide, *Formes élémentaires de la stratification sociale* (Centre de Documentation Universitaire, 1965); Philippe Warnier, *Le phénomène de la communautés de base* (Desclée De Brower, 1973); Richard Sennett, 'La communauté destructrice' in Norman Birnbaum et al. (eds), *Au-delà de la crise* (Seuil, 1976) 86; Patrick Démerin, *Communautés pour le socialisme* (Maspero, 1975).

Territories and their communities hold the vital energy that the administration must have the courage to acknowledge and embrace.

The communities know very well what is needed: because they directly experience those needs, they know the stress factors, they meet the obstacles of the context and try to overcome them, they see the opportunities that are worth taking. The community that lives in a territory knows if it is necessary to organize systems to protect from flooding – as in Barcelona, where underground water depositories were built for the collection of rain water in order to alleviate pressure on the drainage systems during rainstorms – to provide more security – as in San Paolo in Brazil – or, if it is necessary, to improve the efficiency of the transportation system – as in Milan.

Networks of governance are built on the needs and answers of the community. For instance, New Orleans joined Rotterdam in the common interest to find innovative solutions to keep flooding under control in the urban centre.

Thus, networks are created, and partners are sought.

In this direction, public private partnership changes the administration, makes it excellent and makes the difference starting from individuals, entrepreneurship and collective groups, as vehicles of progress and development.

Public private partnership recomposes the formal, juridical, exterior order and unites it into the primitive solidarity of closeness, perspectives and reciprocity.

In the state of rights, legality substituted solidarity; society substituted community. Now, the community returns to playing a direct role in governing the common interests from the bottom up.

It is not the community of consanguinity that plays a leading role in the cultural renaissance that we are describing. The protagonist is the community as defined by spontaneous relationships among individuals, enterprises and administrations. It is the community of shared initiatives.

Public private partnership paves the way for an economy based on reciprocity, in which public values and market reconnect.

Public private partnership is neither a market economy nor a market society, as Sandel defined the modern consumeristic society,[43] but is an ethical, political and economic dimension based on pluralism, on dialogue and on goals, summarized in the expression 'governing common interests'.

The implications of what we observed are enormous.

To renounce this potential would mean, for the administration, to dock Cupid's arrow.

---

[43] Michael Sandel, *What money can't buy: the moral limits of markets* (Penguin, 2013).

Bibliography

Abadzi H, 'Improving adult literacy outcomes: lessons from cognitive research for developing countries' (The World Bank, 2003)

Abbott K, and D Snidal, 'Strengthening international regulation through transnational new governance: overcoming the orchestration deficit' (2009) Vand. J. Transnat'l Law 501

Abbott K, and D Snidal, 'The governance triangle: regulatory standards institutions and the shadow of the state' in W Mattli and N Woods (eds), *The politics of global regulation* (Princeton University Press, 2009) 63

Acar M, *Accountability in public-private partnerships: perspectives, practices, problems, and prospects* (Verlag Dr Müller, 2009)

Agus A, S Barker, and J Kandampully, 'An exploratory study of service quality in the Malaysian public service sector' (2007) International Journal of Quality and Reliability Management 177

Aizawa M, 'A scoping study of PPP guidelines' (DESA Working Paper No. 154, January 2018)

Akhmetshina E, and A Mustafin, 'Public-private partnership as a tool for development of innovative economy' (2015) Procedia Economics and Finance 35

Akintoye A, and M Beck, *Policy, management and finance of public-private partnerships* (Wiley-Blackwell, 2008)

Akintoye A, A Beck, and C Hardcastle, *Public-private partnerships: managing risks and opportunities* (Wiley-Blackwell, 2003)

Albanese A, 'Il principio di sussidiarietà orizzontale: autonomia sociale e compiti pubblici' (2002) Diritto pubblico 51

Alemanno A, 'The shaping of the precautionary principle by European courts: from scientific uncertainty to legal certainty' in L Cuoccolo and L Luparia (eds), *Valori Costituzionali e Nuove Politiche del Diritto* (Bocconi Legal Studies Research Paper No. 1007404, 2007)

Alford J, *Engaging public sector clients: from service-delivery to co-production* (Palgrave Macmillan, 2009)

Alford J, 'The multiple facets of co-production, building on the work of Elinor Ostrom' (2014) Public Management Review 299

Allan J, *Public-private partnership: a review of literature and practice* (Regina, 2001)

Allwinkle S, and P Cruickshank, 'Creating smart-er cities: an overview' (2011) Journal of Urban Technology 1

Alonso-Conde A B, C Brown, and J Rojo-Suarez, 'Public private partnerships: incentives, risk transfer and real options' (2007) Review of Financial Economics 335

Álvarez-Díaz A, L González, and B Radcliff, 'The politics of happiness: on the political determinants of quality of life in the American states' 72 The Journal of Politics (2010) 894

Aman Jr A, 'Privatization and democracy: resources in administrative law' in J Freeman and M Minow (eds), *Outsourcing and American democracy* (Harvard University Press, 2009) 261

Amilhat M, 'Contractualisation, négociation, consensualisme: nouvelles approches du droit public' (2018) Revue française de droit administratif 1

Amorth A, 'Osservazioni sui limiti dell'attività amministrativa di diritto privato' (1939) Archivio di diritto pubblico 89

Amselek P, 'L'évolution générale de la technique juridique dans les sociétés occidentales' (1982) RD Publ. 275

Andonova L, *Governance entrepreneurs: international organizations and the rise of global public-private partnerships* (CUP, 2017)

Appelt S, and F Galindo-Rueda, 'Measuring the link between public procurement and innovation' (OECD Science, Technology and Industry Working Papers, No. 2016/03, OECD Publishing, Paris, 2016)

Arena G, 'Introduzione all'amministrazione condivisa' (1997) Studi parlamentari e di politica costituzionale 29

Arensberg C, 'American communities' (1955) American Anthropologist 241

Arensberg C, 'The community study method' (1954) American Journal of Sociology 109

Arnstein S, 'A ladder of citizen participation' (1969) Journal of the American Institute of Planners 216

Arrowsmith A, 'Public private partnerships and the European procurement rules: EU policies in conflict?' (2000) CML Review 709

Arrowsmith S, 'A taxonomy of horizontal policies' (2010) Journal of Public Procurement 149

Arrowsmith S, 'Modernising the EU's public procurement regime: a blueprint for real simplicity and flexibility' (2012) Public Procurement Law Review 71

Arrowsmith S, 'Revisiting the case against a separate concessions regime in the light of the concessions directive: a specific directive without specificities?' in F Amtenbrink et al. (eds), *The internal market and the future of European integration: essays in honour of Laurence W. Gormley* (CUP, 2019) 370

Arrowsmith S, *The law of public and utilities procurement* (2nd edition, Sweet and Maxwell, 2006)

Arrowsmith S, and P Kunzlik (eds), *Social and environmental policies in EC procurement law* (CUP, 2009)

Arts B, *The political influence of global NGOs: case studies on the climate and biodiversity conventions* (International Books, 1998)

Asian Development Bank, 'Public private partnership handbook' (Manila, 2008)

Asian Development Bank, 'Public-private partnership operational plan 2012–2020' (2012)

Aslam M, S Rawal, and S Saeed, 'Public-private partnerships in education in developing countries: a rigorous review of the evidence' (Ark Education Partnerships Group, London, 2017)

Athias L, and S Saussier, 'Un partenariat public-privé rigide ou flexible? Théorie et application aux concessions routières à péage' (2007) Revue Économique 565

Auby J F, *Les services publics locaux* (Berger-Levrault, 1982)

Auby J F, *Les services publics en Europe* (PUF, 1998)

Auby J B, *Droit de la ville: du fonctionnement juridique des villes au droit à la Ville* (Lexis Nexis, 2013)

Auby J B, 'Contracting out and "public values": a theoretical and comparative approach' in S Rose-Ackerman, P Lindseth, and B Emerson (eds), *Comparative administrative law* (2nd edition, Edward Elgar, 2017) 552.

Audit Commission for Local Authorities and the National Health Service in England and Wales, 'Improving value for money in local government: a compendium of good practice from Audit Commission value for money report' (London, 1995)

Auhagen A E, and H W Bierhoff (eds), *Responsibility: the many faces of a social phenomenon* (Routledge, 2001)

Averch H, *Private markets and public intervention: a primer for policy designers* (University of Pittsburgh Press, 1990)

Badcoe P (ed.), *Public private partnerships and PFI* (Sweet and Maxwell, 1999)

Badcoe P, 'Best value – an overview of the United Kingdom Government's Policy for the Provision and Procurement of Local Authority Services' (2010) Public Procurement Law Review 92

Bahri A, *Public private partnership for WTO dispute settlement* (Edward Elgar, 2018)

Bailey N, 'Towards a research agenda for public-private partnerships in the 1990s' (1994) Local Economy 292

Bain R, 'Public sector comparators for UK PFI roads: inside the black box' (2010) Transportation 447

Bakhsh Malik A, 'Public-private partnerships in education: lessons learned from the Punjab education foundation' (Asian Development Bank, 2010)

Balakrishnan S et al., 'Information asymmetry, market failure and joint ventures: theory and evidence' (1999) Journal of Economic Behavior and Organization 99

Barak-Erez D, 'Three questions of privatization' in S Rose-Ackerman, P Lindseth, and B Emerson (eds), *Comparative administrative law* (2nd edition, Edward Elgar, 2017) 533

Barber B, *Strong democracy* (UC Press, 2004)

Barr N, *Economics of the welfare state* (6th edition, OUP, 2012)

Barrera-Osorio F et al., 'Expanding educational opportunities in remote parts of the world: evidence from a RCT of a public-private partnership in Pakistan' (The World Bank, 2011)

Barry B 'The public interest' (1964) Proceedings of the Aristotelian Society 1

Barth T, 'The public interest and administrative discretion' (1992) American Review of Public Administration 289

Bartling B, and U Fischbacher, 'Shifting the blame: on delegation and responsibility' (2012) The Review of Economic Studies 67

Bason C, *Leading public sector innovation: co-creating for a better society* (The Policy Press, 2010)

Bassanini F et al. (eds), *Il mostro effimero. Democrazia, economia e corpi intermedi* (il Mulino, 2019).

Bastide R, *Formes élémentaires de la stratification sociale* (Centre de Documentation Universitaire, 1965)

Bator F, 'The anatomy of market failure' (1958) The Quarterly Journal of Economics 351

Bauböck R, 'Political community beyond the sovereign state: supranational federalism and transnational minorities' (Austrian Academy of Sciences Research Unit for Institutional Change and European Integration ICE – Working Paper Series 7/2000)

Beckers A, 'Using contracts to further sustainability? A contract law perspective on sustainable public procurement' in B Sjåfjell and A Wiesbrock (eds), *Sustainable public procurement under EU law: new perspectives on the state as stakeholder* (CUP, 2016) 206

Bederman N, and M Trebilock, 'Unsolicited bids for government functions' (1996) Alta. Law Review 903

Bel G, T Brown, and R Cunha Marques (eds), *Public-private partnership: infrastructure, transportation and local services* (Routledge, 2014)

Ben-Porath E, 'Rationality, Nash equilibrium and backward induction in perfect information games' (1997) Review of Economic Studies 23

Benito B, V Montesinos, and F Bastida, 'An example of creative accounting in public sector: the private financing of infrastructures in Spain' (2008) Critical Perspectives on Accounting 963

Bennett R, and A McCoshan, *Enterprise and human resource development* (Paul Chapman, 1993)

Benington J, 'From private choice to public value?' in J Benington and M Moore (eds), *Public value: theory and practice* (Palgrave MacMillan, 2011) 31

Benington J, and M Moore, 'Public value in complex and changing times' in J Benington and M Moore (eds), *Public value: theory and practice* (Palgrave MacMillan, 2011) 8

Benington J, and M Moore (eds), *Public value: theory and practice* (Palgrave MacMillan, 2011)

Bentham J, 'Introduction to the principles of morals and legislation' in J Bowring, *The collected works of Jeremy Bentham* (OUP, 1943) 2

Benvenisti E, 'The future of sovereignty: the nation state in the global governance space' in S Cassese (ed.), *Research handbook on global administrative law* (Edward Elgar, 2016) 483

Benvenuti F, 'Eccesso di potere amministrativo per vizio della funzione' (1950) Rass. dir. pubbl. 1

Benvenuti F, 'Funzione amministrativa, procedimento, processo' (1952) Rivista trimestrale di diritto pubblico 118

Benz A, and Y Papadopoulos (eds), *Governance and democracy: comparing national, European and international experiences* (Routledge, 2006)

Berg S, M Pollitt, and M Tsuji (eds), *Private initiatives in infrastructure: priorities, incentives and performance* (Edward Elgar, 2002)

Bermann G, 'Taking subsidiarity seriously: federalism in the European Community and the United States' (1994) Columbia Law Review 331

Bernstein S, and B Cashore, 'Can non-state global governance be legitimate? An analytical framework' (2007) Regulation and Governance 347

Besley T, 'Public-private partnership for the provision of public goods: theory and an application to NGOs' (LSE STICERD Research Paper No. DEDPS17, London, 2008)

Besley T, and M Ghatak, 'Public-private partnerships for the provision of public goods: theory and an application to NGOs' (2017) Research in Economics 356

Besselink L F M, F Pennings, and S Prechal (eds), *The eclipse of the legality principle in the European Union* (Wolters Kluwer, 2011)

Bexell M, and U Mörth (eds), *Democracy and public-private partnerships in global governance* (Palgrave Macmillan, 2010)

Biber E et al., 'The permit power revisited: the theory and practice of regulatory permits in the administrative state' (2014) Duke Law Journal 133

Biermann F et al., 'The overall effects of partnerships for sustainable development: more smoke than fire?' in P Pattberg et al. (eds), *Public-private partnership for sustainable development* (Edward Elgar, 2012) 45

Biermann F, and K Dingwerth, 'Global environmental change and the nation state' (2004) Global Environmental Politics 1

Blomqvist A, and E Jimenez, 'The public role in private post-secondary education: a review of issues and options' (Policy Research Working Paper 240, The World Bank, 1989)

Bloomfield P, 'The challenging business of long-term public–private partnerships: reflections on local experience' (2006) Public Administration Review 400

Bobbio N, 'Teoria e ideologia nella dottrina di Santi Romano' in N Bobbio, *Dalla struttura alla funzione* (Laterza, 1977) 168

Bobbio N, *Stato, governo, società: Per una teoria generale della politica* (Einaudi, 1985)

Bobbio N, *Democracy and dictatorship: the nature and limits of state power* (University of Minnesota Press, 1989)

Bombardelli M, 'La cura dei beni comuni come via di uscita dalla crisi' in M Bombardelli (ed.), *Prendersi cura dei beni comuni per uscire dalla crisi: Nuove risorse e nuovi modelli di amministrazione* (Editoriale scientifica, 2016) 1

Bombardelli M, *Prendersi cura dei beni comuni per uscire dalla crisi: Nove risorse e nuovi modelli di amministrazione* (Editoriale Scientifica, 2016)

Bombardelli M, 'La cura dei beni comuni: esperienze e prospettive' (2018) Giornale di Diritto Amministrativo 559

Bonhage J, and M Roberts, 'Germany' in B Werneck, and M Saadi (eds), *The public-private partnership law review* (4th edition, London, 2018) 100

Bonvicini G et al. (eds), *A renewed partnership for Europe* (Nomos Verlag, 1996)

Borin E, *Public-private partnership in cultural sector: a comparative analysis of European models* (ENCATC, 2017)

Borins S, 'Leadership and innovation in the public sector' (2002) Leadership and Organization Development Journal 467

Börzel T, 'Policy networks, a new paradigm for European governance?' (1997) RSC 5

Börzel T, 'Organizing Babylon: on the different conceptions of policy networks' (1998) Public Administration 253

Boussabaine A, *Risk pricing strategies for public-private partnership projects* (Wiley-Blackwell, 2013)

Bovaird T, 'Public-private partnerships: from contested concepts to prevalent practice' (2004) Int. Review Adm. Sci. 199

Bovaird T, 'Beyond engagement and participation: user and community co-production of public services' (2007) Public Administration Review 846

Bovens M, P T'Hart, and B Guy Peters (eds), *Success and failure in public governance: a comparative analysis* (Edward Elgar, 2002)

Bovis C, 'The private finance initiative (PFI) as the prelude of public private partnerships (PPPs)' (2006) European Public Private Partnership Law Review 24

Bovis C, *Public-private partnership in the European Union* (Routledge, 2018)

Box R, 'Re-describing the public interest' (2007) The Social Science Journal 585

Boyd J, 'From Rio to Johannesburg: a review of Asian Development Bank environmental practice and policy' (2002) Sing. J. Int'l and Comp. Law 723

Bozeman B, *Public values and public interest: counterbalancing economic individualism* (Georgetown University Press, 2007)

Braibant G, and B Stirn, *Le droit administratif français* (4th edition, Presses de Sciences Po et Dalloz, 1984) 13

Breyer S et al., *Administrative law and regulatory policy: problems, texts and cases* (7th edition, Wolters Kluwer, 2011) 5

Brinkerhoff D, and J Brinkerhoff, 'Public-private partnerships: perspectives on purposes, publicness and good governance' (2011) Public Administration and Development 2

Brinkerhoff J, 'Government-nonprofit partnership: a defining framework' (2002) Public Administration and Development 19

British Department of Transport, *Value for money framework: moving Britain ahead* (London, 2015) 8

Brooks H, L Liebman, and C Schelling (eds), *Public-private partnership: new opportunities for meeting social needs* (Bellinger, 1984)

Brown T, M Potoski, and D Slyke, 'Managing Public service contracts: aligning values, institutions, and markets' (2006) Public Administration Review 323

Brudney J et al., 'Exploring and explaining contracting out: patterns among the American states' (2005) Journal of Public Administration Research and Theory 393

Bruno K, and J Karliner, 'The UN's global compact, corporate accountability and the Johannesburg Earth Summit' (2002) Development 33

Bryson J, and W Roering, 'Applying private sector strategic planning to the public sector' (1987) Journal of the American Planning Association 9

Bull B, and D McNeill, *Development issues in global governance: public-private partnerships and market multilateralism* (Taylor and Francis, 2006)

Burns J, 'Happiness and utility: Jeremy Bentham's equation' (2005) Utilitas 46.

Busch N, and A Givens, *The business of counterterrorism: public-private partnerships in homeland security* (Peter Lang, 2014)

Buse K, and A Harmer, 'Seven habits of highly effective global public-private health partnerships: practice and potential' (2006) Social Science and Medicine 259

Buse K, and G Walt, 'Global public-private partnerships: part II. What are the health issues for global governance?' (2000) Bulletin of the World Health Organization 699

Cahill M, 'Sovereignty, liberalism and the intelligibility of attraction to subsidiarity' (2016) The American Journal of Jurisprudence 109

Caliari A et al., 'What standards for public-private partnerships (PPPs)? Analysing the role of the World Bank Group' (Bretton Woods Project, 2016)

Calliess C, *Subsidiaritäs-und solidaritäsprinzip in der Europäischen Union* (Nomos, 1996)

Calo R, 'Code, nudge, or notice?' (2014) Iowa Law Review 773

Canadian Council for Public-Private Partnerships, 'Public sector accounting for public-private partnership transactions in Canada' (Position Paper by the Accounting Task Force of the Canadian Council for Public-Private Partnerships, 2008)

Cangiano M et al., 'Public-private partnerships, government guarantees, and fiscal risk' (International Monetary Fund, 2006)

Caranta R, 'The changes to the public contract directives and the story they tell about how EU law works' (2015) CML Review 391

Caranta R, and M Trybus (eds), *The law of green and social procurement in Europe* (DJØF Publishing, 2010)

Carbone G, A Ferro, and M Vitale, *Spiritualità nell'Impresa* (Piccola Biblioteca d'Impresa Inaz, 2011)

Carley M et al., *Urban regeneration through partnership: a study in nine urban regions in England, Scotland and Wales* (The Policy Press, 2000)

Carlin R, and S Singh, 'Executive power and economic accountability' (2015) The Journal of Politics 1031

Carozza P, 'Subsidiarity as a structural principle of international human rights law' (2003) American Journal of International Law 38

Carroll A B, 'Corporate social responsibility: evolution of a definitional construct' (1991) Business and Society 1

Cartlidge D, *Public private partnership in construction* (CRC Press, 2006)

Carvalho C, and C Briton, 'Assessing users' perceptions on how to improve public services quality' (2012) Public Management Review 451

Carvalho R, 'As concessionárias dos sistemas multimunicipais' (1997) Revista Direito e Justiça 221

Caselli S, V Vecchi, and G Corbetta (eds), *Public private partnership for infrastructure and business development: principles, practices, and perspectives* (Palgrave Macmillan, 2015)

Cassatella A, 'La responsabilità funzionale nell'amministrare. Termini e questioni' (2018) Diritto Amministrativo 677

Cassese S, 'The rise and decline of the notion of state' (1986) International Political Science Review 120

Cassese S, 'Crisi dell'amministrazione e riforme amministrative' (1996) Giornale Dir. Amm. 869

Cassese S, 'Diritto amministrativo comunitario e diritti amministrativi nazionali' in M P Chiti and G Greco (eds), *Trattato di diritto amministrativo europeo* (Giuffrè, 1997) I

Cassese S, *La crisi dello Stato* (Laterza, 2002)

Cassese S, *Lo spazio giuridico globale* (Laterza, 2003)

Cassese S, 'European administrative proceedings' (2004) Law and Contemporary Problems 21

Cassese S, *Universalità del diritto* (Editoriale Scientifica, 2005)

Cassese S, *The global polity: global dimensions of democracy and the rule of law* (Global Law Press, 2012)

Cassese S, *Chi governa il mondo?* (Il Mulino, Bologna, 2013)

Cassese S, 'Global administrative law: the state of the art' (2015) International Journal of Constitutional Law 465

Cassese S (ed.), *Research handbook on global administrative law* (Edward Elgar, 2016)

Cassese S et al. (eds), *Global administrative law: the casebook* (IRPA-IILJ, 2012)

Cassinelli C, 'Some reflections on the concept of the public interest' (1958) Ethics 48

Castaneda J, 'The World Bank adopts environmental impact assessments' (1992) Pace Y B Int'l Law 241

Castelli A, 'Smart cities and innovation partnership: a new way of pursuing economic wealth and social welfare' (2018) European Procurement and Public Private Partnership Law Review 207

Cavallo Perin R, 'Proprietà pubblica e uso comune dei beni tra diritti di libertà e doveri di solidarietà' (2018) Diritto Amministrativo 839

Centre for Bhutan Studies and GNH, 'A compass towards a just and harmonious society' (2015 GNH Survey Report, 2016)

Chern C, *Public private partnerships: practice and procedures* (Routledge, 2017)

Chevallier J, 'L'intérêt général dans l'administration française' (1975) Revue internationale des sciences administratives 325

Chevallier J, 'Contractualisation et régulation' in S Chassagnard-Pinet and D Hiez (eds), *La contractualisation de la production normative* (Dalloz, 2008) 87

Chevallier J, *L'État post-moderne* (LGDJ, 2008)

Chiti M P, 'Forms of European administrative action' (2004–2005) Law and Contemporary Problems 37

Chiti M P, 'Il partenariato pubblico-privato e la nuova direttiva concessioni' in G F Cartei and M Ricchi (eds), *Finanza di progetto e PPP: temi europei, istituti nazionali e operatività* (Editoriale Scientifica, 2015) 12

Chivers J, and N Flores, 'Market failure in information: the national flood insurance program' (2002) Land Economics 515

Chloros A, 'The doctrine of consideration and the reform of the law of contract: a comparative analysis' (1968) International and Comparative Law Quarterly 137

Chon M et al., *The handbook of public-private partnerships, intellectual property governance, and sustainable development* (CUP, 2018)

Cibinic J et al., *Administration of government contracts* (5th edition, Wolters Kluwer, 2006)

Cirell S, and J Bennett, *Best value: law and practice, for an international overview* (Sweet and Maxwell, 1999)

Cirell S, J Bennett, and R Hann, *Private finance initiative and local government* (London, 1997)

Citroni G, A Lippi, and S Profeti, 'Local public services in Italy: still fragmentation' in H Wollmann, I Koprić, and G Marcou (eds), *Public and social services in Europe: from public and municipal to private sector provision* (Springer, 2016) 103

Clarke L, *Public-private partnerships and responsibility under international law: a global health perspective* (Routledge, 2016)

Claypool M, and J McLaughlin, *We are in this together: public-private partnerships in special and at-risk-education* (Rowman and Littlefield, 2015)

Clive J, 'Agricultural research and development: the need for public-private sector partnerships' (1996) Issues in Agriculture 9

Cochran C, 'Political science and "the public interest"' (1974) The Journal of Politics 327

Coda V et al. (eds), *Valori d'impresa in azione* (Egea, 2012)

Codecasa G, and D Ponzini, 'Public-private partnership: a delusion for urban regeneration? evidence from Italy' (2011) European Planning Studies 647

Cohen J, 'A lawman's view of the public interest' in C Friedrich (ed.), *The public interest* (Atherton Press, 1962) 155

Cohen J, 'Truth and public reason' (2009) Philosophy and Public Affairs 2

Cole D, and M McGinnis (eds), *Elinor Ostrom at the Bloomington School of Political Economy: Vol. 3, A framework for policy analysis* (Lexington Books, 2017)

Colmeiro M, *Derecho administrativo Español* (Eduardo Martinez, 1876) 3

Colombo A, *The principle of subsidiarity and European citizenship* (Vita e Pensiero, 2004)

Comptroller and Auditor General, 'The refinancing of the Fazakerley PFI Prison contract' (Report by the Comptroller and Auditor General, HC 584 Session 1999–2000, 29 June 2000)

Cook B, *Democracy and administration: Woodrow Wilson's ideas and the challenges of public management* (Johns Hopkins University Press, 2007)

Cornu G, *Vocabulaire juridique* (11th edition, PUF, 2016)

Corry O, 'Defining and theorizing the third sector' in R Taylor (ed.), *Third sector research* (Springer, 2010) 11

Cosgrove R A, *The rule of law: Albert Venn Dicey, Victorian jurist* (The University of North Carolina Press, 1980)

Cour des Comptes, 'La Politique immobilière du ministère de la justice, mettre fin à la fuite en avant' (Rapport public thématique, December 2017)

Cowen T (ed.), *Public goods and market failures: a critical examinations* (Transnational Publishers, 1992)

Craig P, 'Dicey, unitary, self-correcting democracy and public law' (1990) Law Quarterly Report 106

Craig P, 'Global networks and shared administration' in S Cassese (ed.), *Research handbook on global administrative law* (Edward Elgar, 2016) 153

Craig P, 'Proportionality and judicial review: a UK historical perspective' in S Vogenauer (ed.), *General principles of law: European and comparative perspectives* (Hart Publishing, 2017) 145

Crawford C, 'Subsidiarity, local government and privatisation of service' (1997) Holdsworth Law Review 12

Crepaldi G, 'Il baratto amministrativo: sussidiarietà, collaborazione ed esigenze di risparmio' (2018) Responsabilità Civile e Previdenza 37

Crètois P, and S Roza, *De l'intérêt général: introduction* (Asterion, Dossier 17/2017)

Crippa L, 'Multilateral development banks and human rights responsibility' (2010) Am. U. Int'l Law Review 533

Crocco C (ed.), *Public private partnerships: the PPP guide* (Cedam, 2018)

Croley S, *Regulation and public interest: the possibility of good regulatory government* (Princeton University Press, 2008)

Cruz C O, and R Cunha Marques, *Infrastructure public-private partnerships: decisions, management and development* (Springer, 2013)

Cruz C O, and J M Sarmento, 'Reforming traditional PPP models to cope with the challenges of smart cities' (2017) Competition and Regulation in Network Industries 94

Cunha Marques R, and S Berg, 'Public-private partnership contracts: a tale of two cities with different contractual arrangements' (2011) Public Administration 1585

Cunha Marques R, and C Oliveira Cruz, *Public-private partnership in the water sector: from theory to practice* (IWA, 2018)

Damon J (ed.), *Intérêt général: Que peut l'entreprise?* (Institut Montaigne, Paris, 2013)

Davidson N, *Affordable housing and public-private partnership* (Intermediate Technology Publications Ltd, 2016)

de Bettignies J E, and T Ross, 'The economics of public-private partnerships' (2004) Canadian Public Policy 135

De Búrca G, 'The principle of proportionality and its application in EC law' (1993) Yearbook of European Law 105

De Búrca G, 'Reappraising subsidiarity's significance after Amsterdam' (Jeanne Monet Working Paper 7/1999)

de Jong M et al., 'Introducing public-private partnerships for metropolitan subways in China: what is the evidence?' (2010) Journal of Transport Geography 301

de Laubadère A, 'Administration et contrat' in *Mélanges offerts à Jean Brethe de La Gressaye* (Editions Bière, 1967) 453

De Lemos T et al., 'From concessions to project finance and the private finance initiative' (2000) Journal of Project Finance 19

De Nardis F, 'Challenges to democracy and the opportunity of a new participatory governance in the era of trans-local societies' (2014) Journal of Communication 71

De Palma A, G Prunier, and L Leruth, 'Towards a principal-agent based typology of risks in public-private partnerships' (International Monetary Fund, 2009)

de Visser M, 'Network-based governance in EC law: the example of EC competition and EC communications law' (Bloomsbury Professional, 2009)

Dehousse R, 'Regulation by networks in the European Community: the role of European agencies' (1997) JEPP 246

Della Cananea G, and A Sandulli, *Global standards for public authorities* (Editoriale Scientifica, 2012)

Della Porta D, *Another Europe* (Routledge, 2009)

Dellenbaugh M et al. (ed.), *Urban commons: moving beyond state and market* (Bau Verlag, 2015)

Delmon J, *Public-private partnership projects in infrastructure: an essential guide for policy makers* (2nd edition, CUP, 2017)

Démerin P, *Communautés pour le socialisme* (Maspero, 1975)

Department of the Treasury and Finance, State Government of Victoria, Australia, 'Public sector comparator' (Supplementary Technical Note, Melbourne, 2003)

Dernbach J, 'Making sustainable development happen: from Johannesburg to Albany' (2004) Alb. Law Envt'l Outlook 173

Dewulf G, A Blanken, and M Bult-Spiering, *Strategic issues in public-private partnership* (2nd edition, Wiley-Blackwell, 2011)

Di Giovanni A, *Il contratto di partenariato pubblico privato tra sussidiarietà e solidarietà* (Giappichelli, 2012)

Di Lascio F, and F Giglioni (eds), *La rigenerazione di beni e spazi urbani: Contributo al diritto delle città* (Il Mulino, 2017)

Di Robilant A, 'Genealogies of soft law' (2006) American Journal of Comparative Law 499

Dixon J, and R Dogan, 'Hierarchies, networks and markets: responses to societal governance failure' (2002) Administrative Theory and Praxis 175

Dixon T, G Pottinger, and A Jordan, 'Lessons from the Private Finance Initiative in the UK' (2005) Journal of Property Investment and Finance 412

Dolan M J, 'Government speech' (2003–2004) Hastings Const. Law Q. 71

Dolovich S, 'How privatization thinks. The case of prisons' in J Freeman and M Minow (eds), *Outsourcing and American democracy* (Harvard University Press, 2009) 128

Domberg S, and P Jensen, 'Contracting out by the public sector: theory, evidence, prospects' (1997) Oxford Review of Economic Policy 67

Domberger S, and C Hall, 'Contracting for public services: a review of Antipodean experiences' (1996) Public Administration 129

Donnelly C, 'Participation and expertise: judicial attitudes in comparative perspective' in S Rose-Ackerman, P Lindseth, and B Emerson (eds), *Comparative administrative law* (2nd edition, Edward Elgar, 2017) 370

Dowd R, and J McAdam, 'International cooperation and responsibility sharing to combat climate change: lessons for international refugee law' (2017) Melbourne J. of Int'l Law 18

Drewry G, 'Public-private partnerships: rethinking the boundary between public and private law' in S Osborne (ed.), *Public-private partnerships: theory and practice in international perspective* (Routledge, 2000) 57

Drucker P, 'Converting social problems into business opportunities: the new meaning of corporate social responsibility' (1984) California Management Review 53

Dunn J, 'Transportation: policy-level partnerships and project-based partnerships' in P Vaillancourt Rosenau (ed.), *Public-private policy partnerships* (MIT Press, 2000) 77

Dutz M et al., 'Public-private partnership units what are they, and what do they do?' (Washington DC, 2006)

Dyzenhaus D, 'Emergency, liberalism and the state' (2011) Perspectives on Politics 69

Easterlin R, 'Happiness, growth, and public policy' (IZA Discussion Paper No. 7234, 2013)

Easton P, 'Enhancing the contributions of adult and non-formal education to achievement of education for all and millennium development goals: Vol. I. Finding improved means of service provision in adult and non-formal education' (The World Bank, 2004).

Edelenbos J, 'Institutional implications of interactive governance: insights from Dutch practice' (2005) Governance 111

Edelenbos J, and I van Meerkerk (eds), *Critical reflections on interactive governance: self-organization and participation in public governance* (Edward Elgar, 2016)

Edelenbos J, and I van Meerkerk, 'Introduction: three reflecting perspectives on the interactive governance' in J Edelenbos and I van Meerkerk (eds), *Critical reflections on interactive governance: self-organization and participation in public governance* (Edward Elgar, 2016) 1

Edquist C et al. (eds), *Public technology procurement and innovation* (Kluwer Academic Publishers, 2000)

Eisenmann C, 'Le droit administratif et le principe de legalité' (1957) C. d'E, Etudes ed documents 29

Emek U, 'Turkish experience with public private partnerships in infrastructure: opportunities and challenges' (2015) Utilities Policy 120

Emiliou N, 'Subsidiarity: an effective barrier against the "enterprises of ambition?"' (1992) EL Review 383

Emiliou N, 'Subsidiarity: panacea or fig leaf?' in D O'Keeffe and P Twomeny (eds), *Legal issues of the Maastricht treaty* (Chancery, 1994) 65

Engel E, R Fischer, and A Galetovic, *The economics of public-private partnerships: a basic guide* (CUP, 2014)

Esping-Andersen G, *Social foundations of postindustrial economies* (OUP, 1999)

Essig M, and A Batran, 'Public-private partnership: development of long-term relationships in public procurement in Germany' (2005) Journal of Purchasing and Supply Management 221

Estlund D et al., 'Democratic theory and the public interest: Condorcet and Rousseau revisited' (1989) American Political Science Association 1317

Etzioni-Halevy E, *Bureaucracy and democracy* (Routledge, 2013)

European Commission, 'Green paper on public-private partnerships and Community law on public contracts and concessions' COM (2004) 327 final

European Commission, 'Guidelines for a successful public-private partnership' COM (2005) 569

European Commission, 'Interpretative communication on the application of Community law on public procurement and concessions to institutionalised public-private partnerships' COM (2007) 6661

European Commission, 'Mobilising private and public investment for recovery and long term structural change: developing public private partnerships' COM (2009) 615

European Commission, 'Buying social: a guide to taking account of social considerations in public procurement' (European Union, 2010)

European Commission, 'Europe 2020; a strategy for smart, sustainable and inclusive growth' COM (2010) 2010 final

European Commission, 'Green paper on the modernisation of EU public procurement policy: towards a more efficient European procurement market' COM (2011) 15 final

European Commission, 'Guide to social innovation' (Regional and Urban Policy, February 2013)

European Commission, 'A global partnership for poverty eradication and sustainable development after 2015' COM (2015) 44 final

European Commission, 'Buying green! A handbook on green public procurement' (3rd edition, 2016)

European Commission, 'Science for Environment policy. Future brief: the precautionary principle: decision-making under uncertainty' (September 2017, Issue 18)

European Commission, 'Public procurement guidance for practitioners' (Brussels, 2018)

European Commission, Directorate-General for Economic and Financial Affairs 'Public finances in EMU – 2014' (2014)

European International Bank, European PPP Expertise Centre, 'A guide to the statistical treatment of PPPs' (September 2016)

European Network for Rural Development, 'Connecting rural Europe' https://enrd.ec.europa.eu/leader-clld/lag-database_en, accessed 30 June 2019

European Parliament, 'Resolution on public-private partnerships and Community law on public procurement and concessions' (2006/2043(INI))

Eurostat, 'New decision of Eurostat on deficit and debt: treatment of public-private partnerships' (Decision No. 18 of 11 February 2004) 1

Evans J, 'Abuse-free development: how the World Bank should safeguard against human rights violations' (Proceedings of the Annual Meeting of the American Society of International Law, Vol. 107: International Law in a Multipolar World, July 2013) 298

Exton C, and M Shinwell, 'Policy use of well-being metrics: describing countries' experiences' (OECD Statistics and Data Directorate, SDD Working Paper No. 94, SDD/DOC(2018)7, 6 November 2018)

Fabi F, R Loiero, and F Profiti, *Il partenariato pubblico-privato nell'ordinamento giuridico nazionale, comunitario ed internazionale* (Dike giuridica, 2015)

Falcon G, *Le convenzioni pubblicistiche: Ammissibilità e caratteri* (Giuffrè, 1984)

Falcon G, 'Convenzioni e accordi amministrativi' *Enciclopedia Giuridica Treccani*, IX (1988) 4

Farley M, and N Pourbaix, 'The EU concessions directive: building (toll) bridges between competition law and public procurement' (2015) Journal of European Competition Law and Practice 15

Farquharson E, C Torres de Mästle, and E Yescombe, 'How to engage with the private sector in public-private partnerships in emerging markets' (The World Bank, 2011) 145

Farrell J, 'Cheap talk, coordination, and entry' (1987) Rand J. Econ. 34

Farrell J, 'Communication, coordination and Nash equilibrium' (1988) Econ. Lett. 209

Farrell J, and M Rabin, 'Cheap talk' (1996) J. Econ. Persp. 103

Fenei G, and A Vàri, 'Partnership between local government and the local community in the area of social policy: a Hungarian experience' in S Osborne (ed.), *Public-private partnership: theory and practice in international perspective* (Routledge, 2000) 265

Ferrarese M R, *Diritto sconfinato: Inventiva giuridica e spazi nel mondo globale* (Laterza, 2006)

Fialaire J, *Le droit des services publics locaux* (Litec, 1998)

Fidone G, 'Il partenariato pubblico-privato: una fuga in avanti del legislatore nazionale rispetto al diritto europeo' (2016) Il Diritto dell'Economia 404

Fidone G, *Proprietà pubblica e beni comuni* (ETS, 2017)

Finer H, 'Administrative responsibility in democratic government' (1941) Public Administration Review 335

Fischbacher M, and P Beaumont, 'PFI, public-private partnerships and the neglected importance of process: stakeholders and the employment dimension' (2010) Public Money and Management 171

Flathman R, *The public interest: an essay concerning the normative discourse of politics* (John Wiley, 1966)

Flinders M, 'The politics of public-private partnership' (2005) The British Journal of Politics and International Relations 215.

Flinders M, 'Public/private: the boundaries of the state' in C Hay, M Lister, and D Marsh (eds), *The state: theories and issues* (Macmillan International, 2006) 223

Florini A, *The third force: the rise of transnational civil society* (Japan Center for International Exchange – Carnegie Endowment for International Peace, 2000)

Flyvbjerg B, *Rationality and power: democracy in practice* (The University of Chicago Press, 1998)

Foldvary F, *Public goods and private communities* (Edward Elgar, 1994)

Fontanari E, and G Piperata (eds), *Agenda re-cycle: Proposte per reinventare la città* (Il Mulino, 2017)

Forrer J et al., 'Public-private partnerships and the public accountability question' (2010) Public Administration Review 475

Foster S, and C Iaione, 'The city as a commons' (2016) Yale Law and Policy Review 281

Fox J, and N Tott, *The PFI handbook* (Jordan Publishing Limited, 1999)

Frankfurter F, 'The tasks of administrative law' (1926–1927) U. Pa. Law Review 614

Freedland M, 'Government by contract and public law' (1994) Public Law 86

Freeman J, 'Collaborative governance in the administrative state' (1997) UCLA Law Review

Freeman J, 'Private parties, public functions and the new administrative law' in D Dyzenhaus (ed.), *Recrafting the rule of law: the limits of legal order* (Hart Publishing, 1999) 331

Freeman J, 'The contracting state' (2000) Florida State University Law Review 155

Freeman J, 'The private role in public governance' (2000) NYULR 543

Freeman J, 'Extending public accountability through privatization: from public law to publicization' in M Dowdle (ed.), *Public accountability: designs, dilemmas and experiences* (CUP, 2006) 83

Freeman J, and M Minow (eds), *Government by contracts: outsourcing and American democracy* (Harvard University Press, 2009)

Freeman J, and M Minow, 'Introduction: reframing the outsourcing debates' in J Freeman and M Minow (eds), *Government by contract: outsourcing and American democracy* (Harvard University Press, 2009) 1

Freund E, *Administrative powers over persons and property: a comparative survey* (University of Chicago Press, 1928)

Friedman M, *Capitalism and freedom* (3rd edition, University of Chicago Press, 2002)

Friedrich C (ed.), *The public interest* (Atherton Press, 1962)

Frilet M, and F Lager, 'Public procurement issues in the European Union' (2010) Eur. Bus. Law Review 21

Fuller L, 'Consideration and form' (1941) Columbia Law Review 799

Garcìa M, S Eizaguirre, and M Pradel, 'Social innovation and creativity in cities: a socially inclusive governance approach in two peripheral spaces of Barcelona' (2018) City, Culture and Society 363

Garner B A, 'Partnership' in *Black's Law Dictionary* (9th edition, Thomson Reuters, 2009) 1230

Garner B A, 'Private' in *Black's Law Dictionary* (9th edition, Thomson Reuters, 2009) 1315

Garner B A, 'Public' in *Black's Law Dictionary* (9th edition, Thomson Reuters, 2009) 1348

Gasiorowski P, and M Marian, 'Optimal capital structure of public-private partnerships' (International Monetary Fund, 2008)

Gaudemet Y, 'Pour une nouvelle théorie générale du droit des contrats administratifs: mesurer les difficultés d'une entreprise nécessaire' (2010) RD Publ. 313

Gaudemet Y, *Droit administratif* (LGDJ, 2018)

Geis M E, *Die öffentliche Förderung sozialer Selbsthilfe* (Sonstiges, 1997)

Geng Y, and B Doberstein, 'Greening government procurement in developing countries: building capacity in China' (2008) Journal of Environmental Management 932

Gerybadze A, 'Strategic alliances and process redesign' (Walter de Gruyter, 1995)

Ghizdeanu I, 'International experiences to stimulate PPPs' (2012) Rom. Pub.-Priv. Partnership Law Review 36

Ghizdeanu I, 'PPP's contribution to economic development – a macroeconomic approach' (2012) Rom. Pub.-Priv. Partnership Law Review 42

Ghizdeanu I, 'Public-private partnerships revival: current European approaches' (2015) Rom. Pub.-Priv. Partnership Law Review 14

Ghobadian A et al. (eds), *Public-private partnership: policy and experience* (Palgrave Macmillan, 2004)

Giannini M S, *Il potere discrezionale della Pubblica Amministrazione: concetto e poteri* (Giuffrè, 1939)

Giglioni F, *Governare per differenza: Metodi europei di coordinamento* (Edizioni ETS, 2012)

Giglioni F, 'Limiti e potenzialità del baratto amministrativo' (2016) Rivista Trimestrale di Scienza dell'Amministrazione 1

Gilbert C, 'The framework of administrative responsibility' (1959) The Journal of Politics 373

Goisis F, 'Il rischio economico quale proprium del concetto di concessione nella direttiva 2014/23/UE: approccio economico versus visioni tradizionali' (2015) Diritto Amministrativo 743

Goodnow F J, *Politics and administration: a study in government* (1900, Taylor and Francis Ltd, 2017)

Gordillo A, *Tratado de derecho administrativo* (Macchi, 1974, III) 9

Graells A, *Public procurement and the EU competition rules* (Hart Publishing, 2011)

Graham A, 'The government speech doctrine and its effects on the democratic process' (2011) Suffolk U. Law Review 703

Grant Long J, *Public-private partnerships for major league sports facilities* (Routledge, 2012)

Grazzini L, and A Petretto, 'Public-private partnership and competition in health-care and education' (2014) Italian Antitrust Review 91

Greenway J, B Salter, and S Hart, 'How policy networks can damage democratic health: a case study in the government of governance' (2007) Public Administration 717

Greve C, and G Hodge, 'Public-private partnership and public governance challenges' in S Osborne (ed.), *The new public governance: emerging perspectives on the theory and practice of public governance* (Routledge, 2010) 149

Greve C, and G Hodge, 'Public-private partnerships: governance scheme or language game?' (2010) Australian Journal of Public Administrations 8

Greve C, and G Hodge (eds), *Rethinking public-private partnerships: strategies for turbulent times* (Routledge, 2016)

Greve C, and G Hodge, 'On public-private partnership performance: a contemporary review' (2017) Public Works Management and Policy 55

Greve C, and G Hodge, 'Contemporary public-private partnership: towards a global research agenda' (2018) Financial Acc. and Man. 3

Grimsey D, and M Lewis, 'Evaluating the risk of public private partnership for infrastructure projects' (2002) International Journal of Project Management 107

Grimsey D, and M Lewis (eds), *The economics of public private partnerships* (Edward Elgar, 2005)

Grimsey D, and M Lewis, *Public private partnerships: the worldwide revolution in infrastructure provision and project finance* (Edward Elgar, 2004)

Grosse Ruse-Khan H, 'A real partnership for development: sustainable development as treaty objective in Europe economic partnership agreements and beyond' (2010) J. Int'l Econ. Law 13

Grossi P, *L'ordine giuridico medievale* (Laterza, 1995)

Grossi P, *L'invenzione del diritto* (Laterza, 2017)

Grossman G, and A Krueger, 'Economic growth and the environment' (1995) Quarterly Journal of Economics 353

Grunewald N, and I Martinez-Zarzoso, 'Did the Kyoto Protocol fail? An evaluation of the effect of the Kyoto Protocol on CO_2 emissions' (2016) Env. and Dev. Econ. 1

Grzymala-Busse A, *Rebuilding the Leviathan: party competition and state exploitation in post-communist democracies* (CUP, 2007)

Guedon M J, *Sur les services publics* (Paris, 1982)

Gulick L, 'Democracy and administration face the future' (1977) Public Administration Review 706

Gwartney J, and R Lawson, 'The concept and measurement of economic freedom' (2003) European Journal of Political Economy 405

Haas P, *Epistemic communities, constructivism, and international environmental politics* (Routledge, 2015)

Habermas J, *The structural transformation of the public sphere: an inquiry into a category of bourgeois society* (MIT Press, 1991)

Habermas J, 'Three normative models of democracy' (1994) Constellation 1

Habermas J, *Droit et démocraties* (Nrf Essais, Gallimard, 1997)

Habermas J, I Aubert, and K Genel, 'La démocratie a-t-elle encore une dimension épistémique? Recherche empirique et théorie normative' (2013) Participations 151

Hall J, 'Private opportunity, public benefit?' (2005) Fiscal Studies 7

Hallo de Wolf A, *Reconciling privatization with human rights* (Intersentia, 2012)

Hansen P, and A Jespersen, 'Nudge and manipulation of choice: a framework for the responsible use of the nudge approach to behaviour change in public policy' (2013) The European Journal of Risk Regulation 3

Haque MS, 'New public management: origin, dimensions and critical implications' (2007) Journal of Public Administration and Public Policy 1

Hardin G, 'The tragedy of the commons' (1968) Science 1243

Harding A, 'Public-private partnership in urban regeneration' in M Campbell (ed.), *Local economic policy* (Cassell, 1990) 89

Harlow C, 'Global administrative law: the quest for principles and values' (2006) EJIL 187

Harlow C, and R Rawlings, *Process and procedure in EU administration* (Hart Publishing, 2014)

Harvey D, *A brief history of neoliberalism* (OUP, 2005)

Hatcher R, 'Getting down to business: schooling in the globalised economy' (2001) Education and Social Justice 45

Hatcher R, 'Privatization and sponsorship: the re-agenting of the school system in England' (2006) Journal of Education Policy 599

Hauriou M, *Précis de droit administrative et de droit public general* (Larose et Forcel, 1933)

Hauser M, and J B Morel, 'Use of unsolicited proposals for new projects – the approaches in Australia' (2006) 2006 Int'l Bus Law Journal 3

Hazell P, and L Haddad, 'Agricultural research and poverty reduction' (International Food Policy Research Institute, Washington, DC, 2001)

Head J, 'Law and policy in international financial institutions: the changing role of law in the IMF and the multilateral developments banks' (2007) Kan. J. Law and Pub. Pol'y 201

Heald D, 'Value for money test and accounting treatment in PFI schemes' (2003) Accounting, Auditing and Accountability Journal 342

Hécquard-Théron M, 'La contractualisation des actions et des moyens publics d'intervention' (1993) AJDA 451

Held D, *Democracy and the global order: from the modern state to cosmopolitan governance* (Stanford University Press, 1995)

Held V, *The public interest and individual interests* (Basic Books, 1970)

Hemming R, G Schwartz, and B Akitoby, 'Public investment and public-private partnerships' (International Monetary Fund, 2007)

Henty P, 'Chandler v Camden Borough Council; Chandler v Secretary of State for Children, Schools and Families' (2009) Public Procurement Law Review 160

Herald M, 'Licensed to speak: the case of vanity plates' (2001) U. Colo. Law Review 595

Hetzel R, *The great recession: market failure or policy failure?* (CUP, 2012)

Hillery G, 'Definitions of community: areas of engagement' (1955) Rural Sociology 20

Hirschman A, and R Frank, *Shifting involvements: private interest and public action* (Princeton University Press, 2002)

Hirst P, *Associative democracy: new forms of economic and social* (Wiley-Blackwell, 1994)

HM Treasury, 'Infrastructure procurement: delivering long-term value' (2008)

HM Treasury, 'Managing public money' (2013)

HM Treasury, 'The choice of finance for capital investment' (Briefing by the National Audit Office, March 2015)

HM Treasury, 'PFI and PF2' (Report by the Comptroller and Auditor General, HC 718 Session 2017–2019, 18 January 2018)

Ho L, N Dickinson, and G Chan, 'Green procurement in the Asian public sector and the Hong Kong private sector' (2010) Natural Resources Forum 24

Hobbes T, *Leviathan* (1651, OUP, 1996).

Hobsbawm E, 'The future of the state' (1996) Development and Change 267

Hodge G, 'Accountability in the privatised state' (2004) Alternative Law Journal 4

Hodge G, 'The risky business of public-private partnerships' (2004) Australian Journal of Public Administration 37

Hodge G, and C Greve, *The challenge of public-private partnership* (Edward Elgar, 2005)

Hodge G, C Greve, and A Boardman (eds), *International handbook on public-private partnerships* (Edward Elgar, 2010)

Höffe O, 'Subsidiarität als Staatsphilosophisches Prinzip' in K W Nörr and T Oppermann (eds), *Subsidiarität: Idee und Wirklichkeit* (Bücher, 1997) 52

Hofmann H, G Rowe, and A Türk, *Administrative law and policy of the European Union* (OUP, 2011)

Holland R, 'The new era in public-private partnership' in Paul Porter and David Sweet (eds), *Rebuilding America's cities: roads to recovery* (Center for Urban Policy Research, 1984)

Holt C, and M Capra, 'Classroom games: a prisoner's dilemma' (2002) The Journal of Economic Education 229

Horga I, A Ivan, and I Gheorghe Bărbulescu, 'Regional and cohesion policy – insights into the role of the partnership principle in the new policy design' (Regional and Cohesion Policy, 2011, 5)

House of Commons, Public Administration and Constitutional Affairs Committee, 'After Carillion: public sector outsourcing and contracting' (HC 748, published on 9 July 2018) https://publications.parliament.uk/pa/cm201719/cmselect/cmpubadm/748/748.pdf accessed 13 March 2019

House of Commons, Public Administration and Constitutional Affairs Committee, 'Sourcing public services: lessons to be learned from the collapse of Carillion' (HC 748, published on 9 July 2018) https://publications.parliament.uk/pa/cm201719/cmselect/cmpubadm/748/748.pdf accessed 13 March 2019

Huang C, and D Law, 'Proportionality review of administrative action in Japan, Korea, Taiwan, and China' in F Bignami and D Zaring (eds), *Research handbook in comparative law and regulation* (Edward Elgar, 2014)

Humphreys P et al., 'Integrating environmental criteria into the supplier selection process' (2003) Journal of Materials Processing Technology 349

Huxham C, and S Vangen, *Managing to collaborate: theory and practice of collaborative advantage* (Routledge, 2005)

Iaione C, 'Governing the urban commons' (2015) Italian J. Public Law 170

Iber S T, *The principle of subsidiarity in Catholic social thought: implications for social justice and civil society in Nigeria* (Peter Lang, 2011)

Idoux P, 'Dynamique contractuelle et dynamique délibérative dans le renouvellement des méthodes d'action publique' in G Clamour and M Ubaud-Bergeron (eds), *Contrats publics: mélanges en l'honneur du professeur Michel Guibal* (Montpellier Université, II, 2006)

Illig P, 'The role of non-government organizations in the development of environmental policy at the Asian Development Bank' (1994) Buff. J. Int'l Law 47

International Bank for Reconstruction and Development, The World Bank, 'Mobilizing Islamic finance for infrastructure public-private partnerships' (Washington DC, 2017)

International Bank for Reconstruction and Development, The World Bank. 'Procuring infrastructure public-private partnerships' (Washington DC, 2018)

International Finance Cooperation, 'IFC supports management of Komodo National Park in Indonesia' (27 June 2005) https:// ifcextapps.ifc.org/ifcext/Pressroom/IFCPressRoom.nsf/0/7B5F1CD 246F58BA18525702D004B681E?OpenDocument, accessed 11 January 2019

International Finance Corporation Advisory Services in Public-Private Partnerships, 'Public-private partnership stories. Bangladesh: Bangladesh dialysis centers' (Washington DC, 2015)

International Monetary Fund, 'Public-private partnership' (Washington DC, 2004)

International Monetary Fund, 'Making public investment more efficient' (Policy Papers, Washington DC, 2015)

International Monetary Fund, 'Public-private partnership fiscal risk assessment model: user guide' (Washington DC, 2016)

International Monetary Fund, 'IMF annual report 2017: promoting inclusive growth' (Washington DC, 2017)

Iossa E, G Spagnolo, and M Vellez, 'Best practices on contract design in public-private partnerships' (World Bank, 2007)

Irwin T, S Mazraani, and S Saxena, 'How to control the fiscal costs of public-private partnerships' (International Monetary Fund, 2018)

Iwata H, and K Okada, 'Greenhouse gas emissions and the role of the Kyoto Protocol' (MPRA Paper No. 22299, Munich Personal RePEc Archive, Munich, 2010)

Jacobs S, R King Jr, and R Sabino, 'The act of state doctrine: a history of judicial limitations and exceptions' (1977) Harv. Int'l Law 677

Jacobson C, and S Ok Choi, 'Success factors: public works and public-private partnerships' (2008) International Journal of Public Sector Management 637

Jamali D, 'Success and failure mechanisms of public private partnerships in developing countries: insights from Lebanon' (2004) Emerald. The International Journal of Public Sector Management 414

James M, 'Public interest and majority rule in Bentham's democratic theory' (1981) Political Theory 49

Jansen O, and B Schöndorf-Haubold (eds), *The European composite administration* (Intersentia, 2011)

Jégouzo Y, 'L'administration contractuelle en question' in *Mouvement du droit public, mélanges F. Moderne* (Dalloz, 2004) 547

Jessop B, 'The dynamics of partnership and governance failure' in G Stroker (ed.), *The new politics of local governance in Britain* (MacMillan, 2000) 11

Jèze G, *Les principes généraux du droit administratif: Tome II: La notion de service public, les individus au service public, le statut des agents publics* (1925, Dalloz, 2003)

Jèze G, 'Le service public' (1926) Revista de drept public 161

Johnston J, *Public relations and the public interest* (Routledge, 2016)

Jonas H, *Das prinzip verantwortung: versuch einer ethik für die technologische zivilisation* (1979; Suhrkamp Taschenbuch, 1984)

Jones J, *The politics of transport in twentieth-century France, Montreal and Kingston* (MQUP, 1984)

Kakabadse A et al. (eds), *Corporate social responsibility: reconciling aspiration with application* (Palgrave Macmillan, 2006)

Kamensky J, and T Burlin (eds), *Collaborations: using networks and partnerships* (IBM Center for the Business of Government, 2004)

Kamolov S, 'Digital public governance: trends and risks' (2017) Giornale di Storia Costituzionale 33

Kaul I, 'Exploring the policy space between markets and states: global public-private partnerships' in I Kaul, and O Conceição P (eds), *The new public finance: responding to global challenges* (OUP, 2006) 219

Keck M, and K Sikkink, *Activists beyond borders: transnational advocacy networks in international politics* (Cornell University Press, 1998)

Kemp S, *Public goods and private wants* (Edward Elgar, 2002)

Kerwer D, 'Rules that many use: standards and global regulation' (2005) Governance 611

Kestenbaum M, and R Straight, 'Procurement performance: measuring quality, effectiveness, and efficiency' (1995) Procuring Productivity and Management Review 200

Kettl D, *The global public management revolution: a report on the transformation of governance* (Brookings Institution Press, 2000)

Kettl D, *The transformation of governance: public administration for the twenty-first century* (Johns Hopkins University Press, 2002)

Keys M, and C Godfrey, 'Common good' in M Bevir (ed.), *Encyclopedia of political theory* (Sage, 2010) 239

Kickert W, 'Expansion and diversification of public administration in the postwar welfare state: the case of the Netherlands' (1996) Public Administration Review 88

King S, and B Chilton, *Administration in the public interest: principles, policies and practices* (Carolina Academic Press, 2009)

Kingsbury B, N Krisch, and R B Stewart, 'The emergence of global administrative law' (2005) Law and Contemp. Problems 15

Kingsford Smith D, 'Governing the corporation: the role of soft regulation' (2012) UNSW Law Journal 378

Kirlin J, 'The big questions of public administration in a democracy' (1996) Public Administration Review 416

Klatt M, and M Meister, *The constitutional structure of proportionality* (OUP, 2012)

Klijn E H, and G Teisman, 'Governing public-private partnerships: Analysing and managing the process and institutional characteristics of public-private partnerships' in S Osborne (ed.), *Public-private partnerships: theory and practice in international perspective* (Routledge, 2000) 84

Koppenjan J, and B Enserink, 'Public-private partnerships in urban infrastructures: reconciling private sector participation and sustainability' (2009) Public Administration Review 284

Kort M, and E H Klijn, 'Public-private partnerships in urban regeneration projects: organizational form or managerial capacity?' (2011) Public Administration Review 618

Kotler P, D H Haider, and I Rein, *Marketing places* (Free Press, 1993)

Koutalakis C, A Buzogany, and T Börzel, 'When soft regulation is not enough: The integrated pollution prevention and control directive of the European Union' (2010) Regulation and Governance 329

Krumm T, *The politics of public-private partnerships in western Europe: comparative perspectives* (Edward Elgar, 2016)

Kunzmann K, 'Smart cities: a new paradigm of urban development' (2014) Crios 9

Kutney G, *Carbon politics and the failure of the Kyoto protocol* (Routledge, 2014)

Kwok T, and K Hampson, 'Building strategic alliances in construction' (Queensland University of Technology, AIPM Special Publication, 1996)

La Chimia A, and P Trepte (eds), *Public procurement and aid effectiveness: a roadmap under construction* (Hart Publishing, 2019)

La Torre M, *Norme, istituzioni, valori: Per una teoria istituzionalistica del diritto* (Laterza, 1999)

Ladner A, 'Switzerland: subsidiarity, power-sharing, and direct democracy' in F Hendriks, A Lidström, and J Loughlin (eds), *The Oxford handbook of local and regional democracy in Europe* (OUP, 2011) 201

Lawther W, *Privatizing toll roads: a public-private partnership* (Pager, 1946)

Le Galès P, 'Aspects idéologiques et politiques du partenariat public-privé' (1995) Partenariat public-privé et développement territorial 51

Le Grand J, 'The theory of government failure' (1991) British Journal of Political Science 423

Leach W, 'Collaborative public management and democracy: evidence from Western Watershed Partnerships' (2006) Public Administration Review 100

Lee A, 'Taming Asia's legal frontiers: the Asian Development Bank's General Counsel explains how the bank's technical assistance programmes are improving the investment framework of the region's emerging markets' (2014) Int'l Fin. Law Review 24

Leeper R, 'The Ku Klux Klan, public highways and the public forum' (2000) Communications and the Law 39

Levi-Faur D, 'The welfare state: a regulatory perspective' (2014) Public Administration 599

Levinson D, R Garcia, and K Carlson, 'A framework for assessing public-private partnerships' in P Rietveld and R Stough (eds), *Institutions and sustainable transport: regulatory reform in advanced economies* (Edward Elgar, 2007) 285

Leys W, and C Perry, 'Philosophy and the public interest' (Committee to Advance Original Work in Philosophy, Chicago, 1959)

Liebman L, and H Brooks (eds), *Public private partnership: new opportunities for meeting social needs* (American Academy of Arts and Sciences, 1984)

Lind A W, *An island community, ecological succession in Hawaii* (University of Chicago Press, 1938)

Lindberg S, 'Mapping accountability: core concepts and subtypes' (2013) International Review of Administrative Science 202

Linder S H, 'Coming to terms with the public-private partnership: a grammar of multiple meanings' in P Vaillancourt Rosenau (ed.), *Public-private policy partnerships* (MIT Press, 2000) 19

Linder S and P Vaillancourt Rosenau, 'Mapping the terrain of the public-private policy partnership' in Pauline Vaillancourt Rosenau (ed.), *Public-private policy partnerships* (MIT Press, 2000) 1

Lindley N, *A treatise on the law of partnership* (1881, 8th edition, Sweet and Maxwell, 1912)

Link A, *Public/private partnerships: innovation strategies and policy alternatives* (Springer, 2006)

Linotte D, and R Romi, *Services publics et droit public economique* (Paris, 1992)

Lipsey R, and C Harbury, *First principles of economics* (2nd edition, OUP, 2004) 169

Locke J, *Two treatises of government* (1689, McMaster University Archive, 1823)

Lokiec P, 'Contractualisation et recherche d'une légitimité procédurale' (Actes du colloque 11, 12 and 13 October 2007 'La contractualisation de la production normative') 95

Long N, 'Power and administration' (1949) Public Administration Review 260

Lorini G, *Dimensioni giuridiche dell'istituzionale* (CEDAM, 2000)

Love P, and A Gunasekaran, 'Learning alliances: a customer–supplier focus for continuous improvement in manufacturing' (1999) Industrial and Commercial Training 88

Lu M, *Corporate social and environmental responsibility: another road to China's sustainable development* (Brill Nijhoff, 2019)

Ludlow A, *Privatising public prisons: labour law and the public procurement process* (Hart, 2015)

Luhmann N, *Theory of society* (1997, translation by Rhodes Barrett, Stanford University Press, 2013)

Lujan Gallegos V et al., 'Sustainable financing for marine protected areas: lessons from Indonesian MPAs: case studies: Komodo and Ujung Kulon National Parks' (Environmental and Resource Management, 2005) http://www.selfpas.it/libreria/Sustainable_Financing_of_MPAs-Komodo.pdf, accessed 11 March 2019.

Maass A, and L Radway, 'Gauging administrative responsibility' (1949) Public Administration Review 182

MacCallum D, *Social innovation and territorial development* (Ashgate, 2011)

Macdonald S, and C Cheong, 'The role of public-private partnerships and the third sector in conserving heritage buildings, sites, and historic urban areas' (The Getty Conservation Institute, 2014)

Maggino F (ed.), *A new research agenda for improvements in quality of life* (Springer, 2015)

Maine H, *Village-communities in East and West* (Murray, 1871)

Mair J, and I Marti, 'Social entrepreneurship research: a source of explanation prediction and delight' (2006) Journal of World Business 36

Majone G, 'The rise of the regulatory state in Europe' (1994) West European Politics 77

Manabu N, 'Triggers of contract breach: contract design, shocks, or institutions?' (The World Bank, 2014)

Mancina C, 'Uso pubblico della ragione e ragione pubblica: da Kant a Rawls' (2008) Diritto e questioni pubbliche 33

Mannori L, and B Sordi, *Storia del diritto amministrativo* (Laterza, 2011)

Marcuzzo M C, *Fighting market failure: collected essays in the Cambridge tradition of economics* (Routledge, 2012)

Marique Y, *Public private partnerships and the law* (Edward Elgar, 2014)

Marquand D, *Decline of the public: the hollowing out of citizenship* (Polity, 2004)

Marques P, K Morgan, and R Richardson, 'Social innovation in question: the theoretical and practical implications of a contested concept' in Environment and Planning C: Politics and Space (July 2017)

Marques Mendes A, and M Meica, 'The quest to justify a long lasting role for multilateral development banks' (SADIF Newsletter and Investment Management Portal, 2005)

Martin R, and S Osberg, 'Social entrepreneurship: the case for definition' (2007) Stanford Social Innovation Review 11

Martin S, and K Scott, 'The nature of innovation market failure and the design of public support for private innovation' (2000) Research Policy 437

Martin Witte J, and C Streck, 'Introduction to progress or peril? Partnership and networks in Global environmental governance: the post-Johannesburg agenda' (Global Public Policy Institute, Washington DC, 2003)

Marzona N, 'Il potere normativo delle autorità indipendenti' in S Cassese and C Franchini (eds), *I garanti delle regole* (Il Mulino, 1996)

Mashaw J, 'Structuring a "Dense Complexity": accountability and the project of administrative law' (Issues in Legal Scholarship, 5/2005)

Mashaw J, 'Accountability and institutional design: some thoughts on the grammar of governance' in M Dowdle (ed.), *Public accountability: designs, dilemmas and experiences* (CUP, 2006) 115

Mashaw J, 'Administration and "The Democracy": administrative law from Jackson to Lincoln, 1829–1861' (2007–2008) Yale Law J. 1928

Mashaw J, *Creating the administrative constitution: the lost one hundred years of American administrative law* (Yale University Press, 2012)

Maslova S, 'The new Russian law on PPP: breakthrough or throwback' (2012) Eur. Procurement and Pub. Private Partnership Law Review 268

Mason M, 'The utility of consideration – a comparative view: cause and consideration' (1941) Columbia Law Review 825

Masters A, *Cultural influences on public-private partnerships in global governance* (Palgrave MacMillan, 2018)

Mathews J, 'Searching for proportionality in American administrative law' in S Ranchordàs and B De Waard (eds), *The judge and the proportionate use of discretion: a comparative study* (Routledge, 2016) 160

Mathews J, 'Proportionality review in administrative law' in S Rose-Ackerman, P Lindseth, and B Emerson (eds), *Comparative administrative law* (2nd edition, Edward Elgar, 2017) 40

Matsukawa T, and O Habeck, 'Review of risk mitigation instruments for infrastructure financing and recent trends and developments' (The International Bank for Reconstruction and Development, The World Bank, 2007)

Matten D, and J Moon, 'Corporate social responsibility' (2004) Journal of Business Ethics 323

Matteucci Ni, 'Bene comune' in N Bobbio, N Matteucci, and G Pasquino (eds), *Dizionario di politica* (UTET, 1990) 74

Maurrasse D, *Strategic public private partnership* (Edward Elgar, 2013)

Mayntz R, 'Common goods and governance' in Adrienne Heritier (ed.), *Common goods: reinventing European and international governance* (Rowman and Littlefield Publishers, 2002) 15

McCann A et al. (eds), *When private actors contribute to public interests: a law and governance perspective* (Eleven, 2014)

McCarthy J, *Partnership, collaborative planning and urban regeneration* (Ashgate, 2007)

McCrudden C, 'Equality and non-discrimination' in D Feldman (ed.), *English public law* (OUP, 2004) 499

McCrudden C, 'Using public procurement to achieve social outcomes' (2004) Natural Resources Forum 257

McDonald D, and G Ruiters (eds), *The age of commodity: water privatization in Southern Africa* (Earthscan, 2005)

McGeorge D, and A Palmer, *Construction management new directions* (2nd edition, Blackwell Science, 2002)

McQuaid R et al., 'European economic development partnerships: the case of Eastern Scotland European Partnership' in L Montanheiro et al. (eds), *Public and private sector partnerships: fostering enterprise* (Sheffield Hallam University Press, 1998) 355

McWilliams A, and D Siegel, 'Corporate social responsibility: a theory of the firm perspective' (2001) Academy of Management Review 1

Medda F, 'A game theory approach for the allocation of risks in transport public private partnerships' (2007) International Journal of Project Management 213

Megginson W, and J Netter, 'From state to market: a survey of empirical studies on privatization' (2001) Journal of Economic Literature 321

Mekata M, 'Building partnerships toward a common goal: experiences of the international campaign to ban landmines' in A Florini (ed.), *The third force: the rise of transnational civil society* (Japan Center for International Exchange – Carnegie Endowment for International Peace, 2000) 143

Meletiadis N, *Public private partnerships and constitutional law: accountability in the United Kingdom* (Routledge, 2018)

Meyerstein A, 'Transnational private financial regulation and sustainable development: an empirical assessment of the implementation of the Equators Principles' (2013) NYU J. Int'l Law and Policy 500

Meziou A, 'The legal framework for public-private partnerships (PPPs) in Nigeria: Untangling the complex web' (2013) Eur. Procurement and Pub. Private Partnership Law Review 324

Micciché C, *Beni comuni: risorse per lo sviluppo sostenibile* (Editoriale Scientifica, 2018)

Millon-Delsol C, *L'etat subsidiaire* (Paris, 1992)

Minow M, 'Partners, not rivals: redrawing the lines between public and private, non-profit, and secular and religious' (2000) BU Law Review 1061

Minow M, *Partners, not rivals: privatization and the public good* (Beacon Press, 2002)

Minow M, 'Outsourcing power: privatizing military efforts and the risks to accountability, professionalism, and democracy' in J Freeman, and M Minow (eds), *Outsourcing and American democracy* (Harvard University Press, 2009) 110

Minsoo L et al., 'Hazard analysis on public-private partnership projects in developing Asia' (2018) ADB Economics Working Paper Series 1

Mitnick B, *The political economy of regulation* (Columbia University Press, 1980)

Mohr J, and R Spekman, 'Characteristics of partnership success: partnership attributes, communication behaviour, and conflict resolution techniques' (1994) Strategic Management Journal 135

Möllers C, 'Braucht das öffentliche Recht einen neuen Methoden-und Richtungsstreit?' (1999) Verwaltungsarchiv 187

Montaner L C, *Manual de Derecho administrativo* (2nd edition, Editorial Civitas, 1991) I

Moor P, 'Définir l'intérêt public: une mission impossible?' in J Ruegg, S Decoutère, and N Mettan (eds), *Le partenariat public-privé: un atout pour l'aménagement du territorie et la protection de l'environement?* (Presses polytechniques et universitaires romandes, 1994) 218

Moore M, *Creating public value: strategic management in government* (Harvard University Press, 1995)

Moore M, *Recognising public value* (Harvard University Press, 2013)

Moravcsik A, 'Preferences and power in the European Community: a liberal intergovernmentalist approach' (1993) Common Market Studies 473

Morbidelli G, *Il diritto amministrativo tra particolarismo e universalismo* (Editoriale Scientifica, 2012)

Morgan B, and K Yeung, *An introduction to law and regulation: text and materials* (CUP, 2007)

Möric K E, *PPP et SEC 2010: La répartition des risques dans les partenariats public-privé et le déficit public* (Larcier, 2018)

Morley M, *The public-private partnership handbook: how to maximize value from joint working* (Kogan Page, 2015)

Mörth U, *Soft law in governance and regulation, an interdisciplinary analysis* (Edward Elgar, 2004)

Mosey D, *Early contractor involvement in building procurement: contracts, partnering and project management* (Wiley-Blackwell, 2009)

Mosey D, 'The origins and purposes of the FAC-1 framework alliance contracts' (2017) International Construction Law Review

Mosey D (ed.), *Collaborative construction procurement and improved value* (Wiley, 2019)

Mouraviev N, and N Kakabadse (eds), *Public-private partnerships in transitional nations: policy, governance and praxis* (Cambridge Scholars Publishing, 2017)

Mulgan G, 'Supply and demand and measurement of value' in J Benington and M Moore (eds), *Public value: theory and practice* (Palgrave MacMillan, 2011) 212

Mulgan R, *Holding power to account: accountability in modern democracies* (Houndmills, 2003)

Munck G (ed.), *Regimes and democracy in Latin America* (OUP, 2007)

Munday S, *Markets and market failure* (Heinemann, 2000)

Münder J, and D Kreft (eds), *Subsidiarität heute* (Votum, 1990)

Mwita JI, 'Performance management model: A systems-based approach to public service quality' (2000) The International Journal of Public Sector Management 19

Nagurney A, and F Toyasaki, 'Supply chain supernetworks and environmental criteria' (2003) Transportation Research Part D: Transport and Environment 185

Napolitano G, *Diritto amministrativo comparato* (Giuffrè, 2007)

Nash R et al., *The government contracts reference book: a comprehensive guide to the language of procurement* (4th edition, Wolters Kluwer, 2013)

Nelson R, 'Multilateral development banks, transparency and corporate clients: "public-private partnerships" and public access to information' (2003) Public Administration and Development 249

Nespor S, 'Tragedie e commedie nel nuovo mondo dei beni comuni' (2013) Riv. giur. ambiente 665

Newman J, *Governing public-private partnership* (MQUP, 2017)

Ng A, and M Loosemore, 'Risk allocation in the private provision of public infrastructure' (2007) International Journal of Project Management 66

Nicholas C, 'Devising transparent and efficient concession award procedures' (2012) Uniform Law Review 97

Nicholls A, and A Murdock, 'The nature of social innovation' (2012) Social Innovation 1

Nicholson G, 'Choosing the right partner for your joint venture, Fletcher construction' (Proceedings of Joint Venture and Strategic Alliance Conference, Sydney, Australia, 1996)

Nielsen R 'The establishment and operations of the Asian Development Bank' (1970) Colum. J. Transnat'l Law 81

Nigro M, *Le decisioni amministrative* (Jovene, 1953)

Nigro M, *Giustizia amministrativa* (Il Mulino, 1976)

Nigro M, 'L'amministrazione tra diritto pubblico e diritto privato: a proposito di condizioni legali' (1961) Foro it. (now in M Nigro, *Scritti giuridici* (Giuffrè 1996) I, 495)

Nigro M, 'Procedimento amministrativo e tutela giurisdizionale contro la pubblica amministrazione (il problema di una legge generale sul procedimento amministrativo)' (1980, now in Mario Nigro, *Scritti giuridici* (Giuffrè, 1996) II, 1427)

Nordtveit B, 'Managing public-private partnership. lessons from literacy education in Senegal' (The World Bank, 2004)

Nordtveit B, 'Use of public-private partnerships to deliver social services: advantages and drawbacks' (Center for International Education Faculty Publications, 2004)

Nose M, 'Enforcing public-private partnership contract: how do fiscal institutions matter?' (International Monetary Fund, 2017)

Novak W J, 'Public private governance: a historical introduction' in J Freeman and M Minow (eds), *Government by contracts: outsourcing and American democracy* (Harvard University Press, 2009)

Oakley D, 'The American welfare state decoded: uncovering the neglected history of public-private partnership' (2006) City and Community 243

Organization for Economic Cooperation and Development, 'Participatory development and good governance, development cooperation guideline series' (OECD Publications, Paris, 1995)

Organization for Economic Cooperation and Development, 'Recommendation of the Council on Improving the Environmental Performance of Government' (20 February 1996, C(96)39/final)

Organization for Economic Cooperation and Development, 'Special issue on public/private partnerships in science and technology' (Science Technology Industry No. 23, 1999)

Organization for Economic Cooperation and Development, 'Environmental strategy for the first decade of the 21st century' (16 May 2001)

Organization for Economic Cooperation and Development, 'Public-private partnerships: in pursuit of risk sharing and value for money' (OECD Publishing, Paris, 2008)

Organization for Economic Cooperation and Development, 'Dedicated public-private partnership units: a survey of institutional and governance structures' (OECD Publishing, Paris, 2010)

Organization for Economic Cooperation and Development, 'Value for money and international development: deconstructing myths to promote a more constructive discussion' (2012)

Organization for Economic Cooperation and Development, 'Effective delivery of large infrastructure projects' (OECD, 2015)

Organization for Economic Cooperation and Development, 'Recommendation on public procurement' (Paris, 2015)

Organization for Economic Cooperation and Development, 'Multi-dimensional review of Uruguay. Volume 2. In-depth analysis and recommendations' (Paris, 2016)

Organization for Economic Cooperation and Development, 'Getting infrastructure right: a framework for better governance' (Paris, 2017) 29

Ogus A, *Regulation: legal form and economic theory* (Bloomsbury Publishing, 2004)

Olivetti A, *L'ordine politico della comunità* (Nuove Edizioni, 1945)

Osborne D, and T Gaebler, *Reinventing government* (Ingrid Schneider Clemson University, 1992)

Osborne S, 'Understanding public-private partnerships in international perspective: globally convergent or nationally divergent phenomena?' in S Osborne (ed.), *Public-private partnerships: theory and practice in international perspective* (Routledge, 2000) 1

Ost F, and M van de Kerchove, *De la pyramide au réseau? Pour une théorie dialectique du droit* (FUSL, 2002)

Ostrom E, *Governing the commons: the evolution of institutions for collective action* (Political Economy of Institutions and Decisions, 1990)

Ostrom E, 'Reflections on the commons' in J Baden and D Noonan (eds), *Managing the commons* (Indiana University Press, 1998) 95

Ostrom E, *Design principles and threats to sustainable organizations that manage commons* (Bloomington, 1999)

Ostrom E, R Gardner, and J Walker, *Rules, games and common-pool resources* (The University of Michigan Press, 1994)

Ostrom E et al., *The future of the commons: beyond market failure and government regulation* (The Institute of Economic Affairs, 2012)

Park S, 'Guarding the guardians: the case for regulating state-owned financial entities in global finance' (2014) U. Pa. J. Bus. Law 739

Pascual A, 'Private sector participation in infrastructure: experience in Asia and the role of the Asian Development Bank.' (2004) Transnat'l Law 107

Pateman C, *Participation and democratic theory* (CUP, 1970)

Patrinos H A, F Barrera-Osorio, and J Guàqueta, 'The role and impact of public-private partnerships in education' (The International Bank for Reconstruction and Development; The World Bank, 2009)

Pattberg P, 'Introduction: partnerships for sustainable development' in P Pattberg et al. (eds), *Public-private partnerships for sustainable development* (Edward Elgar, 2012) 1

Pattberg P et al. (eds), *Public-private partnership for sustainable development* (Edward Elgar, 2012)

Payne G (ed.), *Making common ground: public-private partnerships in land for housing* (London, Practical Action, 1999)

Paz-Fuchs A, R Mandelkern, and I Galnoor (eds), *The privatization of Israel: the withdrawal of state responsibility* (Palgrave MacMillan, 2018)

Peng H, and J Cai, 'Measuring performance of public procurement for innovation' (IEEE, 2008)

Péraldi-Leneuf F, 'Le recours à l'externalité dans le système administratif communautaire: la délégation de la technicité' in P Mbongo (ed.), *Le Phénomène Bureaucratique Européen: Intégration Européenne et 'Technophobie'* (Bruyllant, 2009)

Peters G, *The future of governing: four emerging models* (University Press of Kansas, 1996)

Peters R et al., 'Case study of the Acton Peninsula Development. Research and case study of the construction of the National Museum of Australia and the Australian Institute of Aboriginal and Torres Strait Islander Studies. School of Construction Management and Property' (Queensland University of Technology, 2001)

Peterson G, 'Land leasing and land sale as an infrastructure-financing option' (World Bank, 2006)

Phillips W et al., 'Social innovation and social entrepreneurship: a systematic review' (2014) Group and Organization Management 428

Pierson P, 'The new politics of the welfare state' (1996) World Politics 143

Piga G, and T Tatrai, *Public procurement policy* (Routledge, 2015)

Piperata G, 'Rigenerare I beni e gli spazi della città: attori, regole e azioni' in E Fontanari and G Piperata (eds), *Agenda re-cycle: proposte per reinventare la città* (Il Mulino, 2017) 21

Pitschas R, *Verwaltungsverantwortung und Verwaltungsverfahren* (Monaco, 1990)

Pitt M, N Collins, and A Walls, 'The private finance initiative and value for money' (2006) Journal of Property Investment and Finance 363

Pollitt C, *Managerialism in the public sector: the Anglo-American experience* (Blackwell, 1990)

Pollitt C, 'The new public management: an overview of the current status' (2017) Journal of Public Management 110

Pontier J M, *Le droit administratif et la complexité* (AJDA, 2000) 187

Popescu G, *Agrifood economics and sustainable development in contemporary society* (IGI Global, 2019)

Porat C E, *Proportionality and constitutional culture* (CUP, 2013)

Pototschnig U, *I pubblici servizi* (Cedam, 1964)

Prager J, 'Contracting out government services: lessons from the private sector' (1994) PAR 176

Przeworski A, S Stokes, and B Manin (eds), *Democracy, accountability, and representation* (CUP, 1999)

Quiggin J, 'Risk, PPPs and the public sector comparator' (2008) Australian Accounting Review 51

Quinot G, 'Promotion of social policy through public procurement in Africa' in S Arrowsmith and G Quinot (eds), *Public procurement regulation in Africa* (CUP, 2013)

Ramraj V, 'Transnational non-state regulation and domestic administrative law' in S Rose-Ackerman, P Lindseth, and B Emerson (eds), *Comparative administrative law* (2nd edition, Edward Elgar, 2017) 582

Randall A, 'The problem of market failure' (1983) Natural Resource Journal 131

Rangeon F, *L'ideologie de l'interet general* (Vedel, 1986)

Rankin M et al., 'Public-private partnerships for agribusiness development: a review of international experiences' (Food and Agriculture Organization of the United Nations, Rome, 2016)

Rasche A, M Morsing, and J Moon (eds), *Corporate social responsibility: strategy, communication, governance* (CUP, 2017)

Ratiu M A, 'The decision made by a public partner to implement a project as a PPP' (2012) Rom. Pub.-Priv. Partnership Law Review 6

Rawls J, *A theory of justice* (Belknap Press, 1971)

Rayman-Bacchus L, and P Walsh, *Corporate responsibility and sustainable development: exploring the nexus of private and public interests* (Routledge, 2015)

Rebonato R, *Taking liberties: a critical examination of libertarian paternalism* (Palgrave MacMillan, 2012)

Redford E, 'The protection of the public interest with special reference to administrative regulation' (1954) The American Political Science Review 1103

Rehfuss J, 'Contracting out and accountability in state and local governments: the importance of contract monitoring' (1990) State and Local Government Review 44

Reich M (ed.), *Public-private partnerships for public health* (Harvard University Press, 2002)

Renna M, and V Sessa, 'Commento all'art. 190 del Codice dei contratti pubblici (Baratto amministrativo)' in G M Esposito (ed.), *Codice dei contratti pubblici: Commentario di dottrina e giurisprudenza* (Utet Giuridica, 2017) 2226

Rescigno G U, 'Principio di sussidiarietà orizzontale e diritti sociali' (2002) Diritto Pubblico 5

Reside R, and A Mendoza, 'Determinants of outcomes of public-private partnerships (PPP) in infrastructure in Asia' (School of Economics, University
of the Philippines, Discussion Paper No. 3/2010)

Revel M et al., *Le débat public: une expérience française de démocratie participative* (La Découverte, 2007)

Revet T, 'Droit législatif, droit réglementaire et droit néo-corporatif du contrat'
(2004) Revue des contrats 607

Rich B, 'The multilateral development banks, environmental policy, and the
United States' (1984) Ecology LQ 684

Richer L, and L Lichère, *Droits des contracts administratifs* (LGDJ, 2016) 542

Richter J, '"We the Peoples" or "We the Corporations"? Critical reflections on
UN-business "partnerships"' (IBFAN, Geneva, 2003)

Rivero J, *Droit public et droit privé: conquête ou* status quo? (Dalloz, 1947) 69

Robinson H et al., *Governance and knowledge management
for public-private partnerships* (Wiley-Blackwell, 2009)

Robinson L, *Following the quality strategy: the reasons for the use of quality
management in UK public leisure facilities* (1999) Managing Leisure 201

Rom M C, 'From welfare state to opportunity, Inc.: public-private partnerships
in welfare reform' in P Vaillancourt Rosenau (ed.), *Public-private policy
partnerships* (MIT Press, 2000) 161

Romano A, 'Il ruolo e le funzioni dell'Amministrazione' in L Mazzarolli et
al. (eds), *Diritto amministrativo, i, parte generale* (4th edition, Monduzzi
Editore, 2005) 1

Romano S, *L'ordinamento giuridico* (Quodlibet, 1917)

Romeo A, 'Dalla forma al risultato: profili dogmatici ed evolutivi della decisione amministrativa' (2018) Diritto Amministrativo 551.

Romero M J, 'Where is the public in PPPs? Analysing the World Bank's
support for public-private partnerships' (Bretton Woods Observer, 2014)

Rose-Ackerman S, P Lindseth, and B Emerson (eds), *Comparative administrative law* (2nd edition, Edward Elgar, 2017)

Rosen A, 'The wrong solution at the right time: the failure of the Kyoto
Protocol on climate change' (2015) Politics and Policies 30

Rossi G, 'Pubblico e privato nell'economia semi-globalizzata. L'impresa
pubblica nei sistemi permeabili e in competizione' (2014) Rivista Italiana di
Diritto Pubblico Comunitario 1.

Rothstein B, and J Teorell, 'What is quality of government? A theory of impartial government institutions' (2008) Governance 165

Roumboutsos A (ed.), *Public private partnerships in transport: trends and
theory* (Routledge, 2015)

Roumboutsos A, and S Saussier, 'Public-private partnerships and investments in innovation: the influence of the contractual arrangement' (2014)
Construction Management and Economics 349

Rousseau J J, *Du contrat social, ou Principes du droit politique* (1762)

Ruffert M, 'The Transformation of administrative law as a transnational methodological project' in M Ruffert (ed.), *The transformation of administrative law in Europe* (Sellier, 2007)

Sachs J, *The age of sustainable development* (Columbia University Press, 2015)

Sachs M, 'Bürgerverantwortung im demokratischen Verfassungsstaat' (1995) DVBl 873

Sadka E, 'Public-private partnership: a public economics perspective' (2007) CESifo Economic Studies 466

Sagalyn L, 'Public private development. lessons from history, research and practice' (2007) Journal of the American Planning Association 7

Samii R, L van Wassenhove, and S Bhattacharya, 'An innovative public–private partnership: new approach to development' (2002) GSDRC 991

Sandel M, *Democracy's discontent: America in search of a public philosophy* (Harvard University Press, 1996) 350

Sandel M, *Justice: what's the right thing to do?* (Ferrar, Straus and Firoux, 2009)

Sandel M, *Liberalism and the limits of justice* (2nd edition, CUP, 2010)

Sandel M, *What money can't buy: the moral limits of markets* (Penguin, 2013)

Sanford J, 'US policy toward the multilateral development banks: the role of Congress' (1988) Geo. Wash. J. Int'l Law and Econ. 2

Saruchera F, and M Phiri, 'Technological innovations performance and public-private partnerships' (2016) Corporate Ownership and Control 549

Saunders C, and K Yam, 'Government regulation by contract: implications for the rule of law' (2004) Public Law Review 51

Savas E, *Privatization in the city: successes, failures, lessons* (CQ Press, 2005)

Schaeffer P, and S Loveridge, 'Toward an understanding of types of public-private cooperation' (2002) Public Performance and Management Review 169

Scharpf F W, 'The European social model: coping with the challenges of diversity' (2002) Journal of Common Market Studies 645

Schedler A, L Diamond, and M Plattner (eds), *The self-restraining state: power and accountability in new democracies* (Lynne Rienner Publishers, 1999)

Scherr J, and R Juge Gregg, 'Johannesburg and beyond: the 2002 World Summit on Sustainable Development and the rise of partnership' (2006) Geo. Int'l Envt'l Review 425

Schlemmer-Schulte S, 'The impact of civil society on the World Bank, the International Monetary Fund and the World Trade Organization: the case of the World Bank' (2000) ILSA J. Int'l and Comp. Law 401

Schmidt-Aßmann E S, 'Verwaltungsverantwortung und Verwaltungsgerichtsbarkeit' (1976) VVDStRL 227

Schmidt-Aßmann E, *Verwaltungsrechtliche Dogmatik: Eine Zwischenbilanz zu Entwicklung, Reform und künftigen Aufgaben* (Mohr Siebeck, 2013)

Schubert G Jr, 'The "Public Interest" in administrative decision-making: theorem, theosophy, or theory?' (1957) The American Political Science Review 346

Schuppert G F, 'Verwaltungswissenschaft im Kontext' in Armin von Bogdandy, Sabino Cassese, and Peter M Huber (eds), *Handbuch Ius Publicum Europaeum* (OUP, 2011) 479

Schwartz G, A Corbacho, and K Funke (eds), *Public investment and public-private partnerships* (Palgrave Macmillan, 2008)

Scott C, 'Regulation in the age of governance: the rise of the post-regulatory state' in J Jordana and D Levi-Faur (eds), *The politics of regulation: institutions and regulatory reforms for the age of governance* (Edward Elgar, 2004)

Sedhari A, 'Public-private partnership as a tool for modernizing public administration' (2004) International Review of Administrative Sciences 291

Segal G, 'Testimony to the Utah law enforcement and criminal justice interim committee' in Y Fortin and H van Hassel (eds), *Contracting in the new public management: from economics to law and citizenship* (IOS Press, 1994)

Segan J, 'Exploring the "Best Value" duty' (2013) Judicial Review 93

Senden L, *Soft law in European Community law* (Hart, 2004)

Sennett R, 'La communauté destructrice' in N Birnbaum et al. (eds), *Au-delà de la crise* (Seuil, 1976) 86

Sennett R, *The fall of public man* (CUP, 1977)

Shaffer G, 'Defending interests: public-private partnerships in WTO litigation' (2004) TDM 4

Shaffer G, and M Pollack, 'Hard vs. soft law: alternatives, complements and antagonists in international governance' (2009) Minnesota Law Review 706

Shakya R K (ed.), *Green public procurement strategies for environmental sustainability* (IGI Global, 2019)

Shaoul J, A Stafford, and P Stapleton, 'Accountability and corporate governance of public private partnerships' (2012) Critical Perspectives on Accounting 213

Shapiro S, 'A delegation theory of the APA' (1996) Admin. Law J. Am. U. 89

Shen L, A Platten, and X Deng, 'Role of public private partnerships to manage risks in public sector projects in Hong Kong' (2006) International Journal of Project Management 587

Shinohara F, *Perspectives on private finance initiative (PFI) in Japan: the impact on administrative reform* (1998) Social Infrastructure and Public Services. NLI Research 117

Short Jones S et al., 'The process of developing a cost-effective public-private partnership: the team approach' (1991) Pub. Cont. Law J. 442

Siegan B H, *Economic liberties and the constitution* (2nd edition, Routledge, 2009)

Singh H, *Creating vibrant public-private panchayat partnership (PPPP) for inclusive growth through inclusive governance* (Academic Foundation, 2010)

Sisson K, and P Marginson, 'Soft regulation: travesty of the real thing or new dimension?' (Economic and Social Research Council 'One Europe or Several' Programme, Working Paper 32/01, Brighton, 2001)

Sjåfjell B, and A Wiesbrock (eds), *Sustainable public procurement under EU law: new perspectives on the state as stakeholder* (CUP, 2016)

Skowronek S, *Building a new American state: the expansion of national administrative capacities 1877–1920* (CUP, 1982)

Slaughter A, 'Governing the global economy through government networks' in M Byers (ed.), *The role of law in international politics: essays in international relations and international law* (OUP, 2000) 177

Smith A, *The wealth of nations* (1776, Shine Classics, 2014)

Sanchez-Graells A, 'What need and logic for a new directive on concessions, particularly regarding the issue of their economic balance?' (2012) EPPPL 94

Snellen I, and W van de Donk (eds), *Public administration in an information age: a handbook* (IOS Press, 1998)

Snyder F, 'Soft law and institutional practices in the European Community law' in S Martin (ed.), *The construction of Europe: essays in honour of Emile Noël* (Kluwer Academic Publishers, 1994) 198

Sordi B, '*Rèvolution, Rechtsstaat* and the rule of law: historical reflections on the emergence and development of administrative law' in S Rose-Ackerman, P Lindseth, and B Emerson (eds), *Comparative administrative law* (2nd edition, Edward Elgar, 2017) 23

Sørensen E, and J Torfing, 'Enhancing collaborative innovation in the public sector' (2011) Administration and Society 842

Sorauf F, 'The public interest reconsidered' (1957) The Journal of Politics 616

Sorauf F, 'The conceptual muddle' in C Friedrich (ed.), *Nomos V: the public interest* (Atherton Press, 1962) 183

Spackman M, 'Public-private partnerships: lessons from the British approach' (2002) Economic Systems 283

Spicker P, 'The principle of subsidiarity and the social policy of the European Community' (1991) Journal of Social Policy 3

Starr P, 'The meaning of privatization' (1988) Yale Law and Policy Review 6

Stephenson M, 'Whither the public private partnership: a critical overview' (1991) Urban Affairs Review 109

Stewart R B, 'Vermont Yankee and the evolution of administrative procedure' (1977–1978) Harvard Law Review 1805

Stewart R B, 'Remedying disregard in global regulatory governance: accountability, participation, and responsiveness' (2014) American Journal of International Law 211

Stipo M, 'Itinerari dell'interesse pubblico nell'ordinamento democratico nel quadro generale degli interessi' in F Astone et al. (eds), *Studi in memoria di Antonio Romano Tassone* (Editorial Scientifica, 2017) 2439

Stolleis M, *Geschichte des öffentlichen Rechts in Deutschland* (CH Beck Verlag, 1999)

Stone Montgomery S, 'When the Klan adopts-a-highway: the weaknesses of the public forum doctrine exposed' (1999) Wash. U. Law Q. 557

Stasser G, and W Titus, 'Hidden profiles: a brief history' (2003) Psychological Inquiry 304

Subijanto J, 'Towards a sustainable Komodo National Park Management: a 2002 progress report' (The Nature Conservancy, 2002)

Sugden R, '"Better off, as judged by themselves": a reply to Cass Sunstein' (2017) International Review of Economics 9

Sugden R, 'Do people really want to be nudged towards healthy lifestyles?' (2017) International Review of Economics 113

Sundaram Jomo K et al., 'Public-private partnerships and the 2030 Agenda for Sustainable Development: fit for purpose?' (UN Department of Economic and Social Affairs (DESA) Working Paper No. 148, UN, New York, 2016)

Sunstein C, 'Of Montreal and Kyoto: a tale of two protocols' (2007) Harvard Environmental Law Review 1

Sunstein C, 'Nudges vs. shoves' (2014) Harvard Law Review Forum 210

Sunstein C, 'Do people like nudges?' (2015) Administrative Law Review 1

Sunstein C, *The ethics of influence: government in the age of behavioral science* (CUP, 2016)

Sunstein C, '"Better off, as judged by themselves": a comment on evaluating nudges' (2017) International Review of Economics 1

Sunstein C, 'Nudges that fail' (2017) Notre Dame Journal of Law, Ethics and Public Policy 4

Sunstein C, and L Reisch (eds), *The economics of nudge* (Routledge, 2017)

Sylvia Karlsson-Vinkhuyzen S, and A Vihma, 'Comparing the legitimacy and effectiveness of global hard and soft law: an analytical framework' (2009) Regulation and Governance 400

Syrett S, 'The politics of partnership: the role of social partners in local economic development in Portugal' (1997) European Urban and Regional Studies 99

Tadem T E, 'Transforming the state into a partner in cooperative development: an evaluation of NGO-government partnership in the Philippines' in S Osborne (ed.), *Public-private partnerships: theory and practice in international perspective* (Routledge, 2000) 187

Tarantini M L, *Istituzionalismo e neoistituzionalismo: questioni e figure* (Giuffrè, 2011)

Tardivo G, G Santoro, and A Ferraris, 'The role of public-private partnerships in developing open social innovation: the case of GoogleGlass4Lis' (2017) World Review of Entrepreneurship, Management and Sustainable Development 580

Taylor G, 'Germany: the subsidiarity principle' (2006) International Journal of Constitutional Law 115

Teicher J, and B Van Gramberg (eds), *Sharing concerns: country case studies in public-private partnerships* (Cambridge Scholars Publishing, 2013)

Teisman G, and E Klijn, 'Partnership arrangements: governmental rhetoric or governance scheme?' (2002) Public Administration Review 197

Thaler R, *Misbehaving: the making of behavioural economics* (Penguin, 2015)

Thaler R, and C Sunstein, *Nudge: improving decisions about health, wealth, and happiness* (New Haven, 2008)

Theron C, and M Dowden, *Strategic sustainable procurement: law and best practice for the public and private sectors* (Routledge, 2017)

Thomas R, 'Private finance initiative. government by contract' (1997) EPL 519

Torchia L, *Il governo delle differenze: Il principio di equivalenza nell'ordinamento europeo* (Il Mulino, 2006)

Torchia L (ed.), *Attraversare i confini del diritto: Giornata di studio dedicata a Sabino Cassese* (Il Mulino, 2016)

Torfing J, *Interactive governance: advancing the paradigm* (Oxford Scholarship, 2012)

Toth A, 'The principle of subsidiarity in the Maastricht Treaty' (1992) Common Market Law Review 1079

Toth A, 'A legal analysis of subsidiarity' in D O'Keeffe and P Twomeny (eds), *Legal issues of the Maastricht Treaty* (Chancery, 1994) 39

Treasury Committee, 'Private finance initiative' (17th Report of Session 2010–12, HC 1146)

Trepte P, *Public procurement in the EU: a practitioner's guide* (OUP, 2007)

Tridimas T, 'Proportionality in Community law: searching for the appropriate standard of scrutiny' in E Ellis (ed.), *The principle of proportionality in the laws of Europe* (Hart Publishing, 1999) 65

Trimarchi M, *L'inesauribilità del potere amministrativo: Profili critici* (Editoriale Scientifica, 2018)

Truchet D, *Les fonctions de la notion d'intérêt général dans la jurisprudence du Conseil d'État* (LGDJ, 1977)

Türk A, *The concept of legislation in European Community law: a comparative perspective* (Springer, 2006)

UK Office for Budget Responsibility, Fiscal risks report (July 2017)

Umamil Asri D, and B Hidayat, 'Current transportation issues in Jakarta and its impacts on environment' (National Development Planning Agency, Republic of Indonesia, Jakarta, 2005)

UN Environment, '2017 global review of sustainable public procurement' (New York, 2017)

UNEP, 'Capacity building for sustainable public procurement in developing countries' (December 2009)

Unger B, D van der Linde, and M Getzner (eds), *Public or private goods?* (Edward Elgar, 2017)

United Nations, 'Agenda 21' (United Nations Conference on Environment and Development, Rio de Janeiro, Brazil, 3 to 14 June 1992)

United Nations, 'Annex: Guiding principles for partnership for sustainable development' (Bali, Indonesia, 7 June 2002)

United Nations, 'Johannesburg Declaration on Sustainable Development' (World Summit on Sustainable Development, September 2002)

United Nations, 'Report of the World Summit on Sustainable Development' (New York, 2002)

United Nations, 'Transforming our world: the 2030 Agenda for Sustainable Development' (Resolution adopted by the General Assembly, 25 September 2015)

United Nations Commission on International Trade Law (UNCITRAL), 'Model legislative provisions on privately financed infrastructure projects' (New York, 2004)

United Nations Commission on International Trade Law (UNCITRAL), 'Legislative guide on privately financed infrastructure projects' (New York, 2011)

United Nations Economic and Social Commission for Asia and the Pacific, 'Country guidance. public-private partnerships for sustainable development in Asia and the Pacific' (Washington DC, 2017) 24

United Nations Economic Commission for Europe, 'Revised guiding principles on people-first public-private partnerships for the United Nations sustainable development goals' (New York, 2018)

United Nations Educational Scientific and Cultural Organization (UNESCO), 'The global learning crisis: why every child deserves a quality education' (Programme and Meeting Document, 2013)

United Nations Educational Scientific and Cultural Organization (UNESCO), 'The Hangzhou Declaration placing culture at the heart of sustainable development policies' (Adopted in Hangzhou, People's Republic of China, 17 May 2013).

United Nations General Assembly, 'United Nations Millennium Declaration' (18 September 2000, A/RES/55/2)

United States Trade Center, 1998 http://ustradecenter.com/alliance.html #introduction, accessed 28 June 2019

Urban@it. Centro Nazionale di Studi per le Politiche Urbane, *Terzo Rapporto sulle città: Mind the gap: Il distacco tra politiche e città* (Il Mulino, 2018) 203

USAID policy framework, available at https://www.usaid.gov/ policyframework/documents/1870/usaid-policy-framework, accessed 30 June 2019

Vaillancourt Rosenau P (ed.), *Public-private policy partnerships* (MIT Press, 2000)

Vaillancourt Rosenau P, 'The strengths and weaknesses of public-private policy partnership' in Pauline Vaillancourt Rosenau (ed.), *Public-private policy partnerships* (MIT Press, 2000) 217

Valaguzza S, *La frammentazione della fattispecie nel diritto amministrativo a conformazione europea* (Giuffrè, 2008)

Valaguzza S, *Società miste a partecipazione comunale: ammissibilità e ambiti* (Guiffrè, 2012)

Valaguzza S, 'Pubblico e privato nell'organizzazione' in B Marchetti (ed.), *Pubblico e privato oltre i confini dell'amministrazione tradizionale* (Cedam, 2013) 99

Valaguzza S, 'Le sponsorizzazioni pubbliche: le insidie della rottura del binomio tra soggetto ed oggetto pubblico e la rilevanza del diritto europeo' (2015) Rivista Italiana di Diritto Pubblico Comunitario 1381

Valaguzza S, 'La regolazione strategica dell'Autorità Nazionale Anticorruzione' (2016) RRM

Valaguzza S, *Sustainable development in public contract: an example of strategic regulation* (Editoriale Scientifica, 2016)

Valaguzza S, '*Nudging* pubblico vs. pubblico: nuovi strumenti per una regolazione flessibile di ANAC' (2017) RRM

Valaguzza S, *Governare per contratto: Come creare valore attraverso i contratti pubblici* (Editoriale Scientifica, 2018)

Valaguzza S, *Collaborare nell'interesse pubblico: Perché passare dai modelli antagonisti agli accordi collaborativi* (Editoriale Scientifica, 2019)

Valguzza S, 'How does collaborative procurement operate in Italy?' in D Mosey (ed.), *Collaborative construction procurement and improved value* (Wiley, 2019) 445 van Garsse S, 'Concessions and public procurement' in C Bovis (ed.), *Research handbook on EU public procurement law* (Edward Elgar, 2016) 593

van Jaarsveld I, 'International banking: the World Bank and other financial institutions' (2000) Juta's Business Law 160

Vatn A, and D Bromley, 'Externalities – a market model failure' (1997) Environmental and Resource Economics 135

Vause G, 'The subsidiarity principle in European Union law – American federalism compared' (1995) Case W. Res J. Int'l Law 61

Venn Dicey A, *Introduction to the study of the law of the constitution* (1885, Liberty Fund, 1982)

Ventura C, G Cassalia, and L Della Spina, 'New models of public-private partnership in cultural heritage sector: sponsorships between models and traps' (2016) Procedia – Social and Behavioral Sciences 257

Verger A, and M Moschetti, 'Public-private partnerships as an education policy approach: multiple meanings, risks and challenges' (UNESCO Working Paper, 2017)

Verkuil P, 'Public law limitations on privatization of government functions' (2007) North Carolina Law Review 397

Vermeule A, 'Our Schmittian administrative law' (2008) Harvard Law Review 1095

Verschuere B, and V Pestoff (eds), *New public governance, the third sector and co-production* (Routledge, 2012)

Villamena S, '"Baratto amministrativo": prime osservazioni' (2016) Rivista Giuridica dell'Edilizia

Villata R, *Autorizzazioni amministrative e iniziativa economica privata: Profili generali* (Giuffrè, 1974)

Villata R, *Pubblici servizi: discussioni e problemi* (5th edition, Giappichelli, 2008)

Villey M, 'Esquisse historique sur le mot responsable' in M Boulet-Sautel et al. (eds), *La responsabilité á travers les ages* (Sirey, 1989) 75

Vischer R, 'Subsidiarity as a principle of governance: beyond devolution' (2001) Ind. Law Review 103

Vitale M, *L'impresa irresponsabile: Nelle antiche radici il suo futuro* (ESD, 2014)

Vitale M et al., *Responsabilità nell'impresa* (Piccola Biblioteca d'Impresa Inaz, 2010)

Vittadini G, 'Subsidiarity: a new partnership between state, market and civil society' in A Brugnoli and A Colombo (eds), *Government, governance and welfare reform: structural changes and subsidiarity in Italy and Britain* (Edward Elgar, 2012) 17

von Bogdandy A, and P Dann, 'International composite administration: conceptualizing multi-level and network aspects in the exercise of international public authority' (2008) German Law Journal 2013

von Hippel E, *Democratizing innovation* (MIT Press, 2005)

von Mehren A, 'Civil-law analogues to consideration: an exercise in comparative analysis' (1959) Harvard Law Review 1009

Voorberg W, V Bekkers, and L Tummers, 'A systematic review of co-creation and co-production, embarking on the social innovation journey' (2015) Public Management Review 1333

Voorberg W et al., 'Does co-creation impact public service delivery? The importance of state and governance traditions' (2017) Public Money and Management 365

Voßkuhle A, 'The reform approach in the German science of administrative law' in Matthias Ruffert (ed.), *The transformation of administrative law in Europe* (Sellier, 2007) 89

Voßkuhle A, and T Wischmeyer, 'The "*Neue Verwaltungsrechtswissenschaft*" against the backdrop of traditional administrative law scholarship in Germany' in S Rose-Ackerman, P Lindseth, and B Emerson (eds), *Comparative administrative law* (2nd edition, Edward Elgar, 2017) 85

Wade W, and C Forsyth, *Administrative law* (11th edition, OUP, 2010)

Waldo D, *The administrative state* (The Ronald Press Company, 1948)

Walker-Said C, and J D Kelly (eds), *Corporate social responsibility? Human rights in the new global economy* (University of Chicago Press, 2015)

Wall A, *Public-private partnerships in the USA: lessons to be learned for the United Kingdom* (Routledge, 2013)

Wall D, *The sustainable economics of Elinor Ostrom: commons, contestation and craft* (Routledge, 2014)

Wallis J, and B Dollery, *Market failure, government failure, leadership and public policy* (Palgrave Macmillan, 1999)

Walsh K, *Public services and market mechanisms: competition, contracting and the new public management* (Macmillan International Higher Education, 1995)

Warnier P, *Le phénomène de la communautés de base* (Desclée De Brower, 1973)

Webb A, 'Co-ordination: a problem in public sector management' (1991) Policy and Politics 19

Weingast B R, 'The economic role of political institutions: market-preserving federalism and economic development' (1995) Journal of Law, Economics and Organization 1

Weintraub J, and K Kumar, *Public and private in thought and practice: perspectives on a grand dichotomy* (University of Chicago Press, 1997)

Weisbrod B A, 'Conceptual perspective on the public interest: an economic analysis' in B A Weisbrod, J Handler, and N Komesar (eds), *Public interest law, an economic and institutional analysis* (University of California Press, 1978) 4

Weitzenbock E, *A legal framework for emerging business models: dynamic networks as collaborative contracts* (Edward Elgar, 2012) 5

Whiteside H, *Purchase for profit: public-private partnerships and Canada's public health care system* (University of Toronto Press, 2015)

Widdus R, 'Public-private partnerships for health: their main targets, their diversity and their future directions' (2001) Bulletin of the World Health Organization: the International Journal of Public Health 713

Williams-Elegbe S, *Public procurement and multilateral development banks* (Hart Publishing, 2017)

Williamson O, *Dominant firms and the monopoly problem: market failure considerations* (Brookings Institution, 1972)

Willoughby W, *The government of modern states* (The Century Company, 1919)

Wilson W, 'The study of administration' (1887) Political Science Quarterly 2

Winston C, *Government failure versus market failure: microeconomics policy research and government performance* (AEI-Brookings Joint Center Regulatory Studies, 2006)

Witters L, R Marom, and K Steinert, 'The role of public-private partnerships in driving innovation' in S Dutta, *The Global Innovation Index 2012: stronger innovation linkages for global growth* (INSEAD and World Intellectual Property Organization, 2012) 81

Wittgenstein L, *Philosophical investigations* (1953, Wiley, 2009)

Wolf C, 'Market and non-market failures: comparison and assessment' (1987) Journal of Public Policy 43

Woodley M, 'Partnership' in *Osborn's concise law dictionary* (11th edition, Thomson Reuters, 2009) 300

Woodley M, 'Public authority' in *Osborn's concise law dictionary* (11th edition, Thomson Reuters, 2009) 332

World Bank, 'Working with NGOs: a practical guide to operational collaboration between the World Bank and non-governmental organizations'. Operations Policy Department (World Bank, 1995)

World Bank Group, Independent Evaluation Group, 'World Bank Group support to public-private partnerships: lessons from experience in client countries' (Washington DC, 2015)

World Bank, International Bank for Reconstruction and Development, 'Public-private partnership reference guide' (Version 3, Washington DC, 2017)

World Economic Forum, 'African food security: a role for public private partnership' (World Economic Forum Africa Economic Summit, 2003)

Wouters J, 'Government by negotiation' in S Cassese (ed.), *Research handbook on global administrative law* (Edward Elgar, 2016) 196

Wright G, 'Legal paternalism and the eclipse of principle' (2016) Miami Law Review 194

Wrong M, *In the footsteps of Mr. Kurtz: living on the brink of disaster in Mobutu's Congo* (Harper Collins, 2002)

Wyman K, and D Spiegel-Feld, 'The urban environmental renaissance' (2020) California Law Review, forthcoming

Yamamoto H, 'Multi-level governance and public private partnership: theoretical basis of public management' (2007) Interdisciplinary Information Sciences 65

Yeung J, A Chan, and D Chan, 'The definition of alliancing in construction as a Wittgenstein family-resemblance concept' (2007) International Journal of Project Management 219

Yeung K, 'Nudge as fudge' (2012) The Modern Law Review 122

Yoan S 'Proportionality in French administrative law' in S Ranchordàs and B De Waard (eds), *The judge and the proportionate use of discretion: a comparative study* (Routledge, 2016) 43

Young M, and S Sullivan, 'Evolution through the duty to cooperate: implications of the whaling case at the International Court of Justice' (2015) Melbourne Journal of Int'l Law 327

Zahran A et al., 'Ecological development and global climate change: a cross-national study of Kyoto Protocol ratification' (2007) Society and Natural Resources 37

Zapatrina I, 'Sustainable Development Goals for developing economies and public-private partnership' (2006) Eur. Procurement and Pub. Private Partnership Law Review 39

Zen F, and M Regan (eds), *ASEAN public private partnership guidelines* (Jakarta, 2014)

Zerbe R Jr, and H McCurdy, 'The failure of market failure' (1999) Journal of Policy Analysis and Management 558

Index

accountability xvi, 21, 22, 89, 138, 152, 171
activism 46, 98–9
administrative action 140–141, 142
    mutation of expected results
        from compliance to better response to social needs 166–7
        from economy principle to value for money 167–70
    mutation of modalities of awarding procedures 162–4
        from direct intervention to co-administration 154–62
        public interest to common interests 164–5
    mutations of principles of competition and consistency 150–151
        from good administration to sustainable development 146–9
        from reason-giving duty to reinforced motivation 152–4
    integrity, awareness and flexibility 151–2
    non-discrimination 144–6, 153
    public image 150, 152
    mutations of public administration's liability 170–172
administrative authorization or permits 98–100, 111, 165

administrative law 19, 21, 25, 99–100, 120, 123–4, 128, 152, 166, 171
    efficacy and efficiency 146, 147, 167
    European xviii–xix
    general principles enriched 148–9
    governing from bottom up 141–4
advantages of PPP 28–9
    participatory democracy 22, 23–5
    public authorities and isolation 19–23
    responsible enterprises 25–8
advocacy groups 39
Agenda 21 38–9
agent-principal relationship 97
agreement: element of PPP 108, 110–111
agriculture 33–4, 46
alliancing 156–9, 161
Aquinas, Thomas 119
Aristotle 119
Asian Development Bank 43, 52
Australia xiii, 95
authorization or permits 98–100, 111, 165
awarding procedures 150–152, 162–4

background: strengths and weaknesses of PPPs 2–8
Bangladesh 34–5
banks, multilateral development 42–5
    criticism 52–3
barter, administrative 72, 109
behavioural economics 126
Bentham, Jeremy 119–20

bias(es) 22, 78
biodiversity
　　Indonesia: Komodo National Park
　　　xii–xiii
bottom up approach xiii, xxiv, 23–4, 53,
　　54, 67, 71, 107, 108, 129, 172,
　　173
　　from traditional administrative law
　　　to 141–4
　　governing common interests 164–5
　　new paradigm for administrative
　　　action 138–41
Brazil 113, 114, 173
Burkina Faso xii, 13, 24, 113

Cambodia xxiii
Chile xxiii
China xxiii
cities 33
　　innovation in smart 75–7
　　smart 60
civil law countries 141–2, 171
civil society, transnational 39
climate change 32, 129
　　greenhouse gas emission reduction
　　　35
co-creation of value 24, 134
co-management 69, 107, 134, 139
　　definition of PPP 111, 113
　　of public tasks vs horizontal
　　　subsidiarity 88–100
　　　co-management explained
　　　　93–100
co-owned company 58
collaborative contracting xxiii, 156,
　　157–62
Colombia 65, 114
common good 118, 119, 122
common goods xiv, xx, 71, 74, 84–5
common interests 116–37, 145, 152, 153,
　　172, 173
　　complexity of social needs 127, 133

　　from pursuing public interest to
　　　governing 164–5
　　governance of the 139–40
　　governing from bottom up 138–41
　　need to expand concept of public
　　　interest 116–17
　　public administration and public
　　　interest 133–5
　　　contrast with PPP 123–8
　　　origin and development 118–23
　　towards objective view of
　　　governance 128–35
　　welfare provision 127–8
community xiv, 172–3
competition and consistency 150–151
compromise 28, 85–6, 100, 103–4,
　　105–6, 152
　　definition of PPP 108, 110
　　public private antinomy and logic
　　　of 16–19
concession contracts xxii, xxiii, xxiv, 4,
　　8, 13, 52, 151
　　award of 163
　　definition of PPP 109, 111
　　health care 34
　　local dimension 56–7, 61–7, 80
　　　ex ante value for money
　　　　analysis 65–7
　　　risk allocation 61–4, 67
　　privately funded build and operate
　　　11
confidentiality 141
consensualism 79, 130, 134, 143, 150,
　　154–5
consistency and competition 150–151
contracting out 16, 58, 93–4, 95, 96, 97,
　　113, 138
contracts 58, 59, 87, 106, 110, 143, 155,
　　165
　　alliance 158–9
　　collaborative contracting xxiii, 156,
　　　157–62

concession *see separate entry*
  horizontal contractual relations 130
  liability 171
  model 49
  renegotiation of terms 51, 62
cooperation xxiii, 3–4, 10, 22, 47, 54,
    106, 107, 128, 133, 134, 161, 162
  contract 155, 156–7
  duty of loyal 145
  element of PPP 108, 113–14
  governing common interests 164–5
  market failures vs 82–8
    single aim 85–8
  partnership: juxtaposition vs 14–16
  relational dynamics 155–6
corporate social responsibility 19, 26–7,
    28–9, 67, 145, 150
corruption 28, 41, 45, 53, 71, 129
cost-benefit analysis 169
cost-efficiency analysis 65, 114
Costa Rica xxiii
critiques 7–8, 10–11, 13–14, 52–3
  private finance initiative projects
    11–13
Croatia xxiii
cultural heritage 70, 98
  Australia: North Head Quarantine
    Station xiii
  Italy 77
cultural organizations 52

definition of PPP 13, 108–15, 137, 164
  elements
    agreement 108, 110–111
    common interests 137
    joint management 108, 113–14
    left out 109–10
    public entity and private
      operator 108, 111–13
    public interest 108, 114–15
  soft law, international 52

OECD: Committee for Science
    and Technology Policy
    37–8
  vagueness of discourse 9–14
delegation 16, 58
democracy 54, 75, 79, 80, 89, 120,
    122–3, 165
  legitimacy xvi, 22
  participatory 22, 23–5, 28, 71,
    107–8, 139, 146
developing countries xv, xxiv, 31–2, 33,
    39, 68
  agriculture 34
  multilateral development banks
    42–5
disabled persons 25
disease xvi
duration 109–10

e-governance platforms 38
economic added value 140
economic crisis 26
economic development 35
economic incentives 99
education 33, 35, 46, 68, 98, 109–10
  school construction 77
  women's literacy programme xi–xii
Egypt 113
  Smart Village Cairo 76
elements of PPP 105–8
employment 35
endangered species xvi
  Indonesia: Komodo National Park
    xii–xiii
energy xv, xvii, 32, 33, 113
environment 17, 25, 26, 29, 32, 41, 53,
    54, 60, 98
  climate change 32, 35, 129
  Indonesia
    Komodo National Park xii–xiii
    rapid transit bus line 35
  precautionary principle 149

equal treatment 72
Estonia Rural Connectivity 76
ethics 27, 28, 151, 173
European Bank for Reconstruction and
        Development 43
European Union 72
    Commission xxii, 13
    Concession Contracts Directive
        (2014/23/EU) xxii, 163–4
    European Court of Auditors 10–11
    Eurostat 62, 63, 64
    Fiscal Stability Treaty (2012) 4
    government deficit and debt 62, 63
    precautionary principle 149
    subsidiarity 91
expertise centres 48

family resemblance (Wittgenstein) 157–8
features of PPP 105–8
financing 68, 69, 109–10
    international finance institutions *see
        separate entry*
    see also concession contracts
food 32
    security 34
Food and Agriculture Organization
        (FAO) 34
formalism 19, 171
fragmentation 19
France xviii–xix, 120, 141, 170
    concierge de cartier 74
    consensualisme 130
    marché de partenariat xxiv
    public debate 139
    railways 4
freedom of economic initiative 141

Gambia xii
game theory 155–6
Germany 170
globalization of governance 128–9
goal-oriented networks 38–41, 54

governance 164
    of the common interests 139–40
    globalization of 128–9
    good 25, 37, 48, 54, 108
    and government 138
    networks of 173
government 138, 165
    deficit and debt 62–4
Greece: definition of public subject 112
Greenpeace 112
Guinea xii

health care xvii, 33, 34, 46, 68, 98, 151
    dialysis capacity: Bangladesh 34–5
    disease xvi
    remote 38
Hobbes, Thomas 119
horizontal contractual relations 130
horizontal subsidiarity *see* subsidiarity
housing
    adequate 32
    affordable xvii
    social 99
        management of 71
human dignity 32
human rights 32, 98, 147

image of private operators 24, 28–9,
        77–8, 86, 116, 150–151
inclusion 57, 61, 67, 79, 108
    social 37, 59, 72, 104
    social innovation and market 68–77
    smart cities 75–7
    solidarity and participation
        71–5
income equality 35
India: e-Mitra 76
Indonesia
    bus line in Jakarta, rapid transit 35
    Komodo National Park xii–xiii
    scope of application of PPP 113
inequality of power 53

information 147, 167
  asymmetry 19
  right to access 141
  unshared 156
information and communication
    technologies (ICT) 37, 38, 76
infrastructure xv, 11, 13, 52–3, 68, 69,
    114
  agriculture 34
  energy xv, xvii
  highways
    adopt-a-highway programmes
      x, 77
  railways 4, 68
  UNCITRAL Model Legislative
    Provisions on Privately
    Financed Infrastructure
    Projects 49
  water xvi
innovation 5, 8, 18, 37–8, 60
  smart cities 75–7
  social 24, 57, 59, 67, 79, 80, 108
    market inclusion and 68–77
institutional partnership 58
intergovernmentalism 41
international dimension 30–55, 104, 106,
    107–8
  actors 38, 41–2
    international finance
      institutions *see separate*
      entry
    non-governmental
      organizations *see*
      separate entry
  goal-oriented networks 38–41, 54
  people first approach 52–5
  soft regulation 47–52
  sustainable development 32, 33–8,
    146
international finance institutions 39,
    42–5, 47, 48, 51
  criticisms 52–3

International Finance Corporation
  Bangladesh: dialysis capacity
    34
  Indonesia: Komodo National
    Park xii–xiii
international law xvi
International Monetary Fund (IMF) 31,
    52
  PPP Fiscal Risk Assessment Model
    48–9
  'Public Private Partnerships' 49
  value for money 65
international organizations 40, 41, 42,
    47, 48, 53
Italy xix, xxiv, 131, 170, 173
  balanced budget 4
  risks 64
  solidarity and participation 72–4,
    109
  value for money analysis, *ex ante*
    65–6

Johannesburg Summit (2002) 32, 53
joint and several liability 171
judicial review 142, 171
justice 118, 120

Kant, I. 118
know-how 7, 37, 77

legality principle 17, 141, 142, 143, 173
legitimacy xvi, 108, 123, 146
  democratic xvi, 22
  local government 79
  subsidiarity 90
liability 170–172
liberalization 95–6
Liberia xxiii
libertarian paternalism 126
literacy programme xi–xii
literature review xv–xxi
Lithuania xxiii

local dimension 56–80, 104, 107–8, 146
    concessions 56–7, 61–7, 80
        ex ante value for money
            analysis 65–7
        risk allocation 61–4, 67
    cultural and political choice 57–61,
        83
    market inclusion and social
        innovation 68–71
            innovation in smart cities 75–7
            solidarity and participation
                71–5
    methodological premise 56–7
    sponsorships 70, 77–9
    value for money analysis, *ex ante*
        65–7
Locke, John 119

market failures vs cooperation 82–8
migration 129
multilateral development banks 42–5
    criticisms 52–3
multilevel governance 67

negotiation 79, 88, 111, 130, 134, 163
neo-liberalism 96, 97
networks 130, 139, 159–61, 173
    goal-oriented 38–41, 54
    organizational 157
New Public Management 5, 95
New Zealand 95
non-discrimination 72, 78, 88, 144–6,
    153
non-governmental organizations 39, 42,
    45–7, 54, 112, 113
    definition 46
nudging 126

objective view of governance 128–35
objectives 85–8, 105–6

OECD (Organization for Economic
    Cooperation and Development)
        30–31
    Committee for Science and
        Technology Policy 37–8
    value for money 65
off-balance-sheet 62–3
outsourcing 57–8, 95–6, 138, 165

participatory democracy 22, 23–5, 28,
    71, 107–8, 139, 146
partnership and cooperation vs
    juxtaposition 14–16
people first approach 52–5
permits or authorization 98–100, 111,
    165
Plato 118
pollution 35
poverty eradication 32
pre-feasibility verification 65, 114
precautionary principle 149
principal-agent relationship 97
principles 19, 49, 53, 63, 72, 78, 122,
    140, 141
    from economy principle to value for
        money 167–70
    legality 17, 141, 142, 143, 173
    mutations of principles of
        administrative action 144–54
    non-discrimination 72, 78, 88,
        144–6, 153
    precautionary 149
    proportionality 148–9
    subsidiarity *see separate entry*
    transparency 72, 78, 88, 116, 125,
        141, 153, 159
privatization 16, 93–6, 97, 113
proportionality 148–9
public authorities and isolation 19–23,
    88, 99, 107, 133
public consultation 139

public image of private operators 24,
  28–9, 77–8, 86, 116, 150–151
public interest(s) xiv, 3, 13, 19, 54, 78,
  106
  co-management of 69, 97
  definition of PPP 108, 111, 114–15
  essential element of partnership
    agreement 87–8
  from public interest to common
    interests *see* common
    interests
  non-governmental organizations 46
  outsourcing and contracting out 58
  participation in formation of 23,
    58, 97
  private bias 22
  public bodies 17, 79, 86, 97
  shaped through consensual
    negotiation 79
  shared choice and management 25
  traditional identification of public
    administration with 118–23
public and private law boundaries xvii–
  xviii, 3
public procurement xxii, xxiii, 8, 12–13,
  33, 36, 44, 95, 97, 107, 151, 165
  green and social 26, 36
  public sector comparator 66
  risks 63
public sector comparator 66, 169
public service, objectification of notion
  of 128–35
public value, co-creation of 134
Puerto Rico 113

quality 5, 7, 20, 35, 43, 44, 47–8, 59,
  147, 163, 169

Rawls, J. 118
reasons for and advantages of PPP 28–9
  participatory democracy 22, 23–5,
    28

public authorities and isolation
  19–23
responsible enterprises 25–9
reciprocity 173
reconstructing juridical identity of PPP
  108–15
Red Cross 112
responsible enterprises 25–9
risk(s) 51, 109–10
  allocation 10, 11, 51, 61–4, 67
  evaluation of benefits and 80
  international financial institutions
    42–3
  mitigation 44
  PPP Fiscal Risk Assessment Model
    48–9
Rousseau, J.-J. 118
rule of law 120, 142
Russia 59–60

sanitation 32
scientific research 98
security 173
  homeland xvii
  resource 32
selection of private partner 150–152,
  162–4
semantic approach 28, 100, 103
  partnership: cooperation vs
    juxtaposition 14–16
  public private antinomy and logic of
    compromise 16–19, 100
    collective and altruistic
      dimension 18
    individual and egoistic
      dimension 18
Senegal
  *Projet d'Alphabétisation Priorité
    Femme* xi–xii
Singapore 113
size of private enterprises xv
Slovenia 4, 114

social added value 140
social cohesion 75, 79, 80, 85, 142
social enterprises 71, 92, 99, 112, 113
social entrepreneurship 98
social inclusion 37, 59, 72, 104
social partnership 69, 74–5, 111
social responsibility 17, 34
soft regulation, international 47–52
sovereignty 3, 19, 117, 121, 124, 129,
        132, 139, 146, 152, 166, 167
Spain 170, 173
sponsorships 70, 77–9, 109, 111
sport facilities xvii
strengths and weaknesses of PPPs 2–8
subsidiarity 90–1, 113
        co-management of public tasks vs
                horizontal 88–100
        co-management explained
                93–100
supply chain 159
sustainable development xxiv, 29, 33–8,
        39, 54
        administrative action: from good
                administration to 146–9
        goals (SDGs) xvi, 32, 38, 46, 53,
                106
        non-governmental organizations
                46, 47
        UN 2030 Agenda for 32

taxation 73, 99, 150
telecommunications 68, 113
tenders 88, 162–4
terminology
        community xiv
terrorism 129
third sector 98, 112, 113
        see also non-governmental
                organizations
torts 143, 171
tourism 98
tragedy of the commons 84

training 48
transaction costs 12, 50
transnational partnerships xvi, xxiv
transparency 72, 78, 88, 116, 125, 141,
        153, 159
transport xvii, 33, 35, 37, 173
        highways
                adopt-a-highway programmes
                        x, 77
                Indonesia 113
                bus line in Jakarta, rapid transit
                        35
                intelligent 38

UNCITRAL (UN Commission on
        International Trade Law) 31
        Model Legislative Provisions
                on Privately Financed
                Infrastructure Projects 49
UNESCO 31
United Kingdom 95
        definition of PPPs xxii–xiii
        lighthouses 4
        Private Finance Initiative 5, 11–12
                public sector comparator 66
                risk allocation 63–4
                value for money 65, 66
        privately funded build and operate
                concession contracts 11
        school construction 77
United Nations 30
        2030 Agenda for Sustainable
                Development 32
        Agenda 21 38–9
        Economic Commission for Europe
                54
        guiding principles 53
United States 6, 95
        Harvard's Kennedy School of
                Government47 131
        highways

adopt-a-highway programmes
          x, 77
New York: public phones replaced
          with Wi-Fi connected contact
          points 76
oil wells 4
urban spaces 37, 60, 68, 71, 72–5, 147
     cities 33, 60, 75–7
     social partnership agreements 69
utilitarianism 119–20

value for money
     ex ante analysis 65–7
     from economy principle to 167–70

water xvi, 32, 33, 113
     management xvii
welfare state 19
Wittgenstein, L. 157–8
women
     literacy programme xi–xii
World Bank Group 42
     definition of PPP 52
     International Finance Corporation
          see separate entry
     Reference Guide 49
World Bank
          PPP Fiscal Risk Assessment
               Model 48–9
WWF 112